HOSPITALITY
MANAGEMENT
LIBRARY

Accounting I

Raymond Cote

Disclaimer

The author, Raymond Cote, is solely responsible for the contents of this publication. All views expressed herein are solely those of the author and do not necessarily reflect the views of the Educational Institute of the American Hotel & Motel Association (the Institute) or the American Hotel & Motel Association (AH&MA). Nothing contained in this publication shall constitute an endorsement by the Institute or AH&MA of any information, opinion, procedure, or product mentioned, and the Institute and AH&MA disclaim any liability with respect to the use of any such information, procedure, or product, or reliance thereon.

Neither AH&MA nor the Institute make or recommend industry standards. Nothing in this publication shall be construed as a recommendation by the Institute or AH&MA to be adopted by, or binding upon, any member of the hospitality industry.

Library of Congress Cataloging-in-Publication Data
Cote, Raymond.
   Understanding hospitality accounting I.

   Includes index.
   1. Hotels, taverns, etc.—Accounting. 2. Motels—
Accounting. 3. Restaurants, lunch rooms, etc.—
Accounting. 4. Food service—Accounting. I. Title.
HF5686.H75C63   1987   657'.837   87-15724
ISBN 0-86612-035-1

Editor: Kent F. Premo

Contents

Preface

Over the years, the hospitality sector has been searching for a financial accounting text which combines a clear and straightforward approach with an awareness of the industry's unique requirements. The publication of the *Understanding Hospitality Accounting* series provides an affirmative response to this search by relating fundamental accounting principles to the hospitality industry in a practical and user-friendly mode. In presenting accounting principles and procedures, the series assumes no previous background in bookkeeping or accounting.

The series is composed of two volumes: *Understanding Hospitality Accounting I* and *Understanding Hospitality Accounting II*. This, the first volume, presents the accounting concepts and procedures used in the accounting cycle. The second volume provides in-depth coverage of more advanced accounting topics.

The authoritative source for the series is the *Uniform System of Accounts and Expense Dictionary for Small Hotels, Motels, and Motor Hotels* published by the Educational Institute of the American Hotel & Motel Association (AH&MA). Where appropriate, references are made to pronouncements of the Financial Accounting Standards Board (FASB) and the American Institute of Certified Public Accountants (AICPA).

Understanding Hospitality Accounting I is a comprehensive financial accounting text that integrates the specialized requirements of the hospitality industry with generally accepted accounting principles. It may be used by professionals as a reference source and by students as a learning tool.

This text uses an approach that concentrates on hospitality accounting principles, yet is authoritative in scope. Each topic is introduced with a basic presentation which gradually builds to more complex areas. The presentation is structured for easy learning and retention by the extensive use of definitions, concepts, illustrations, and pertinent discussion questions and problems.

Understanding Hospitality Accounting I builds a business vocabulary using a modular, step-by-step approach. It combines elements of financial and managerial accounting, emphasizing the mastery of accounting concepts in addition to actual problem solving.

Chapters 1, 2, 3, and 4 introduce the field of hospitality accounting and its relation to the hospitality industry as a whole, and the characteristics of financial information systems. In this manner, *Understanding Hospitality Accounting I* not only teaches the principles of accounting but also recognizes that accounting is part of the larger sphere of business activities. Topics such as starting a business, securing proper business insurance coverage, and safeguarding business assets by internal control are introduced to broaden the reader's awareness of the business environment.

Understanding Hospitality Accounting I gradually builds the essential foundation for understanding the overall accounting process. Chapters 5 and 6 detail the bookkeeping accounts which compose the five major accounting classifications, and the latter chapter addresses the two basic systems for inventory accounting. Chapter 7 analyzes the effects of business transactions, while Chapter 8 relates this analysis to the correct application of debits and credits.

Later chapters emphasize practical accounting procedures and the actual use of special journals in the hospitality industry. Chapters 9 and 10 concentrate on the recording of business transactions in the accounting records. Chapters 11 and 12 follow the accounting cycle through the monthly and end-of-year processes. These four chapters also employ a case study which begins with the recording of business transactions and continues through the completion of the accounting cycle.

As this text fulfills the special requirements of the hospitality industry and educators alike, I feel it fitting to offer my gratitude to industry personnel, fellow educators, and others who made its publication possible.

My colleagues who field-tested the text and course materials were especially helpful in providing comments and suggestions. Many thanks are due the students and hospitality accounting faculty of Johnson & Wales College.

I gratefully acknowledge two reviewers for their generous contributions of time and constructive comments: Ian Patrick Griggs, CPA, Partner/Director of Audit Operations, the Honolulu office of Touche Ross & Company; and Raymond S. Schmidgall, CPA, Associate Professor of Hotel, Restaurant, and Institutional Management at Michigan State University.

Thanks are also extended to Jim M. Mulrooney, Vice President/ Treasurer of Chi-Chi's, Inc., for furnishing his company's annual report, which serves as an illustration of actual financial statements.

Raymond Cote, CPA
Associate Professor, Coordinator of
Hospitality Accounting
Johnson & Wales College
Providence, Rhode Island

With honor and remembrance, I dedicate this book to my father and mother: Raymond E. Cote and Alice E. Cote.

1
Accounting Theory and Practice

Accounting is often referred to as "the language of business." Executives, investors, bankers, creditors, and governmental officials use this language in their day-to-day activities. In order to effectively communicate in today's business world, a fundamental grasp of the theory and practice of accounting is required.

Many of those presently employed within the hospitality industry and many students new to the field of hospitality sometimes feel that the language of business is understood only by specialists who seem to thrive on "number crunching." This misconception arises from an unfamiliarity with the fundamental purpose of accounting and the logic which lies behind basic accounting activities.

This introductory chapter will dispel many misconceptions about basic accounting activities while providing answers to such questions as:

1. Why should managers and supervisors understand the theory and practice of accounting?

2. What is the fundamental purpose of accounting?

3. How extensive a background in mathematics is needed to understand accounting activities?

4. What is the difference between bookkeeping and accounting?

5. What career opportunities are there in the field of accounting?

6. Are there fundamental principles of accounting that apply to every kind of business enterprise?

This chapter addresses the importance of understanding the theory and practice of accounting for managers, supervisors, and those students who are new to the field of hospitality. The major branches of the accounting profession are defined and organizations which serve the professional accountant are identified. Special attention is given to the generally accepted accounting principles which ensure that consistent accounting procedures are followed in the preparation of financial statements. The chapter closes with a brief discussion of the differences between generally accepted accounting principles and specific accounting procedures dictated by income tax law.

Why Study Accounting?

A knowledge of the basic theory and practice of accounting is a valuable tool with which to achieve success not only in the hospitality industry but in the management of your personal finances as well. However, students planning careers in the hospitality industry often tend to neglect the accounting aspects of their field of study. Some believe that they will be able to "pick up" the essentials of accounting once they are out of school and on the job. But, once on the job, many find that day-to-day responsibilities confine them to specific areas of a property's operation. Increased specialization within the hospitality industry at times creates a situation in which relatively few, outside of those actually employed within accounting departments, have opportunities to learn the theory and practice of accounting at a level required by the demands of today's business world.

Most colleges require accounting as part of a business curriculum because the future managers of any type of business need to grasp the essentials of accounting in order to make sound business decisions. Managers need to understand how basic decisions regarding operational matters (such as replacing equipment or changing policy regarding the extension of credit to customers) will affect the financial statements of the business.

Managers and supervisors working in the hospitality industry realize the importance of understanding the basic theory and practice of accounting. In the highly competitive field of hospitality, successful careers often depend on an ability to make daily operating decisions based upon analyses of financial information. In order to achieve satisfactory profit objectives for their areas of responsibility, managers must thoroughly understand how the accounting system accumulates and processes financial information. The increasing use of computers to record accounting information and to prepare financial statements has not diminished the necessity of mastering this business language.

Some individuals are reluctant to learn the fundamentals of accounting because they mistakenly believe that accounting is "numbers oriented," requiring a sophisticated background in mathematics. Accounting theory and practice is not based on complicated mathematics; it is based on *logic* and emphasizes basic terminology, fundamental concepts, and relatively straightforward procedures. Applying the logic of accounting requires only the most basic math skills: addition, subtraction, multiplication, and division. Once the terminology, concepts, and procedures of accounting are mastered, accounting practices are not as difficult to understand as some people tend to believe.

The Function of Accounting

The fundamental purpose of accounting is to provide useful and timely financial information. The American Institute of Certified Public Accountants offers a definition of accounting which emphasizes its functional nature.

> Its function is to provide quantitative information, primarily financial in nature, about economic entities that is intended to be useful in making economic decisions.[1]

Quantitative information may take the form of financial statements, forecasts, budgets, and many types of reports which can be used to evaluate the financial position and operating performance of a hospitality business. Two major financial statements prepared by accounting departments are the balance sheet and the statement of income.

The balance sheet provides important information regarding *the financial position of the hospitality business on a given date*. This financial statement reports the assets, liabilities, and equity on a given date. Simply stated, assets represent anything a business owns which has commercial or exchange value, liabilities represent the claims of outsiders (such as creditors) to assets, and equity represents the claims of owners to assets.

The statement of income provides important information regarding *the results of operations for a stated period of time*. Because this statement reveals the bottom line (net income for a specified period), it is one of the most important financial statements used by managers to evaluate the success of operations.

Chapter 3 discusses basic financial statements in great detail. The balance sheet and the statement of income are mentioned here only to indicate that the financial information prepared by accounting departments is used by a number of different groups with various interests. These groups may be classified as either external or internal users of financial information.

External Users. These groups are those outside of the business who require accounting and financial information. Suppliers want financial information prior to extending credit to the hospitality operation. Bankers require financial statements prior to lending funds for building, remodeling, or major purchases. Investors and stockholders make decisions to buy, sell, or hold based on information in the financial statements. Various governmental agencies, such as the Internal Revenue Service, also require specific kinds of financial information.

Internal Users. These groups include those inside the hospitality business such as the board of directors, the general manager, departmental managers, and other staff involved in the day-to-day and long-range analysis, planning, and control of the hospitality operation. Hospitality managers require much more detailed information regarding day-to-day operations than is provided by the major financial statements. Exhibit 1.1 lists some of the reports generally prepared by an accounting department for various levels of management. The exhibit identifies the frequency, content, comparisons, recipient, and purpose of each report. In general,

Exhibit 1.1 Management Reports

Report	Frequency	Content	Comparisons	Who Gets It	Purpose
Daily Report of Operations	Daily, on a cumulative basis for the month, the year to date.	Occupancy, average rate, revenue by outlet, and pertinent statistics.	To operating plan for current period and to prior year results.	Top management and supervisors responsible for day to day operation.	Basis for evaluating the current health of the enterprise.
Weekly Forecasts	Weekly.	Volume in covers, occupancy.	Previous periods.	Top management and supervisory personnel.	Staffing and scheduling; promotion.
Summary Report — Flash	Monthly at end of month (prior to monthly financial statement).	Known elements of revenue and direct costs; estimated departmental indirect costs.	To operating plan; to prior year results.	Top management and supervisory personnel responsible for function reported.	Provides immediate information on financial results for rooms, food and beverages, and other.
Cash Flow Analysis	Monthly (and on a revolving 12-month basis.)	Receipts and disbursements by time periods.	With cash flow plan for month and for year to date.	Top management.	Predicts availability of cash for operating needs. Provides information on interim financing requirements.
Labor Productivity Analysis	Daily Weekly Monthly	Dollar cost; manpower hours expended; hours as related to sales and services (covers, rooms occupied, etc.)	To committed hours in the operating plan (standards for amount of work to prior year statistics).	Top management and supervisory personnel.	Labor cost control through informed staffing and scheduling. Helps refine forecasting.
Departmental Analysis	Monthly (early in following month.)	Details on main categories of income; same on expense.	To operating plan (month and year to date) and to prior year.	Top management and supervisors by function (e.g., rooms, each food and beverage outlet, laundry, telephone, other profit centers.	Knowing where business stands, and immediate corrective actions.
Room Rate Analysis	Daily, monthly, year to date.	Actual rates compared to rack rates by rate category or type of room.	To operating plan and to prior year results.	Top management and supervisors of sales and front office operations.	If goal is not being achieved, analysis of strengths and weaknesses is prompted.
Return on Investment	Actual computation, at least twice a year. Computation based on forecast, immediately prior to plan for year ahead.	Earnings as a percentage rate of return on average investment or equity committed.	To plan for operation and to prior periods.	Top management.	If goal is not being achieved, prompt assessment of strengths and weaknesses.
Long-Range Planning	Annually.	5-year projections of revenue and expenses. Operating plan expressed in financial terms.	Prior years.	Top management.	Involves staff in success or failure of enterprise. Injects more realism into plans for property and service modifications.
Exception Reporting	Concurrent with monthly reports and financial statements.	Summary listing of line item variances from predetermined norm.	With operating budgets.	Top management and supervisors responsible for function reported.	Immediate focusing on problem before more detailed statement analysis can be made.
Guest History Analysis	At least semi-annually; quarterly or monthly is recommended.	Historical records of corporate business, travel agencies, group bookings.	With previous reports.	Top management and sales.	Give direction to marketing efforts.
Future Bookings Report	Monthly.	Analysis of reservations and bookings.	With several prior years.	Top management, sales and marketing, department management.	Provides information on changing guest profile. Exposes strong and weak points of facility. Guides (1) sales planning and (2) expansion plans.

Source: *Lodging,* July 1979, pp. 40-41.

the more frequently managers must make decisions, the more frequent will be their need for specific kinds of financial and operational information.

Financial statements and accounting reports which are prepared for external and internal users are the end result of basic accounting activities. In order to fully understand financial statements and accounting reports, it is first necessary to understand how accounting activities transform "raw data" into useful and timely information. All accounting activities flow from events which are created by business transactions.

Business Transactions

Business transactions initiate the accounting process. A business transaction can be defined as the exchange of merchandise, property, or services for cash or a promise to pay. Specific accounts are set up to record the results of business transactions which involve promises to pay.

For example, if a restaurant buys merchandise or supplies on open account, this promise to pay is classified as an *Accounts Payable*. If a guest purchases food and beverage items from the restaurant on open account, the guest's promise to pay is classified as an *Accounts Receivable*. Promises to pay may also involve the use of legal documents. If, in order to purchase certain equipment, a restaurant obtains funds by signing a promissory note, the liability is classified as a *Notes Payable*. If realty (land or buildings) is involved, the liability is classified as a *Mortgage Payable*.

A business transaction creates events which affect two or more bookkeeping accounts in the accounting records. The following examples present very basic business transactions, describe the events created by those transactions, and identify the bookkeeping accounts which are affected by those events.

Example #1

When a guest enjoys a dinner at a restaurant and pays for the meal with cash, the business transaction that occurs is the exchange of food and services for cash. This business transaction creates the following events which affect the restaurant:

1. The cash received increases the assets of the restaurant.

2. A sale is made, thus increasing the sales volume (revenue).

These events affect the following bookkeeping accounts:

1. Cash

2. Food Sales

Example #2

When a guest enjoys a dinner at a restaurant and pays for the meal by charging the amount of the guest check to an open account maintained for him or her by the restaurant (no credit card is involved), the business transaction that occurs is similar to the previous example. However, in this case, food and services are exchanged not for cash, but for a promise to pay. The change in the method of payment does not affect the basic events created by the business transaction:

1. The guest's promise to pay increases the assets of the restaurant.

2. A sale is made, thus increasing the sales volume (revenue).

However, the change in the method of payment does change one of the accounts affected by the events. The promise to pay and the sale affect the following bookkeeping accounts:

1. Accounts Receivable

2. Food Sales

Example #3   When a restaurant buys food provisions on open account from a supplier, the business transaction which occurs is also an exchange of food and services for a promise to pay. However, the events created by this transaction which affect the restaurant are as follows:

1. The increase in food provisions increases the assets of the restaurant.

2. The restaurant's promise to pay increases the liabilities of the restaurant.

The bookkeeping accounts which are affected by these events are as follows:

1. Food Inventory

2. Accounts Payable

Every business transaction affects two or more bookkeeping accounts. This *double-entry system of accounting*, which is prevalent in recording business transactions, takes its name from the fact that equal amounts of debits and credits are entered for each business transaction. If more than two bookkeeping accounts are affected by a transaction, the sum of the debit amounts must be equal to the sum of the credit amounts.

The double-entry system does not relate to addition and subtraction, and should not be confused with the misconception that for every "plus" there must be a "minus." Pluses and minuses do not have any application in the recording of business transactions.

Business transactions are recorded in terms of whether their associated events have an increase or decrease effect on affected business accounts. Increases are not necessarily offset by decreases, or vice versa. One type of business transaction may increase all affected accounts; another type of transaction may decrease all affected accounts; yet another type may produce a combination of increases and decreases.

Most people know that accountants are concerned with debits and credits, which, indeed, play an important role in accounting. To apply debits and credits correctly, however, it is first necessary to learn the different types of accounts and understand the increase/decrease effect of business transactions.

It is a mistaken conclusion that a debit will add and a credit will subtract. Such a conclusion is in error and will make it difficult to comprehend debits and credits when they are presented later.

For the first part of this text, the use of debits and credits will not be addressed to any extent. The foundation for debits and credits is the increase/decrease effect which is based on the types of accounts affected by a particular business transaction. It is more important to understand the effect and content of business transactions than to learn how to record them in an accounting format. This approach enables the student to analyze how a business transaction affects the bookkeeping accounts.

Basic Accounting Activities

A major objective of accounting is to provide financial information that is timely and useful. The definition of accounting depends on whether the emphasis is on the accounting function or the accounting process.

Earlier in this chapter, we learned that the definition of accounting offered by the American Institute of Certified Public Accountants emphasizes the *function* of accounting, "to provide quantitative information, primarily financial in nature, about economic entities that is intended to be useful in making economic decisions."

The traditional definition of accounting emphasizes the *process* of recording, classifying, and summarizing financial information. Recording business transactions refers to the procedure of actually entering the results of transactions in an accounting document called a journal. Classifying refers to the process of assembling the numerous business transactions into related categories. Summarizing refers to the actual process of preparing financial information according to the formats of specific reports or financial statements.

Individuals with little exposure to accounting activities often believe that bookkeeping and accounting are one and the same activity. However, there are many important differences between the two. Bookkeeping is only one part of the overall accounting function. While bookkeepers routinely record and classify business transactions, accountants supervise the work of bookkeepers and also interpret accounting data. Since the demands which are placed upon accountants are much greater than those placed upon bookkeepers, the required training is much more extensive.

Accountants must be able to design accounting systems which will meet the needs and requirements of various kinds of businesses. Before designing an accounting system, the accountant first surveys the transactions of a particular business and also determines how accounting data will be used. After the accounting system has been designed and implemented, the accountant must be able to supervise the activity of the bookkeepers, review their work for accuracy, and report to management and others on the business's activity for the period and its financial position at a given time. Other responsibilities of accountants may include:

- Designing and monitoring internal controls
- Budgeting and forecasting
- Performing cost and feasibility studies

Exhibit 1.2 Responsibilities of Hotel Controllers

Area	Percentage Reporting Responsibility
Payroll	89%
Accounts Receivable	95
Accounts Payable	93
Electronic Data Processing	46
Night Auditors	86
Cashiers	65
Food Controls	54
Purchasing	51
Receiving	51
Storage	36
Security	9

- Preparing tax returns
- Analyzing operations
- Advising management

Exhibit 1.2 summarizes the results of a recent survey of 278 hotel property controllers (not hotel corporation controllers) and reflects their wide range of reported responsibilities.

The Accounting Profession

Accounting is a dynamic and growing profession that must keep pace with computer technology, governmental regulations, and the changing economic and hospitality business environment. Career opportunities exist for accountants in public accounting, private industry, government, and other fields.

A certified public accountant (CPA) is an independent accountant providing services to clients in areas such as accounting, taxes, estate planning, auditing, consulting, and other management advisory services. A principal role of a CPA is the attest function, which involves issuing an opinion, generally called an audit report, on the fairness and reliability of a company's financial statements. The CPA performing the attest function for a particular business must be independent. That is, he or she cannot be an employee of that company.

Branches of Accounting

While accountants may differ in terms of how they classify various accounting activities, most agree that there are distinct, yet overlapping, branches of accounting. These branches of accounting include financial accounting, managerial accounting, cost accounting, tax accounting, auditing, and accounting systems design.

Financial Accounting. This branch of accounting is primarily concerned with recording and accumulating accounting information to be used in the preparation of financial statements for external users. Financial accounting involves the basic accounting processes of recording, classifying, and summarizing business transactions. It also includes accounting for assets, liabilities, equity, revenue, and expenses. The focus of this book is primarily directed toward financial accounting.

Managerial Accounting. This branch of accounting is primarily concerned with recording and accumulating accounting information in order to prepare financial statements and reports for internal users. Managerial accounting provides various management levels of a hospitality organization with detailed information, such as performance reports which compare the actual results of operations with budget plans. Since managerial and financial accounting are closely connected branches of accounting, this text will, at times, address various managerial accounting activities, but only as they relate to the basic functions of financial accounting. Raymond S. Schmidgall's *Hospitality Industry Managerial Accounting*, published by the Educational Institute of the American Hotel & Motel Association, offers interested readers a detailed approach to managerial aspects of accounting.[2]

Cost Accounting. This branch of accounting relates to the recording, classification, allocation, and reporting of current and prospective costs. Cost accountants determine costs in relation to products and services offered by a hospitality business and in relation to the operation of individual departments within the property. One of the primary purposes of cost accounting is to assist management in controlling operations.

Tax Accounting. This branch of accounting relates to the preparation and filing of tax forms required by various governmental agencies. A significant part of the tax accountant's work involves tax planning to minimize the amount of taxes which must be paid by a business. Although the emphasis of tax accounting lies in minimizing income tax payments at the federal, state, and local levels, this branch of accounting also involves other areas such as sales, excise, payroll, and property taxes.

Auditing. This branch of accounting is most often associated with the independent, external financial audit. As mentioned previously, financial audits may be conducted only by independent certified public accountants. The financial audit of a hospitality operation renders an opinion of the property's financial statements based upon a review of (a) the accounting records (vouchers, invoices, canceled checks, bank statements, journals, etc.), (b) the underlying internal control system of the property, and (c) the financial statements themselves. Hospitality operations are increasingly employing accountants as internal auditors to review and evaluate the property's internal control systems. Large hospitality firms may have a full staff of internal auditors who assist the managers of individual properties to be more effective in controlling their day-to-day operations.

Accounting Systems Design. This branch of accounting focuses primarily on the information system of a hospitality organization. This information system includes not only accounting, but other areas as well, such as reservations. As more and more hospitality operations become computerized, accounting systems experts will necessarily become electronic data processing specialists, such as programmers and systems analysts.

These branches of accounting clearly indicate that the accounting profession covers a broad range of activities. An in-depth analysis of each branch of accounting is beyond the scope of this text. Our primary focus will be on the basic activities involved in financial accounting.

Professional Organizations

The practice of any profession requires a certain level of specialized education and training. Also, a profession requires its members to conform to certain standards of performance and to abide by a code of conduct. Various accounting organizations and accounting policy-making boards have developed standards for professionals in the accounting field.

American Institute of Certified Public Accountants (AICPA). This professional organization is the authoritative body for certified public accountants. Its members must have a CPA certificate. This certificate is awarded to individuals on the basis of certain educational requirements and successfully passing a uniform national CPA examination. The examination is a rigorous two-and-one-half-day comprehensive series of tests covering accounting problems, accounting theory, auditing, and business law.

AICPA is the primary source of statements on auditing standards. Because its members certify the fairness of financial statements, AICPA exerts a powerful influence on accounting practices.

Based on the accounting principles and standards developed by AICPA, two national accounting firms serving the hospitality industry and various hospitality trade associations have been instrumental in standardizing reporting procedures in the hospitality industry: Pannell Kerr Forster and Laventhol & Horwath collect and publish statistical data on hotels, restaurants, and private clubs.

Exhibits 1.3 and 1.4 graphically illustrate what happens to the average revenue dollar in the lodging and food service industries. Exhibit 1.5 also indicates the kind of statistical data collected and published by national accounting firms. These kinds of industry reports may serve as general standards against which to compare the results of individual operations. These reports are possible only because of an industry-wide adoption of generally accepted accounting principles and standardized reporting procedures.

Financial Accounting Standards Board (FASB). In 1959, AICPA established the Accounting Principles Board (APB) whose primary purpose was to review and refine generally accepted accounting principles. In 1973, the Financial Accounting Standards Board replaced APB but retained the same general purpose and function. FASB is an independent, non-governmental body that develops and issues statements of financial accounting standards.

International Association of Hospitality Accountants (IAHA). This association was organized in 1953 and today is headquartered in Austin, Texas. The constitution of the organization states that its purpose is "to do any and all things to further enhance and develop the profession of accounting in the following industries: hotels, motels, clubs, restaurants,

Exhibit 1.3 The U.S. Lodging Industry Dollar

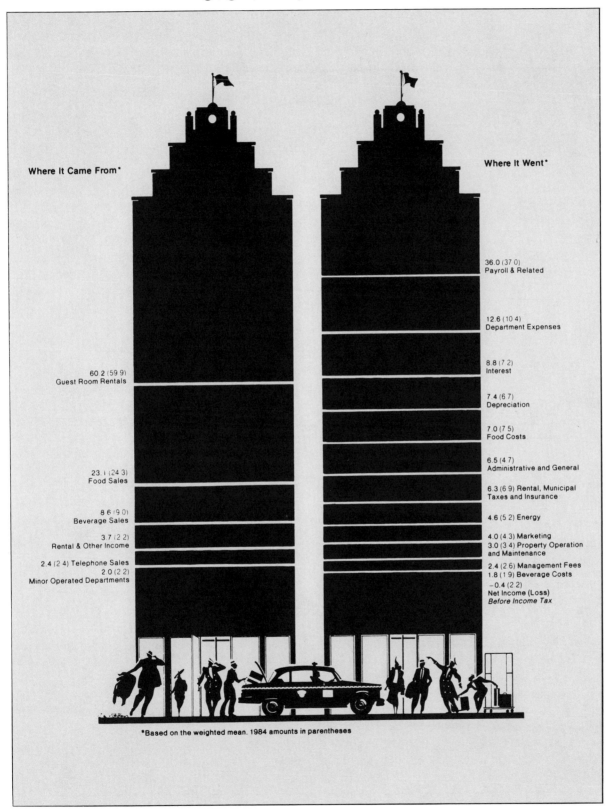

Where It Came From*

Where It Went*

60.2 (59 9)
Guest Room Rentals

23.1 (24 3)
Food Sales

8 6 (9 0)
Beverage Sales

3.7 (2 2)
Rental & Other Income

2.4 (2 4) Telephone Sales
2.0 (2 2)
Minor Operated Departments

36.0 (37 0)
Payroll & Related

12.6 (10 4)
Department Expenses

8.8 (7 2)
Interest

7.4 (6 7)
Depreciation

7.0 (7 5)
Food Costs

6.5 (4 7)
Administrative and General

6.3 (6 9) Rental, Municipal
Taxes and Insurance

4.6 (5 2) Energy

4.0 (4 3) Marketing
3.0 (3 4) Property Operation
and Maintenance

2.4 (2 6) Management Fees
1.8 (1 9) Beverage Costs
−0.4 (2 2)
Net Income (Loss)
Before Income Tax

*Based on the weighted mean. 1984 amounts in parentheses

Source: Laventhol & Horwath, *U.S. Lodging Industry*, 54th Annual Report on Hotel and Motor Hotel Operations, 1986, p. 15.

Exhibit 1.4 The Restaurant Industry Dollar

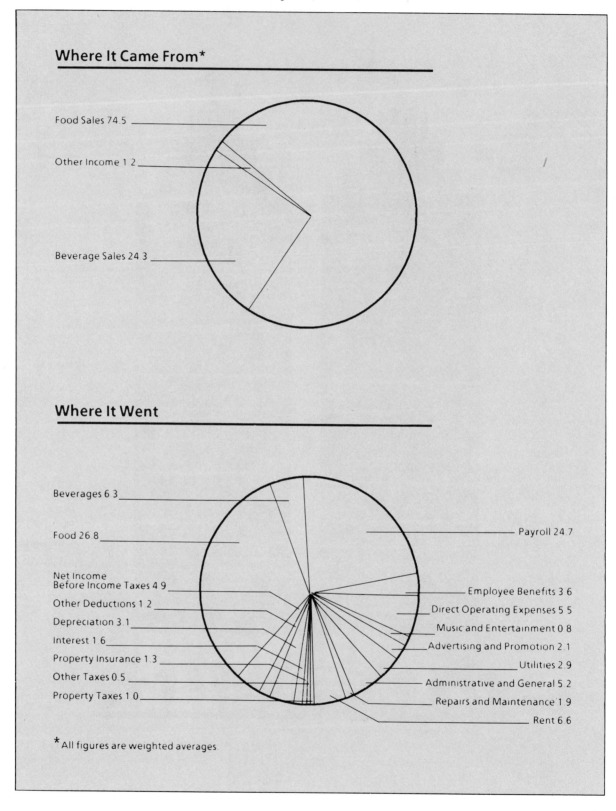

Where It Came From*

Food Sales 74.5

Other Income 1.2

Beverage Sales 24.3

Where It Went

Beverages 6.3

Food 26.8

Net Income
Before Income Taxes 4.9

Other Deductions 1.2

Depreciation 3.1

Interest 1.6

Property Insurance 1.3

Other Taxes 0.5

Property Taxes 1.0

Payroll 24.7

Employee Benefits 3.6

Direct Operating Expenses 5.5

Music and Entertainment 0.8

Advertising and Promotion 2.1

Utilities 2.9

Administrative and General 5.2

Repairs and Maintenance 1.9

Rent 6.6

*All figures are weighted averages.

Source: National Restaurant Association and Laventhol & Horwath, *Restaurant Industry Operations Report '86*, Chart B-1, p. 53.

Exhibit 1.5 Monthly Occupancy Rates

	1st Quarter 1986	Average for Year 1985	Dec.	Nov.	Oct.	Sept.	Aug.	July	June	May	April	Mar.	Feb.	Jan.
							1985							
Albuquerque	54 %	66 %	41 %	54 %	79 %	N/A	74 %	73 %	75 %	73 %	73 %	69 %	63 %	58 %
Atlanta	63	64	44	60	69	62	62	67	70	67	68	73	62	63
Austin	66	67	42	62	65	60	69	67	74	75	80	78	71	60
Baton Rouge	51	51	38	54	56	47	56	54	56	57	52	50	50	44
Boston	55	69	48	69	90	79	77	67	79	75	74	62	51	50
Chattanooga	53	63	44	50	67	64	75	80	71	60	66	63	55	50
Chicago	57	68	52	72	78	69	71	70	79	75	72	68	57	47
Colorado Springs	38	58	N/A	44	58	64	79	70	70	65	49	47	47	41
Corpus Christi	50	55	31	39	51	49	75	74	75	60	58	60	48	40
Dallas/Fort Worth	60	64	44	57	69	54	63	64	75	67	62	69	65	64
Denver	52	58	39	49	56	59	74	66	66	58	57	62	55	51
Fort Lauderdale	83	67	69	62	52	44	53	48	50	58	80	92	86	71
Houston	43	46	34	43	48	42	45	45	47	55	49	56	46	46
Knoxville	58	57	40	54	70	62	65	66	60	55	65	60	51	46
Los Angeles	69	67	53	64	70	66	72	71	69	67	68	76	72	63
Memphis	58	69	49	66	70	67	76	80	85	73	70	68	60	55
Miami	80	65	60	64	55	51	54	60	52	61	66	78	79	73
Nashville	60	70	44	59	77	73	84	84	86	74	69	65	55	52
New Orleans	60	52	41	61	56	49	50	42	54	54	50	57	60	41
New York City	66	72	69	78	83	74	72	63	73	77	73	70	68	57
Orlando Area:														
Disney/Kissimmee	83	72	56	59	60	51	85	89	86	78	91	87	71	46
International Drive	80	66	48	50	57	44	66	77	73	67	86	87	73	62
City of Orlando	60	57	38	38	39	37	55	68	60	46	69	82	71	51
Palm Beach	88	66	59	66	57	53	55	54	61	63	68	89	88	71
Philadelphia	51	57	41	59	73	63	56	64	65	69	61	57	50	50
Phoenix	81	67	55	65	68	58	46	52	68	68	74	89	86	70
San Antonio	63	67	44	57	70	59	77	71	74	70	74	72	71	58
San Francisco	60	68	46	67	83	74	81	77	78	75	65	67	59	56
Scottsdale	74	58	47	51	67	46	34	31	47	56	59	82	81	62
Tampa Bay	82	65	47	55	60	48	61	76	69	74	81	94	78	51
Tucson	82	68	56	65	71	55	64	58	62	63	72	86	92	75
Washington, D.C.	N/A	70	41	68	81	67	73	71	76	82	81	73	65	55
Alabama	62	65	46	63	66	63	75	72	71	67	69	68	63	59
Arizona	78	64	52	60	66	54	48	48	60	64	69	86	84	66
Colorado	52	58	N/A	46	52	58	73	65	63	56	54	63	56	53
Hawaii	86	76	67	75	74	67	81	75	66	67	73	87	92	84
Illinois	56	57	41	50	64	60	71	60	69	63	64	63	57	57
Louisiana	55	52	40	57	55	50	53	48	56	56	51	55	60	42
Mississippi	49	58	38	51	57	60	63	68	66	60	62	60	49	42
New Mexico	49	63	41	50	74	63	75	71	70	68	63	67	62	56
New York State	63	70	64	73	81	73	72	64	71	75	71	68	65	56
North Carolina	59	64	44	60	75	66	67	66	66	68	68	65	61	55
Northern California	60	69	47	65	77	71	79	75	77	76	70	73	67	64
South Carolina	56	64	38	55	70	68	75	69	77	73	79	73	58	49
Tennessee	57	65	44	58	73	67	78	79	78	66	66	63	54	50
Texas	54	58	40	52	61	51	61	59	65	63	60	65	59	55
Virginia	N/A	62	42	56	71	62	65	69	72	71	67	57	48	41
Wyoming/ Montana/Nebraska	49	58	36	46	58	64	77	76	69	57	56	54	62	45
Utah	60	57	47	44	50	60	69	59	59	49	58	69	63	56
Nationwide Averages*	62 %	63 %	47 %	58 %	66 %	59 %	67 %	66 %	68 %	66 %	67 %	70 %	64 %	55 %

* Estimated occupancies for nation's total hotel-motel industry.

Source: Pannell Kerr Forster, *Trends in the Hotel Industry*, USA Edition, 1986, Figure No. 9, p. 36.

and other related industries." Membership in this association includes financial managers of hotels, motels, clubs, restaurants, and condominium associations; members of professional organizations; educators; and students who are involved with the hospitality industry. IAHA's Certified Hospitality Accountant Executive Program offers an industry-recognized certification (CHAE) for hospitality financial managers.

American Hotel & Motel Association (AH&MA). This organization is the national trade association representing the lodging industry. A trade association is an organization of business firms with similar interests organized to foster cooperative action in advancing, by all lawful means, the common purpose of its members, and to promote activities designated to enable the industry to be conducted with the greatest economy and efficiency.

AH&MA is a federation of state associations and is governed by a Board of Directors comprising representatives from each member association. With headquarters in New York City, AH&MA pursues a threefold mission:

- To foster, through positive leadership, conditions in which the lodging industry will be free to operate throughout the world in an open market and will be profitable.

- To promote high quality hospitality services which meet the needs and expectations of the traveling public.

- To provide challenging and rewarding opportunities for people entering and working in the lodging industry through education.

Educational Institute of AH&MA. This organization is a non-profit educational foundation located on the campus of Michigan State University in East Lansing, Michigan. The Educational Institute was established in 1952 to provide essential educational and training resources for the expanding hospitality industry. The stated mission of the Educational Institute is to increase the professionalism of the industry by providing educational opportunities, materials, research, and supportive services for those who are now or may in the future be employed in the hospitality industry.

The Educational Institute develops and produces textbooks and courses, how-to manuals, seminars, instructional videotapes, and other educational materials. The Institute also provides professional certifications which include the Certified Rooms Division Executive (CRDE), Certified Food and Beverage Executive (CFBE), Certified Hospitality Housekeeping Executive (CHHE), Certified Engineering Operations Executive (CEOE), and the prestigious Certified Hotel Administrator (CHA).

The Institute also publishes the *Uniform System of Accounts and Expense Dictionary for Small Hotels, Motels, and Motor Hotels.*[3] Chapter 4 will discuss the importance of this publication in great detail.

National Restaurant Association (NRA). Headquartered in Washington, D.C., NRA is the food service industry's leading trade association with members representing more than 100,000 food service outlets. NRA provides its members with a wide range of programs covering such areas as education, research, communications, and government relations. NRA is governed by an elected Board of Directors representing all types of food service establishments from many areas of the United States and from a dozen foreign countries. NRA publishes the *Uniform System of Accounts for Restaurants.*[4]

Generally Accepted Accounting Principles

For almost every profession there are guidelines and rules to ensure that members carry out their responsibilities in accordance with accepted quality standards. Professional accounting standards have evolved from commonly adopted practices and in response to changes in the business environment. These accounting standards are known within the profession as generally accepted accounting principles, and are commonly referred to by the acronym GAAP. They have received substantial authoritative support and approval from professional accounting associations such as AICPA and IAHA and also from governmental agencies such as the Securities and Exchange Commission.

The application of these generally accepted accounting principles ensures that consistent accounting procedures are followed in recording the events created by business transactions and in preparing financial statements. This consistency makes it possible for internal and external users of financial statements to make reasonable judgments regarding the overall financial condition of a business and the success of business operations from period to period.

Unit of Measurement

Since the value exchanged in a business transaction is expressed in monetary terms, the prevailing monetary unit is used to record the results of business transactions. For businesses in the United States, the common unit of measurement is the U.S. dollar.

A common unit of measurement permits the users of accounting data to make meaningful comparisons between current and past business transactions. Imagine the difficulties that would arise if the accounting records of a hospitality operation recorded food purchases in terms of the British pound and food sales in terms of the U.S. dollar!

Historical Cost

The principle of historical cost states that the value of merchandise or services obtained through business transactions should be recorded in terms of actual costs, not current market values.

For example, assume that a truck having a market value of $15,000 is purchased from a distressed seller for $12,800. The amount recorded as the cost of the truck is $12,800. As long as the truck is owned, the value (cost) shown in the accounting records and on the financial statements will be $12,800. Accumulated depreciation on property and equipment will be discussed in a later chapter.

Going-Concern

The principle of going-concern, also known as continuity of the business unit, states that financial statements should be prepared under the assumption that the business will continue indefinitely and thus carry out its commitments. Normally, a business is assumed to be a going concern unless there is objective evidence to the contrary.

The going-concern assumption can be used to defend the use of historical costs in the presentation of financial statements. Since there is no evidence of liquidation of the business in the near future, the use of liquidating or market values would not be appropriate unless the principle of conservatism applies.

Conservatism

The principle of conservatism serves to guide the decisions of accountants in areas which involve estimates and other areas which may call for professional judgment. However, it is important to stress that this principle is applied only when there is uncertainty in reporting factual results of business transactions.

FASB states that assets and income should be fairly presented and not overstated. This does not in any way suggest that income or assets should be deliberately understated. The purpose of the principle of conservatism is to provide the accountant with a practical alternative for situations which involve doubt. When doubt is involved, the solution or method that will not overstate assets or income should be selected.

For example, if a hotel is the plaintiff in a lawsuit and its legal counsel indicates that the case will be won and estimates the amount which may be awarded to the hotel, the amount is not recorded until a judgment is rendered.

Other examples of the principle of conservatism involve the valuation of inventories, marketable securities, and accounts receivable. Determining the net realizable value of these items requires professional judgment. Following the principle of conservatism, inventories and marketable securities are presented in the financial statements at either cost or market value, whichever is lower. Accounts receivable are presented along with an offsetting account (contra account) that provides for accounts which are judged to be uncollectible:

Accounts Receivable	$255,000
Less: Allowance for Doubtful Accounts	5,000
Accounts Receivable (Net)	$250,000

Objectivity

The principle of objectivity states that all business transactions must be supported by objective evidence proving that the transactions did in fact occur. Obtaining objective evidence is not always a simple matter. For example, a canceled check serves as objective evidence that cash was paid. However, it is not evidence of the reason for which the check was issued. An invoice or other form of independent evidence is necessary to prove the reason for the expenditure.

When independent evidence is not available to document the results of a business transaction, estimates must be made. In these cases, the choice of the best estimate should be guided by the principle of objectivity. Consider the case of the owner of a restaurant who contributes equipment, purchased several years before for personal use, to the business in exchange for 100 shares of company stock. Let's further assume that there is no known market value of the restaurant corporation's stock. Ambiguity arises as the owner believes that the equipment is worth $1,200, while the catalog used by the owner when the equipment was purchased several years ago shows the cost to have been $1,400, and an appraiser estimates the current value of the equipment at $850. In this case, the principle of objectivity determines the amount to record. The most objective estimate of the current value of the equipment is the appraiser's estimate of $850.

Time Period

This generally accepted accounting principle, also known as the *periodicity assumption*, recognizes that users of financial statements need timely information for decision-making purposes. Therefore, accountants are charged with preparing more than just annual financial statements.

The accounting departments of many hospitality operations prepare financial statements not only on an annual basis, but quarterly and monthly as well. Financial statements which are prepared during the business year are referred to as *interim financial statements*. Because accountants may not have all the information at hand in order to complete accurate interim financial statements, they must often proceed on the basis of assumptions and make estimates based on their professional judgment.

Realization

The realization principle states that revenue resulting from business transactions should be recorded only when a sale has been made *and* earned.

The simplest example of the principle of realization involves a customer paying cash for services rendered. When a hotel receives cash from a guest served in the dining room, a sale has been made *and* earned. The results of the transaction are recorded in the proper accounts.

What about the guest served in the dining room who charges the bill to an open account maintained by the hotel? In this case, even though cash is not received at the time of performance, a sale has been made *and* earned. The revenue and the account receivable are recorded at the time of the sale.

However, according to the principle of realization, if a hotel receives cash for services which have not yet been earned, then the transaction cannot be classified as a sale. For example, if a hotel receives an advance deposit of $500 for a wedding banquet which is to be held two months later, the cash received must be recorded—but the event cannot be classified as a sale. This is because the business has not yet earned the revenue; services have not been performed or delivered. In this case, receiving cash creates a liability account called Unearned Revenue. The full amount of the advance deposit is recorded in this account.

Matching

The matching principle states that all expenses must be recorded in the same accounting period as the revenue which they helped to generate. When expenses are matched with the revenue they helped to produce, external and internal users of financial statements and reports are able to make better judgments regarding the financial position and operating performance of the hospitality business. There are two accounting methods for determining when to record the results of a business transaction: cash accounting and accrual accounting.

Cash Accounting. The cash accounting method records the results of business transactions only when cash is received or paid out. Small businesses usually follow cash accounting procedures in their day-to-day bookkeeping activities. However, financial statements which are prepared solely on a cash accounting basis may not necessarily comply with generally accepted accounting principles. If expenses are recorded on the basis of cash disbursements, then expenses will not necessarily match the revenue which they helped to generate. This may occur for any number of reasons.

For example, let's assume that each month begins a new accounting period for a particular restaurant. During each month, the restaurant follows the principle of realization and records revenue only as sales are made and earned. The restaurant also records expenses only as cash payments (which include payments by check) are made to various suppliers and vendors. This cash accounting method will not ensure that expenses will match the revenue generated during the month because many expenses will be incurred during each month but not paid until the following month. These expenses include utility bills, laundry bills, and telephone bills which the restaurant may not even receive until the first week of the following month.

The Internal Revenue Service generally will accept financial statements prepared on a cash accounting basis only if the business does not sell inventory products and meets other criteria. Since food and beverage operations sell inventory products, these establishments must use the accrual method.

Accrual Accounting. In order to conform to the matching principle, most hospitality operations use the accrual method of accounting. The accrual accounting method adjusts the accounting records by recording expenses which are incurred during an accounting period but which (for any number of reasons) are not actually paid until the following period. Once the adjusting entries have been recorded, financial statements and reports for the accounting period will provide a reasonable basis for evaluating the financial position and operating performance of the hospitality business.

Materiality

The generally accepted accounting principle of materiality states that material events must be accounted for according to accounting rules; however, insignificant events may be treated in an expeditious manner. Decisions concerning the materiality of events vary. Most of these decisions call for professional judgment on the part of the accountant.

In general, an event (or information) is material depending on its magnitude and the surrounding circumstances. The general criterion is based on whether in the judgment of a reasonable person, that person would be affected by its omission. Information is material if it can make a difference in the decision process of a reasonable user of the financial statements. For example, a pending lawsuit for $150 against a million-dollar corporation would not be considered a material item.

Consistency

There are several accounting methods by which to determine certain values that are used as accounting data. For example, there are several methods for determining inventory values and for depreciating fixed assets. The choice of which accounting method to use is the responsibility of high-level management officials of the hospitality operation.

The generally accepted accounting principle of consistency states that once an accounting method has been adopted, it should be consistently followed from period to period. In order for accounting information to be comparable, there must be a consistent application of accounting methods and principles. When circumstances warrant a change in the method of accounting for a specific kind of transaction, the change must be reported along with an explanation of how this change affects other items shown on the operation's financial statements.

Full Disclosure

The generally accepted accounting principle of full disclosure states that the financial statements of a hospitality operation should be accompanied by explanatory notes. These notes should describe all significant accounting policies adopted by the operation and should also report all

Exhibit 1.6 Types of Disclosure and Examples

Type of Disclosure	Example
Accounting methods used	Straight-line method of depreciation
Change in the accounting methods	A change from depreciating a fixed asset using the straight-line method to using the double declining balance method
Contingent liability	A lawsuit against the company for alleged failure to provide adequate security for a guest who suffered personal injury
Events occurring subsequent to the financial statement date	A fire destroys significant uninsured assets of the hotel company one week after the end of the year
Unusual and nonrecurring items	A hotel firm in Michigan suffers significant losses due to an earthquake

significant conditions or events which materially affect the interpretation of information presented in the financial statements.

Commonly required disclosures include, but are not limited to, policies regarding the accounting method used to depreciate fixed assets and the methods used to determine the value of inventory and marketable securities. Commonly disclosed items which affect the interpretation of information reported in financial statements include, but are not limited to, changes in accounting methods, extraordinary items of income or expense, and significant long-term commitments. Exhibit 1.6 presents examples of the types of disclosures which may be found in notes accompanying the financial statements of a hospitality property.

Accounting Income vs. Taxable Income

The Treasury Department is an executive branch of the United States Government charged with responsibility in tax matters. The Internal Revenue Service (IRS) is a branch of the Treasury Department assigned to the collection of income taxes and enforcement of tax law. The Internal Revenue Code (IRC) is a codification of income tax statutes and other federal tax laws.

Not all generally accepted accounting principles are used in determining the amount of income tax that a business must pay. Differences arise because the objectives of financial accounting under generally accepted accounting principles are not the same as the objectives which may lie behind the IRC.

The objectives of financial accounting are:

- To provide accurate, timely, and relevant information to help users of financial information make economic, financial, and operational decisions regarding the business.

- To satisfy the common interests of the many users of financial statements, rather than satisfying the specific interests of any single group.

- To select from various accounting alternatives those methods which will fairly present the financial condition of the business and the results of business operations.

These objectives focus solely on the interests and needs of internal and external users of financial information. The generally accepted accounting principles do not attempt to influence business transactions. The overall objective is to ensure that the results of business transactions are fairly presented in the financial statements of a business.

The objectives of the IRC, on the other hand, are guided by large-scale political, economic, and social concerns. Some of the major objectives of the IRC could be:

- To influence change in the economy.

- To promote policies that are in the public interest.

- To achieve social objectives.

These political, economic, and social objectives can powerfully influence business activities. For example, governmental economic policy may lower taxes during an economic recession in an attempt to increase consumer demand for products and services, which eventually may increase production and decrease unemployment. Or, governmental economic policy may raise taxes during a period of high inflation in an attempt to decrease consumer spending and eventually reduce spiraling prices. Political policy may direct legislators to grant tax credits during an energy crisis in an attempt to stimulate purchases of energy-saving equipment. Also, social policy may legislate tax incentives for private businesses to hire the elderly, the handicapped, or individuals from disadvantaged social groups.

An important practical result of the difference in objectives is that the method of accounting for revenue and expenses under generally accepted accounting principles differs from procedures dictated by income tax law. Consequently, the income shown on a business's financial statements *(income before income taxes)* may not be the same figure which appears as *taxable income* on the business's income tax return.

For example, some revenue items, such as interest earned on certain state or municipal bonds, are included on financial statements as income before income taxes, but are excluded on tax returns as part of the taxable income figure. The end result is that the amount of income before income taxes reported on a business's financial statements will differ from the amount of taxable income reported on the business's income tax return.

Some expense items, such as goodwill, are not deductible in the same way for financial accounting purposes as they are for income tax purposes. Goodwill is an accounting term which may apply to situations in which businesses are purchased. Businesses own both tangible and intangible assets. Tangible assets include cash, marketable securities, inventory, and other items which are reported on the business's financial statements. Businesses may own certain intangible assets which do not appear anywhere on financial statements. Such unrecorded intangible assets might include the knowledge, skill, and teamwork of those employed by the company, as well as the company's name, reputation, location, and customer loyalty. Although these intangible assets might not appear on financial statements, they are clearly assets of the business.

When a business is purchased, any consideration paid for goodwill must be separately stated and recorded. The computation of goodwill is technical and can be complex. The following example presents a simplified illustration of how goodwill may be calculated:

Price to acquire business		$300,000
Value of items acquired:		
Land and Buildings	150,000	
Furniture and Equipment	40,000	
Inventories	10,000	
Other Assets	5,000	205,000
Difference		$ 95,000
Payment to seller for no-compete agreement		30,000
Goodwill portion		$ 65,000

Note that goodwill is the excess paid for the assets of an acquired business over the fair market value of its assets.

Under generally accepted accounting principles, the amount paid for goodwill is proportionately allocated to expense (amortized) over a specified number of years. However, under the Internal Revenue Code, the amount paid for goodwill is not considered to be a business operating expense and, therefore, is not deductible until the business is sold. The end result of this difference in accounting for goodwill is that the amount of income before income taxes that is reported on a business's financial statements will be less than the amount of taxable income reported on the business's income tax return.

These examples illustrate only a few of the differences between generally accepted accounting principles and accounting procedures dictated by income tax law. It is not necessary to keep one set of books for financial reporting purposes and another set for income tax reporting purposes. In practice, the financial information from accounting records is transferred to an accounting worksheet and the information is adapted to conform to procedures dictated by income tax law.

The important point is that generally accepted accounting principles prevail in the reporting of financial information to management, stockholders, investors, creditors, and financial institutions.

Use of Dollar Signs, Commas, and Zeros

Dollar signs are not used in journals or ledgers. Some accountants use dollar signs in the trial balance, but this is not necessary. The use of dollar signs is required in financial statements or other published financial information.

While dollar signs are required in financial statements, there are no set rules for where or when they should appear. Some accountants limit the use of the dollar sign to the first number of the financial statement, others put a dollar sign by the first number and final total, and some accountants place a dollar sign by each subtotal or other amount shown below an underline.

Commas and periods are not used on columnar paper. However, they are required if unruled paper is used.

If columnar paper is used, amounts ending in "00" cents may be entered with a "-" or "00" in the cents column.

Notes

1. Statements of the Accounting Principles Board, No. 4, "Basic Concepts and Accounting Principles Underlying Financial Statements of Business Enterprises" (New York: American Institute of Certified Public Accountants, 1970), par. 40.

2. Raymond S. Schmidgall, *Hospitality Industry Managerial Accounting* (East Lansing, Mich.: Educational Institute of the American Hotel & Motel Association, 1986).

3. *Uniform System of Accounts and Expense Dictionary for Small Hotels, Motels, and Motor Hotels*, 4th ed. (East Lansing, Mich.: Educational Institute of the American Hotel & Motel Association, 1987).

4. *Uniform System of Accounts for Restaurants* (Washington, D.C.: National Restaurant Association, 1983).

Discussion Questions

1. What is the fundamental purpose of accounting?

2. What are some examples of external and internal users of financial statements?

3. What is the definition of a business transaction?

4. What is the definition of accounting based on its function?

5. What is the difference between accounting and bookkeeping?

6. How is financial accounting different from managerial accounting?

7. How do generally accepted accounting principles serve the accounting profession?

8. What are the eleven generally accepted accounting principles presented in this chapter? Identify and describe them.

9. Why is the income figure shown on a business's financial statements (income before income taxes) not necessarily the same figure that is reported as taxable income on the business's income tax return?

Problems

Problem 1.1
A lodging operation purchases a parcel of land with cash. What bookkeeping accounts are affected?

Problem 1.2
A restaurant purchases land and buildings with a cash down payment and the balance financed by a mortgage. What bookkeeping accounts are affected?

Problem 1.3
Match the following situations with the accounting principle which best applies. In some cases, more than one principle may apply.

A. Unit of Measurement   G. Realization

B. Historical Cost   H. Matching

C. Going-Concern   I. Materiality

D. Conservatism   J. Consistency

E. Objectivity   K. Full Disclosure

F. Time Period

1. A large hotel corporation is preparing its year-end financial statements. Management has informed the certified public accountant that in two months it will begin closing 15 of its hotel properties. The accountant will provide information of this future event on the current year-end financial statements because of the _____ principle and the _____ principle.

2. A hotel purchases a van for $5,000 from a distressed rental agency. Due to the _____ principle, it is recorded at $5,000, even though the hotel could resell it for $6,500.

3. A motel receives an advance deposit of $150 for reserving guestrooms and meeting room space. This transaction cannot be classified as a sale because of the _____ principle.

4. A resort hotel has used the straight-line method to depreciate its recreation equipment. This year it decides to use another type of depreciation method on these same assets. This violates the _____ principle.

5. A medium-size hotel with an extensive food and beverage operation records business transactions on a cash accounting basis. This violates the _____ principle.

2
Business Organization

The lodging industry was traditionally composed of properties operated by individual owners called proprietors. Since the average hotel was small, a sole proprietor (or a partnership of two or more owners) was able to own and manage the operation in many cases. In the last 30 years, however, properties have increased in size and more and more hotels and motels are owned or franchised by corporations. In some cases, independent management firms operate the property for absentee owners or at the direction of corporate executives.

For those with managerial, executive, and ownership aspirations, the hospitality industry ranks high in opportunity among all American businesses. The modern hotel represents a sophisticated array of management, financial, and operating systems. Students and entrepreneurs interested in this field are concerned with answers to such questions as:

1. What factors should be considered before starting or buying a business?

2. How can a business protect itself against casualty losses and legal claims resulting from its activities?

3. Which form of business organization is best for a given situation?

4. Why is it important for a business to design a management information system?

5. What factors determine whether a hotel department is categorized as a revenue or support center?

This chapter introduces basic entrepreneurial decisions faced by businesspersons starting a hospitality operation. The impact of choosing one form of business organization over another is weighed and compared for each case. Important aspects of the financial information systems used by lodging operations are also discussed in some detail.

To build the foundation for later chapters, the equity structure and related bookkeeping accounts are considered for each of the three forms of business organization. Introducing this topic at an early stage makes it easier to understand the similarities and differences among corporate, partnership, and proprietorship accounting.

Basic Business Considerations

Starting a business can be a complex and difficult undertaking. A great deal of persistence and diligence is needed, as well as significant investments of time and capital. Before starting or purchasing a business, one needs to carefully consider and resolve many questions. Omitting even the simplest item from consideration may cause great complications later.

Business Checklist

The federal government and many states publish guides designed to help the beginning business. For example, the Michigan Department of Commerce publication *Guide to Starting a Business in Michigan* contains general information as well as information specific to Michigan. It includes such topics as establishing a basic business plan; securing adequate financial support; complying with federal, state, and local tax obligations; and obtaining necessary licenses and permits.

For entrepreneurs starting a business, the preparation of a checklist helps to arrange in an orderly fashion those items requiring research and action. A thorough checklist can form the basis for discussing business plans with an attorney, accountant, banker, or insurance agent. Exhibit 2.1 is a checklist from *Guide to Starting a Business in Michigan*, while Exhibit 2.2 is a more in-depth business plan from the same publication.

No one text or individual can provide all of the specific assistance needed in starting a business. A developing business should make full use of qualified and expert assistance. The cost of such advice is small compared to the potential benefits and substantial risks involved.

Business Licenses

Before starting any business, an entrepreneur needs to know about the particular local, state, and federal requirements for that type of business. While states and municipalities have their own specific requirements for businesses, it is possible to make general statements about the types of basic licenses, permits, and registrations most new businesses require.

Local. It may be necessary to obtain a business license from the city, town, or county in which the business is located. In addition, the business must comply with applicable zoning laws and building codes.

State. Unless the business is specifically exempt, most state governments require the business to file for a "sales and use tax" number associated with a sales tax permit. Particular types of businesses (for instance, liquor stores, barber shops, real estate agencies, restaurants, and hotels) may require certain additional licenses which are granted by the state.

Sometimes, a business operates under a name which is different from the legal name of its corporation or owner. In this case, the company's business name may require registration under a state's "fictitious name" statute.

Federal. For new businesses, the Internal Revenue Service (IRS) provides the "Going into Business Kit." This kit is free and is available at any IRS office. It contains forms and other information about federal requirements affecting businesses.

If a business will have one or more employees, it must file a request form with the IRS in order to receive an Employer Identification Number

Exhibit 2.1   Checklist for Starting a Business

This checklist is designed to be used as "helpful hints" for beginning businesses. Frequently, when the decision to start a business moves from an idea to reality, everything seems to demand immediate attention. Important steps may be overlooked. Completing the essential steps included in the checklist will increase the efficiency and organization of a new business.

1. **Personal Assessment**

   _____ Motivation and energy. Willingness to put in long hours with an unpredictable financial return.

   _____ Business experience, background and training for the operation.

   _____ Leadership and organizational abilities. Willingness to assume decision-making responsibilities.

   _____ Interest in working with many different types of people.

2. **Planning**

   _____ Determine and define the products or service to be provided.

   _____ Develop a business plan.

   _____ Develop a financial plan.

   _____ Develop a marketing and/or promotion plan.

3. **Establishment**

   _____ Secure financing.

   _____ Contact the Office of the Michigan Business Ombudsman and/or federal, state and local agencies for regulatory information and permit and license applications.

   _____ Review federal, state and local tax laws.

   _____ Obtain management assistance from resource organizations such as Small Business Centers (SBC), Small Business Development Centers (SBDC) and/or Service Corps of Retired Executives (SCORE).

   _____ Get necessary professional advice and assistance from attorneys and accountants.

   _____ Complete all forms and pay all fees.

4. **Implementation**

   _____ Register the business name.

   _____ Obtain adequate insurance coverage.

   _____ Hire and train employees.

   _____ Initiate marketing plan.

Source: *Guide to Starting a Business in Michigan*, Michigan Department of Commerce, p. iv.

Exhibit 2.2 Business Plan

One of the most important steps in starting a business is the development of a business plan. Not only will the plan provide much needed direction to help guide the business owner, it will also serve as an essential introduction to the business for financial investors and others who must be informed about its operation and convinced of its prospects. A business plan should always be tailored to the specific circumstances of the business, emphasizing the strengths of the venture and addressing the problems.

1. **Cover Sheet**

    Name of business, address and telephone number, and the name(s) of principal(s).

2. **Statement of Purpose**

    A summary of the business covering at least the following items: business concept; product information; current stage of business (start-up, developing or existing); and anticipated financial results and other benefits.

3. **Table of Contents**

4. **The Business**

    a. Description of business: What product or service will you provide?

    b. Historical development: List the name, date of formation, legal structure, subsidiaries and degrees of ownership of your business.

    c. Product/service lines: What is the relative importance of each product/service? Include sales projections if possible.

    d. Market segment: Who will buy your product?

    e. Competition: Describe competing companies and how your business compares.

    f. Location: Where will you locate; why is it the best location?

    g. Marketing: What marketing methods will you use?

5. **Management**

    a. Business format: Is your business a proprietorship, partnership or corporation?

    b. Organizational chart: What is the personnel sructure and who are the key individuals and planned staff additions?

    c. Personnel: What are the responsibilities and past experiences of partners and employees?

6. **Finance**

    a. Funding: What are your sources of financing and percentage from each source?

    b. Advisors: What are the names and addresses of accountant, legal counselor, banker, insurance agent and financial advisor?

    c. Cash requirements: What are your initial cash requirements, and what will they be over the next five years?

    d. Controls: What budget and cost systems do you/will you use?

    e. Sales and profit picture: What is your historical financial statement and/or financial projection?

Source: *Guide to Starting a Business in Michigan*, Michigan Department of Commerce, p. 1.

Exhibit 2.2 (continued)

7. **Production**

   a. Description: How will production or delivery of services be accomplished?

   b. Capacities: What physical facilities, suppliers, patents, labor and technology do you have or will you use?

   c. Capital equipment: What type and amount of machinery and durable equipment will you need to operate your business?

   d. Supplies: Where and how will you obtain your components and day-to-day supplies and services?

8. **Supporting Documents**

   Include personal resumes, personal financial statements, cost of living budget, letters of reference, job descriptions, letter of intent, copies of leases, contracts and other legal documents that you believe convey an accurate picture of your business.

(EIN). Exhibit 2.3 is IRS Form SS-4 used to request an EIN, which is included in the "Going into Business Kit."

General Insurance Requirements

Without proper protection, a hospitality business could be subject to financial ruin due to casualty losses and legal claims resulting from its activities. Insurance can help shield a business from those risks that have little chance of happening, but, if they do, carry the most potential for a damaging loss.

When considering insurance, owners should prioritize their insurance needs and determine the type of coverage needed. For example, some insurance may be considered imperative to protect the property from catastrophic loss. At the same time, lower and upper limits should be established to determine whether the operation has the right amount of coverage.

The types of insurance required by a hotel or restaurant are complex and the assistance of a qualified insurance consultant is typically needed. The four broad classes of insurance coverage that a hospitality operation needs to consider are:

- Liability Insurance
- Crime Insurance
- Property Damage Insurance
- Business Interruption Insurance

This section concludes with a discussion of multi-peril insurance—a special-purpose coverage which combines elements of these broad classes under a single policy.

Liability Insurance. Liability insurance provides a hospitality business with coverage for property damage or personal injury claims arising from

Exhibit 2.3   IRS Form SS-4, Request for EIN

For clear copy on both parts, please type or print with ball point pen and press firmly.

Form **SS-4** (Rev. November 1985) Department of the Treasury Internal Revenue Service	**Application for Employer Identification Number** (For use by employers and others. Please read the separate instructions before completing this form.) For Paperwork Reduction Act Notice, see separate instructions.	OMB No. 1545-0003 Expires 8-31-88

1 Name (True name. See instructions.)		2 Social security no., if sole proprietor	3 Ending month of accounting year

4 Trade name of business if different from item 1	5 General partner's name, if partnership; principal officer's name, if corporation; or grantor's name, if trust

6 Address of principal place of business (Number and street)	7 Mailing address, if different

8 City, state, and ZIP code	9 City, state, and ZIP code

10 Type of organization ☐ Individual ☐ Trust ☐ Partnership ☐ Plan administrator ☐ Governmental ☐ Nonprofit organization ☐ Corporation ☐ Other (specify)	11 County of principal business location

12 Reason for applying ☐ Started new business ☐ Purchased going business ☐ Other (specify)	13 Acquisition or starting date (Mo., day, year). See instructions.

14 Nature of principal activity (See instructions.)	15 First date wages or annuities were paid or will be paid (Mo., day, year).

16 Peak number of employees expected in the next 12 months (If none, enter "0") ▶	Nonagricultural	Agricultural	Household	17 Does the applicant operate more than one place of business? ☐ Yes ☐ No

18 Most of the products or services are sold to whom? ☐ Business establishments (wholesale) ☐ General public (retail) ☐ Other (specify) ☐ N/A	19 If nature of business is manufacturing, state principal product and raw material used.

20 Has the applicant ever applied for an identification number for this or any other business? ☐ Yes ☐ No If "Yes," enter name and trade name. Also enter approx. date, city, and state where the application was filed and previous number if known. ▶	

Under penalties of perjury, I declare that I have examined this application, and to the best of my knowledge and belief it is true, correct, and complete. | Telephone number (include area code)

Signature and Title ▶   Date ▶

Please leave blank ▶	Geo.	Ind.	Class	Size	Reas. for appl.	**Part I**

guests, employees, and others. It does not insure the business against damages to its property and other assets.

A lawsuit involving a liability claim could mean a catastrophic loss to an uninsured business. Therefore, it is vital that a business consider carrying some form of liability protection in the event of lawsuits. A liability policy generally will provide for the policyholder's legal defense and pay claims up to the limits of the policy.

Several different types of liability coverage may be necessary to protect the hospitality business from property or injury claims made by others. Exhibit 2.4 lists and describes a number of important types of liability coverage which may be carried by lodging operations. Some types (particularly automobile insurance and workers' compensation) may be required by law.

Crime Insurance. A hospitality business always runs the risk of losses brought about by a criminal act such as robbery, burglary, employee embezzlement, or theft.

Several different types of crime insurance policies may be necessary to protect the hospitality business from these and other criminal activities. Exhibit 2.4 describes three different types: Fidelity Bonds, Money & Securities Insurance, and Innkeeper's Liability Insurance.

Exhibit 2.4   Specific Types of Insurance Policies

Class/Policy	Description of Coverage
Liability Insurance	
Automobile Liability Insurance	Claims from guests or the general public for bodily injury or property damage resulting from the operation of business vehicles; may be expanded to include coverage for the use of employees' cars for business purposes.
Workers' Compensation Insurance	Claims involving personal injury or death incurred by employees in the course of their employment; mandatory in most states; compensation amounts are prescribed by law.
General Liability Insurance	Claims of others (employees excluded) for injuries sustained on the premises or resulting from activities of the business (automobiles excluded).
Product Liability Insurance	Claims for bodily injury or property damage caused by the consumption of food, beverages, or other products of the business.
Garage Coverage	Claims involving bodily injury or property damage on premises of public or guest garage or parking lot.
Garage Keeper's Legal Liability	Liabilities for fire or theft of vehicles on premises of public or guest garage or parking lot.
Crime Insurance	
Fidelity Bonds	Losses of cash due to theft by employees.
Money & Securities Insurance	Losses due to theft or other reasons caused by persons other than employees.
Innkeeper's Liability Insurance	Claims for damage or destruction of guest property on the premises.
Property Damage Insurance	
(General)	Property losses due to fire, theft, accidents and other types of casualties; may be expanded to include buildings, contents and vehicles.
Business Interruption Insurance	
(General)	Reimbursement for loss of earnings and continuing charges and expenses when an operation is forced to interrupt business; payrolls may be covered or excluded.

Instead of providing separate policies for each type of crime, insurance companies may provide optional crime coverage packages to policyholders. Crime insurance can be expensive, so most policies have a "deductible" in order to keep costs down; for each claim by a policyholder (insured), an insurance company (insurer) would be liable only for the loss in excess of a stated deductible amount. For example, assume a hotel has an insurance policy with a $500 deductible clause and it files a loss claim for $1,200. The insurance company would pay only $700 on this claim—the actual loss claimed less the deductible amount.

Property Damage Insurance. Property damage insurance protects the insured business against direct losses to its property (such as buildings, contents, and vehicles) due to fire, theft, accidents, and other types of casualties. Other casualties covered by such policies may include lightning, windstorms, hail storms, aircraft crashes, riots, and actions associated with strikes and civil disturbances.

It is important to carefully read a property damage policy to determine exactly what is covered and what is excluded from coverage. A given policy cannot reasonably be expected to cover all possible losses. "Riders" are special provisions added to the policy to extend coverage. Such provisions may be needed to protect against *indirect property losses*; for instance, damage caused by smoke or water from a fire in a building adjacent to (but not owned by) the hospitality property.

Business Interruption Insurance. In the event of fire or other disasters, a property may be forced to interrupt its business while repairs are being made. Strikes or civil disturbances may prevent the hospitality business from conducting its normal business activities. Business interruption insurance provides the insured with coverage for loss of earnings and continuing expenses until the business can resume operations. Depending on the policy, payroll may be covered or excluded.

Restoration of the business activities should proceed with the same concern as if no insurance was involved. It is better to earn business revenue than to collect business interruption insurance.

Multi-Peril Insurance. A single business operation could purchase many separate insurance policies to cover its insurance requirements. Rather than shopping for each type of insurance needed, a business may secure coverage by purchasing a multi-peril policy. Under this policy, the owner has the benefit of broad coverage for losses arising from on-site conditions relating to ownership, maintenance, or use of the property. However, the standard multi-peril package provides no coverage for problems that occur off the property or that arise from contract obligations.

In recent years, the whole concept of insurance has become increasingly complex. As a result, the typical multi-peril policy has become less useful than it was in the past. A business needs to work closely with its insurer or agent to obtain the best possible coverage for all of its potential losses.

Finally, insurance policies and programs must be reviewed periodically to ensure their effectiveness at keeping costs to a minimum while providing sufficient coverage of potential losses. The Educational Institute has published a how-to manual, *Reducing Liability Costs in the Lodging Industry*, which addresses the topic of insurance in greater depth.[1]

Legal Forms of Business Organization

A basic decision facing any person starting a business is the choice of the legal form of business organization. Many legal considerations and government regulatory requirements bear on this decision. Deciding on the legal form for any business should be done only after consulting with an accountant and an attorney.

There are three major forms of business organization: proprietorship, partnership, and corporation. In sheer numbers, proprietorships are the most prevalent form of business organization in the hospitality industry. However, in a recent year, revenues from corporate lodging businesses totaled nearly two-thirds of the total lodging revenue across the United States.[2]

Each of the three forms of business organization has both benefits and limitations. Exhibit 2.5 compares them on several basic points, including management control and personal liability for business debts. The following sections discuss differences and similarities among proprietorship, partnership, and corporate forms of business organization.

Proprietorship

A proprietorship is a business owned by a single person who has complete control over business decisions. It is the easiest and quickest form in which to organize a business. As illustrated in Exhibit 2.5, a proprietorship has no formal organizational documents (for instance, articles of incorporation); it is an unincorporated business.

From a legal point of view, the owner of a proprietorship is not separable from the business and is personally liable for all debts of the business. From an accounting perspective, however, the business is an entity separate from the owner (proprietor). Therefore, the financial statements of the business present only those assets and liabilities pertaining to the business.

The owner of a proprietorship cannot be paid any salary or wage from the business. Instead, the owner may withdraw funds (or other property) from the business; such withdrawals are not tax deductible by the business. Withdrawals are treated as reductions of owner's equity (financial interest of the owner in the business). The business itself does not pay any income taxes. The income or loss of the business is reported on the owner's personal income tax return on a supporting schedule (IRS Form 1040, Schedule C).

Furthermore, life insurance, health insurance, and other fringe benefits are deductible business expenses *only* if they are for the benefit of employees. The owner of a proprietorship cannot be classified as an employee of the business. Any payments made by the business for the benefit of the owner are treated as withdrawals by the owner.

A major disadvantage of the proprietorship form is the unlimited liability factor. The owner is personally responsible for meeting business obligations, even beyond the life of the business. However, adequate insurance covering casualty losses and legal claims can at least partially alleviate this problem.

Another drawback to a proprietorship is difficulty in raising needed capital. An owner cannot sell ownership interests in the business and still maintain the proprietorship form of business organization. Re-

Exhibit 2.5 Legal Forms of Business Organization

	Human Resources			Initial Funding			Government Regulation	Revenue	
	Management Control	Personnel and Expertise	Continuity / Transferability	Requirements and Costs	Ability to Raise Capital	Losses/Debts		Profits	Growth Potential
Proprietorship	One owner in total control	Depends mainly on owner's skills; hard to obtain quality employees	Ends on death of owner; free to sell or transfer	Costs are lowest (filing fee required if business held under name other than owner's)	Limited-- all equity (funding) must come from proprietor; loans based on credit-worthiness of owner	Owner liable for all debts	Little regulation; few records needed	All profits to owner	Limited options-- reinvest profits, obtain loans on owner's line-of-credit
Partnership	Divided among two or more partners; decisions made by majority or prearranged agreement (limited partner cannot manage the business)	Depends mainly on partners' skills; hard to find suitable employees	Ends on death of partner (unless otherwise agreed in writing); transfer conditions vary with agreement	Costs low; general partnership agreement optional but recommended (limited means that agreement stating liabilities and responsibilities of each partner is required)	Limited to resources of each of the partners and the ability of each to aquire loans and/or investors	Partners liable for all debts (limited partner has restricted liability and involvement per partnership agreement)	Subject to limited regulation; few records needed; articles of partnership should be drawn up	Divided among partners	Limited options-- reinvest profits, obtain loans on owners' lines-of-credit
Corporation	Corporation acts as one person, but Board of Directors holds legal, formal control; working control held by those who manage the business day-to-day	Allows for flexible management; easier to secure quality employees with the necessary expertise	Continues with overlapping; most flexible in terms of transfer of interest (i.e., ownership) from one shareholder to another	Costs are highest, legal forms, documents, professional fees required	Greatest equity potential -- can sell new stock; loans based on corporate financial strength and expertise, thus providing larger borrowing base	Corporation liable for all debts (i.e., shareholders are liable only for amount invested; are liable for more only if personal guarantees were given)	Extensive record-keeping required; must have articles of incorporation, by-laws and filing fees	Retained in corporation; shareholders receive dividends	Flexible--can reinvest profits (at discretion of Board of Directors); sell additional shares; obtain loans on corporate credit

Source: *Minding Your Own Small Business: An Introductory Curriculum*, Department of Health, Education and Welfare, 1979. Contract Number 300-7000330.

sources may be limited to the assets of the owner, and growth may depend on his or her ability to borrow money.

In many ways, a proprietorship is limited by the owner's resources, skills, and talents. In particular, any business organized as a proprietorship has a limited life—upon death or retirement of the owner, the form of business organization must be dissolved.

However, the proprietorship may be an ideal form of business organization when the following conditions hold true:

- The anticipated risk is minimal and is covered by insurance.

- The owner is either unable or unwilling to maintain the necessary organizational documents and tax returns of more complicated business entities.

- The business does not require extensive borrowing.

Partnership

A partnership is an unincorporated business owned by two or more individuals. A partnership is a very complex form of business organization, and requires extreme caution in selecting partners and drafting the partnership agreement. Compared to corporations, however, partnerships are relatively easy to organize and subject to fewer governmental regulations.

A partner may be classified in either of two categories: general or limited. A general partner has a right to manage and control the business, but, like a proprietor, is personally liable beyond the life of the business. Each general partner is legally and individually liable for the business actions of the other general partners.

By contrast, a limited partner does not actively participate in the management of the business. A limited partner is basically an investor whose liability may be restricted according to the terms of the partnership agreement. In any case, at least one partner must be a general partner. The remainder of this discussion will address general partnerships only.

Many features and limitations described for proprietorships generally apply to partnerships. A partnership, like a proprietorship, does not pay any income taxes. The income or loss of the business is distributed among the partners in accordance with the partnership agreement. Each partner reports his or her portion on a personal income tax return.

Despite its complex nature and the risk of personal liability, the partnership form of business organization provides an excellent means of pooling resources and expertise. As with the proprietorship form, however, partnerships have a limited life. Unless otherwise agreed in writing, partnerships are subject to dissolution upon the death of a partner. Transfer of ownership varies with conditions set forth in the partnership agreement.

Corporation

A corporation is a separate legal entity organized under law and distinct from its owners. As such, a corporation has many of the rights and responsibilities of a person. It can buy, sell, or own property; sue and be sued; enter into contracts; and engage in business activity. A corporation is responsible for its own debts and must pay income taxes just as a person does.

The owners of a corporation are referred to as stockholders or shareholders. The stockholders' ownership in a corporation is represented by shares of stock as evidenced by a stock certificate (Exhibit 2.6). One or more stockholders may account for all shares of stock in a corporation. The fact that only one stockholder owns all of the stock does not alter the legal form of business organization. It is still a corporation, not a proprietorship.

Stock carries certain rights and privileges, namely the election of a board of directors. The board selects the corporate officers who manage the day-to-day activities of the business. Stockholders may be directors, officers, or employees of a corporation. Many small incorporated businesses are owned by a limited number of stockholders and are referred to as closely held corporations.

Usually, a corporation must issue common stock which gives the stockholder ownership and voting rights. A corporation may also issue preferred stock, which usually provides preferential treatment on dividends, but may not give the stockholder the privilege of voting.

A corporation is formed by filing the prescribed articles of incorporation with the state division dealing with corporations. Each state has its particular requirements and various incorporation fees, making this form of business organization more costly to organize than proprietorships and partnerships. Usually, the articles of incorporation contain the following:

- Name and address of the corporation

- A description of the general nature of the business to be conducted by the corporation

- Names and addresses of the board of directors and officers

- The number of authorized shares the corporation intends to issue

The management organization chart for a corporation depends upon its size and type of business. Exhibit 2.7 shows an organization chart for a corporate lodging operation. As a result of the complex relationships among the board of directors, corporate officers, and management, decision-making processes for corporations are typically more involved than those for proprietorships or partnerships.

An important distinction between a corporation and the two other forms of business organization is that the stockholders do not actually own the assets of the business, although they do have legal claims to them. A corporation is responsible for its own actions and liabilities. This limited liability of stockholders means that their losses are normally restricted to their investments.

However, limited liability is not all-encompassing. Governments may pass through the corporate shield to collect unpaid taxes. Also, it is not uncommon for creditors to require that major stockholders personally co-sign for credit extended to the corporation. Thus, upon default by the business, the creditors may sue both the corporation and stockholders who have co-signed.

Besides the protection of limited liability, another advantage of the corporate form is that stockholders may be hired as employees of the

Exhibit 2.6 Stock Certificate

EN 55320

LESS THAN 100 SHARES

SHARES

COMMON STOCK

INCORPORATED UNDER THE LAWS
OF THE STATE OF DELAWARE

Loews Corporation

THIS IS TO CERTIFY THAT

IS THE OWNER OF

SEE REVERSE FOR
CERTAIN DEFINITIONS

CUSIP 540424 10 8

TENS	UNITS
1	1
2	2
3	3
4	4
5	5
6	6
7	7
8	8
9	9
0	0

FULL PAID AND NON-ASSESSABLE SHARES OF THE COMMON STOCK OF THE PAR VALUE OF ONE DOLLAR ($1⁰⁰) PER SHARE OF

Loews Corporation *(hereinafter called the Corporation) transferable on the books of the Corporation in person or by duly authorized attorney upon surrender of this certificate properly endorsed. This certificate and the shares represented hereby are issued and shall be held subject to all the provisions of the Certificate of Incorporation and the amendments thereto (to all of which the holder by acceptance hereof assents) copies of which are on file with the Transfer Agent. This certificate is not valid until countersigned by the Transfer Agent and registered by the Registrar.*

Witness the seal of the Corporation and the signatures of its duly authorized officers.

Dated:

CERTIFICATE OF STOCK

Barry Hirsch
SECRETARY

Laurence A. Tisch
CHAIRMAN OF THE BOARD

COUNTERSIGNED AND REGISTERED:

CITIBANK, N. A.
(NEW YORK)

TRANSFER AGENT
AND REGISTRAR

BY

AUTHORIZED OFFICER

LESS THAN 100 SHARES

NUMBER

LOEWS CORPORATION
CORPORATION
SEAL
1969
INCORPORATED DELAWARE

Exhibit 2.7 Organization Chart for a Corporation

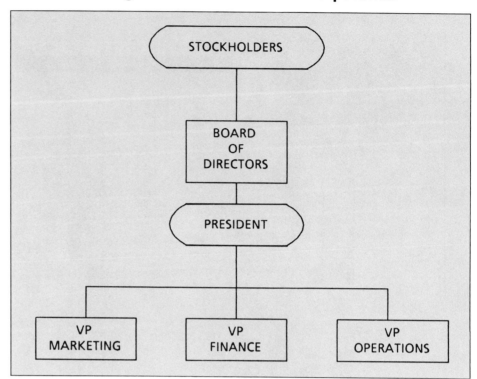

business, and, as such, would be entitled to salaries and wages, life insurance, health insurance, and other employee fringe benefits. The business may deduct these payments as business operating expenses for income tax purposes.

However, the corporate form has its share of disadvantages as well. Corporations are subject to greater government regulation than other forms of business organization, and are often taxed more heavily. Also, although dividends are taxable to the stockholders, the corporation cannot deduct them as a business expense. The complexity of the subject of taxation demands the advice of a qualified tax accountant.

Compared to the owner of a proprietorship, the stockholder of a corporation has less flexibility in the withdrawal of assets from the business. Stockholders may receive corporate assets only when dividends are declared, and these amounts may be subject to limits imposed by law.

Regardless of its drawbacks, the corporate form of business organization offers one important advantage over the other forms: ownership interest can be partially or fully sold by the sale of shares without affecting the legal form of business organization. This enables a corporation to continue business while ownership transfers are taking place. The ability to sell stock provides corporations with a stronger financial base and the capital needed for expansion.

Accounting for Business Transactions

The generally accepted accounting principles discussed in Chapter 1 apply equally to all three forms of business organization. It is not necessary to study separate accounting practices for corporations, partnerships, and proprietorships, provided that one understands the distinct manner in which equity transactions are handled for each.

Equity is defined as the financial interest of the owner(s) in a business. The equity transactions for a proprietorship are simpler than those for other forms of business organization, and therefore offer a good starting point for our discussion.

It should be noted, however, that accounting entries for any form of business organization are concerned only with the effects of transactions on businesses. The personal effects on owners are ignored, since accounting procedures treat businesses as entities separate from owners.

Proprietorship Equity Accounts

Among the types of equity transactions that may occur for a proprietorship form of business organization are:

- The owner invests personal cash or property into the business.

- The owner withdraws cash or property from the business for personal use.

- The business has either an operating profit or loss for the accounting period.

A proprietorship requires only two equity accounts, one to record the owner's equity in the business and another to record withdrawals made by the owner from the business. The titles of these accounts are:

- Capital, (owner's name)

- Withdrawals, (owner's name)

The Owner's Capital account is a business account reflecting the equity transactions between the business and the owner. When an owner personally invests funds, equipment, or property in a proprietorship business, the effect is that the owner has *increased* his or her equity in the business. Each time the owner makes a personal investment, the Owner's Capital account is increased.

When an owner personally withdraws funds, equipment, or property from a proprietorship business, the effect is that the owner has *decreased* his or her equity in the business. The Withdrawals account is a temporary account used during the accounting period to separately record transactions of this type. At the end of the accounting period, the Withdrawals account is charged against the Owner's Capital account and set to zero (closed) so that the next accounting period starts with a new "accumulator." (The Withdrawals account is referred to as a *contra account* because it is used to offset another account upon which it has an opposite effect.)

Owner's Investments in a Proprietorship. An owner may invest his or her personal cash, land, and building in the proprietorship. This transaction affects the following business accounts:

- The account Cash is *increased*.
- The account Land is *increased*.
- The account Building is *increased*.
- The account Capital, (owner's name) is *increased*.

The account called Cash is increased because the business now has more money. Likewise, the accounts called Land and Building are increased. The Owner's Capital account is also increased because the owner's equity in the business has been increased.

Owner's Withdrawals from a Proprietorship. Since an owner of a proprietorship cannot be paid any salary or wage, it is not unusual for the owner to withdraw funds from the business. When cash is withdrawn by the owner for personal use, the accounts affected are as follows:

- The account Withdrawals is *increased*.
- The account Cash is *decreased*.

Proprietorship Net Income or Net Loss. At the end of the accounting period, the operations of the business may show a net income or a net loss. If a net income results, the Owner's Capital account is increased. If a net loss results, the Owner's Capital account is decreased. The other accounts that are affected are discussed in the chapter covering closing entries.

Partnership Equity Accounts

Accounting for a partnership follows the same principles as accounting for other forms of business organization with the exception of ownership equity. Each partner has a separate account for Capital and a separate account for Withdrawals. The net income or loss of the business is distributed among the partners in a proportion specified by the partnership agreement.

Corporation Equity Accounts

As discussed previously, a corporation is a separate legal entity distinct from its stockholders. Therefore, its equity accounts are more involved than those for a proprietorship or a partnership. An important distinction is that a corporation retains its earnings until dividends are declared by the board of directors.

Because corporations are unique with respect to the transfer of ownership interest and the treatment of dividends, corporate equity transactions are quite different from those of either proprietorships or partnerships. The following major equity accounts apply to corporate forms of business organization:

- Common Stock Issued
- Additional Paid-In Capital
- Retained Earnings

Common Stock Issued. A corporation issues stock from its authorized shares at either par value or no par value. Par is not indicative of the price or market value of the stock. Par is an arbitrarily selected amount that is referred to as *legal value*. Par value per share may be set at 1¢, 10¢, $1, or any amount approved by the state division of corporations at the time the articles of incorporation were filed.

Stock may be issued at any price regardless of its par value. The issue price of a closely held corporation is usually determined by mutual agreement of the investors (stockholders). In a publicly issued stock, price is affected by market factors. If stock is issued at less than the par value, stockholders buying this stock are potentially liable for any claims against the corporation for the difference between what they paid and the par value.

Additional Paid-In Capital. When stock is sold above par value, it is called issuing stock at a premium. This premium is recorded in the bookkeeping account called Additional Paid-In Capital.

An example of this type of transaction illustrates the accounting procedures involved. Assume that 10,000 shares (of an authorized 50,000 shares) of $1 par value common stock are issued at $7 per share. This transaction affects the following accounts:

- The account Cash is *increased* by $70,000.

- The account Common Stock Issued is *increased* by $10,000.

- The account Additional Paid-In Capital is *increased* by $60,000.

With the sale of 10,000 shares issued at $7 per share, the corporation receives $70,000 cash. At a $1 par value, this sale of stock results in $10,000 worth of stock issued at legal value.

The premium can be calculated by one of two methods. The cash price of $70,000 less $10,000 par value equals a total premium of $60,000. By an alternative method, the issue price of $7 per share minus the par value of $1 results in a per share premium of $6, giving a total premium of $60,000 when multiplied by 10,000 shares sold.

Retained Earnings. Retained Earnings is an account that represents the earnings retained by the corporation. At the end of each accounting period, a corporation's net income is recorded as an *increase* to the Retained Earnings account. This process is performed during the closing entries procedure, which will be discussed thoroughly in Chapter 12.

Cash dividends represent a sharing of the corporation's profits (retained earnings), rather than an expense. Before any dividends may be payable to the stockholders, they first must be declared. Dividends are declared by the board of directors and generally are stated as a specified amount per share. The declaration of dividends produces the following entries:

- The account Retained Earnings is *decreased*.

- The account Dividends Payable is *increased*.

The Dividends Payable account is a liability account and represents a debt due by the corporation.

Types of Lodging Operations

Entrepreneurs starting a business must carry out a number of preliminary activities. Securing the proper business licenses, satisfying insurance requirements, and choosing the best form of business organization are a few initial tasks. In addition, successful ventures in the hospitality field require careful assessment of potential markets and existing competition before the ideal type of lodging operation for a given area can be chosen.

From an accounting standpoint, all businesses can be neatly classified into any one of three forms of business organization. In actuality, lodging operations (even those with the same form of business organization) can vary greatly according to a number of factors. For instance, take size. Lodging properties range in size from small roadside operations to giant mega-hotels with over 1,200 rooms.

Today, the lodging industry is primarily made up of commercial lodging establishments traditionally identified as hotels, motels, and resorts. A hotel is typically defined as a multi-story building with its own dining rooms, meeting rooms, and other public spaces. A motel is usually described as a "low-rise" building with limited dining facilities and other public spaces. Resorts are almost always located within tourist destination areas and may offer such recreational facilities as golf courses, tennis courts, and ski slopes.

Compounding the structure of today's lodging industry is the appearance of special-purpose hotels which reach out to capture new markets. These hotels have introduced innovative concepts in the lodging industry, including executive floor hotels, bed and breakfast operations, conference centers, and all-suite hotels.

Although every property has its own unique characteristics and distinctive style, lodging operations can be grouped into broad classifications based on service level, location, type of guests, and affiliation.

Service Level. One way of classifying lodging properties is by the level of service offered. Service level is a measure of the benefits provided to guests. It is comparable to the quality level of a manufactured product in the sense that the design and performance characteristics of the service are specified. Hotels may be categorized according to service level as economy (limited service), mid-range service, and world-class.

The service level of a hotel may also be classified by the type of meal plan offered. General meal plans are classified as European or American, but may include modified versions of these two types. In the European plan, room prices are *exclusive* of meals. Guests pay regular prices for meals served in the hotel dining room. In the American plan, meals are included in the price of the room. Some hotels offer a modified version of an American plan. Under this plan, only certain meals are included in the price of the room.

Location. Lodging properties may also be categorized according to their locations in relation to cities, transportation facilities, suburbs, and tourist destinations. For instance, properties may be classified as city-center hotels, airport hotels, highway hotels, suburban hotels, or destination (resort) hotels. City-center hotels are usually located in downtown or commercial districts, and their primary market is the business traveler. Airport hotels are popular because of their convenience for travelers. Highway hotels typically include food and beverage service, room service, banquet and catering facilities, and a gift shop or newsstand.

Among suburban hotels, almost half of total sales comes from food and beverage services.

Type of Guests. A hotel may cater to guests classified as either permanent or transient. Transient guests include business travelers, vacationers, and other visitors to an area. Hotels serving transient guests include motels, motor hotels, highway hotels, and airport hotels.

Other hotels may appeal to the permanent guest. Some of these hotels are purely residential, while others are semi-residential in that they serve permanent guests as well as transient guests. The residential hotel can be characterized as an apartment house with hotel services. Rooms are sold on a yearly or monthly basis, furnished or unfurnished. Rents are usually collected in advance, while other charges are billed weekly.

Affiliation. Another method by which to analyze the structure of the lodging industry is ownership or affiliation. Two basic classifications are possible—independent hotels and chain-affiliated hotels. Hotels in the first group are independently owned and operated. Chain-affiliated operations are often associated with franchise agreements and/or management contracts.

Franchising involves a long-term contract wherein the franchiser agrees to lend its name, goodwill, and back-up support to the franchisee in exchange for the franchisee's agreement to maintain required quality standards for design, decor, equipment, and operating procedures. Another type of chain-affiliated organization involves hiring a management company to operate the property on an ongoing basis.

A number of advantages may be offered by chain affiliation, including expanded financing options, nationwide or international reservations systems, and operational expertise. However, independent property owners avoid certain disadvantages associated with franchising, such as membership fees, conformity to the chain's standards, and cost of renovation or modernization required by a franchise agreement.

Financial Information Systems for Lodging Operations

Certain aspects of the hospitality industry create special considerations for businesspersons. For example, a single lodging operation may comprise several separate facilities working under the same roof simultaneously. Such a situation requires a high degree of coordination and a well-designed system for the management of financial information.

Hospitality managers deal with vast amounts of information on a daily basis. Without the proper organization, unmanaged financial data can overwhelm decision-makers and impair their judgments. Financial information systems must be designed to enable management to closely monitor business operations and accurately measure the performance of particular departments. Each department must be managed effectively if the overall operation is to achieve the greatest possible success.

Large organizations use the concept of *responsibility* in managing and controlling the business. According to responsibility accounting, each department under management's control reports revenue and expense data *separately* from other areas of the organization. A given department is directed by an individual who is held responsible for its operation.

Exhibit 2.8 Financial Information System for a Lodging Operation

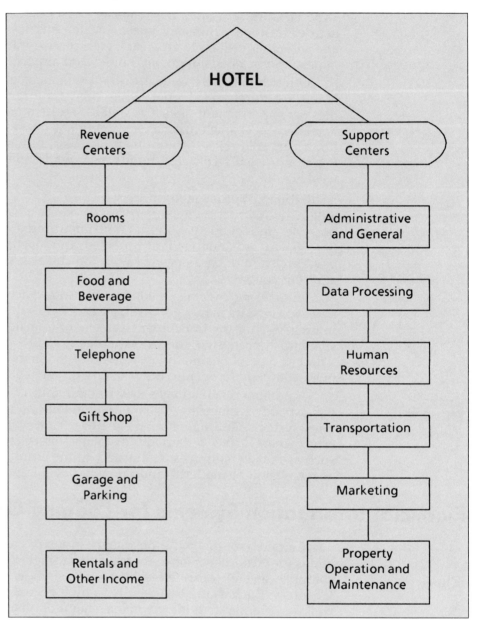

For purposes of financial reporting and data collection, departments may be classified as revenue centers or support centers. Simply stated, revenue centers generate revenue through sales of products and/or services to guests. Revenue centers include such areas as Rooms, Food and Beverage, Telephone, Gift Shop, and Garage and Parking operations.

In contrast, support centers are not directly involved in generating revenue. Instead, they provide supporting services to revenue-

Exhibit 2.9 Major Categories of a Hotel's Statement of Income

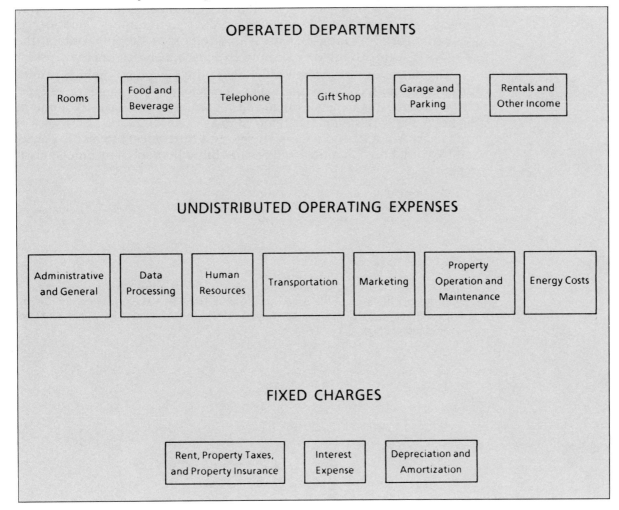

producing departments within the hospitality operation. Support centers include such areas as Administrative and General, Data Processing, Human Resources, Transportation, Marketing, and Property Operation and Maintenance. These departments do not serve guests directly; instead, their main function is to support the operation's revenue centers.

Financial information systems vary from operation to operation depending on the size of the property, the number of revenue and support centers, and the type of management information needed. A hotel may have its departments assigned as in Exhibit 2.8.

Categorizing hotel departments as revenue centers and support centers not only reflects organizational structure but also has a direct bearing on the format of the business's statement of income. Detailed statements of income developed for internal users provide information regarding the performance of operations for a specified period of time.

Exhibit 2.9 presents the major accounting categories which compose a hotel's statement of income. A statement of income refers to revenue centers as Operated Departments and to support centers as Undistributed Operating Expenses. In addition to support centers, the category of Undistributed Operating Expenses includes Energy Costs.

The statement of income must also reflect expenses which cannot easily be attributed to any particular department. The category of *Fixed Charges* represents expenses incurred regardless of the sales volume of the hotel; they are sometimes referred to as *Occupancy Costs*. Examples of fixed charges are Rent, Property Taxes, and Insurance; Interest Expense; and Depreciation. Chapter 3 will discuss the statement of income in great detail.

Notes

1. John Tarras, *Reducing Liability Costs in the Lodging Industry* (East Lansing, Mich.: Educational Institute of the American Hotel & Motel Association, 1986), pp. 21-29.
2. Albert J. Gomes, *Hospitality in Transition* (New York: American Hotel & Motel Association, 1985).

Discussion Questions

1. What are the four broad classes of insurance coverage? Briefly describe each class.

2. What are the advantages and disadvantages of the proprietorship form of business organization?

3. How is the income of a proprietorship taxed?

4. What are the three types of equity transactions that may occur for a proprietorship?

5. What are the names and purposes of the two equity bookkeeping accounts for a proprietorship?

6. What are the advantages and disadvantages of the corporate form of business organization?

7. What are the names and purposes of the three major equity accounts for corporations?

8. How are lodging operations broadly classified according to the following characteristics: service level, location, type of guests, and affiliation?

9. What are the revenue and support centers of a hotel?

Problems

Problem 2.1
A corporation sells 50,000 shares of an authorized 200,000 shares of 10¢ par value common stock issued at $20 per share.

a.   What amount is recorded as Cash?

b.   What amount is recorded as Common Stock Issued?

c.   What amount, if any, is recorded as Additional Paid-In Capital?

Problem 2.2
A corporation sells 200,000 shares of an authorized 500,000 shares of 25¢ par value common stock for a total of $50,000.

a.   What amount is recorded as Cash?

b.   What amount is recorded as Common Stock Issued?

c.   What amount, if any, is recorded as Additional Paid-In Capital?

Problem 2.3
A corporation's board of directors declares a dividend of 20¢ per share on 500,000 shares of issued and outstanding common stock.

a.   What is the total amount of the dividends declared?

b.   What two bookkeeping accounts are affected? Specify whether they are increased or decreased by this transaction.

3
Financial Statements

Financial statements represent the end result of the financial accounting cycle. Their purpose is to communicate various kinds of financial information to both internal and external users. Owners, managers, creditors, and governmental agencies use financial statements to answer a variety of questions regarding a hospitality business. Such questions include:

1. What was the operation's ability to meet its current obligations?

2. What was the total debt of the operation?

3. How much equity did stockholders have in the assets of the business?

4. What was the amount of total revenue generated by the operation during the last accounting period?

5. How profitable was the operation during the last accounting period?

This chapter explains the fundamental format and components of basic financial statements for proprietorship and corporate forms of business organization. Although the preparation of financial statements is not the first step in the accounting cycle, it is advantageous to study these statements now in order to understand the logic behind procedures for recording and posting business transactions.

A portion of the chapter focuses on the different roles performed by independent certified public accountants in auditing, reviewing, or compiling the financial statements of a business. The chapter closes by clarifying the interrelationships among terms most often confused by beginning students of accounting—inventory, sales, and cost of sales.

Basic Financial Statements

The basic financial statements prepared by hospitality businesses are:

- Statement of Income
- Equity Statement:

    Proprietorship—Statement of Owner's Equity

    Partnership—Statement of Partners' Equity

    Corporation—Statement of Retained Earnings

- Balance Sheet
- Statement of Changes in Financial Position
- Statement of Cash Flow

The statement of income provides important information regarding the results of operations for a stated period of time. Because this statement reveals the bottom line (net income for a stated period), it is one of the most important financial statements used by managers to evaluate the success of operations.

The kind of equity statement for a hospitality operation will depend upon its form of business organization. A statement of owner's equity is prepared for a proprietorship, a statement of partners' equity for a partnership, and a statement of retained earnings for a corporation. These statements reflect changes in equity which occurred during an accounting period. The statements are not always prepared as separate financial statements. In some cases, they are incorporated into the other statements as follows:

- The statement of owner's equity may be incorporated at the bottom of the balance sheet prepared for a proprietorship form of business organization.

- The statement of partners' equity may be incorporated at the bottom of the balance sheet prepared for a partnership form of business organization.

- The statement of retained earnings may be incorporated at the bottom of the statement of income prepared for a corporate form of business organization.

The balance sheet provides important information regarding the financial position of a hospitality business by showing the assets, liabilities, and equity on a particular date. Simply stated, assets represent anything a business owns which has commercial or exchange value, liabilities represent the claims of outsiders (such as creditors) to assets, and equity represents the claims of owners to assets.

The statement of changes in financial position and the statement of cash flow report financial information not directly provided by either the balance sheet or the statement of income. The statement of changes in financial position: (a) reveals the extent to which the business has provided funds to operations or used funds from operations and, (b) summarizes financing and investing activities of the property for the period covered by successive balance sheets. The statement of cash flow summarizes the sources of cash and the uses of cash during the period covered by successive balance sheets.

This chapter focuses on the two most widely used financial statements—the statement of income and the balance sheet. The financial statements illustrated in this chapter are for a small restaurant. Except for the inclusion of rooms revenue, a slight variation in format, and an emphasis on departmental reports, hotel financial statements are similar to those prepared for restaurants.

Statement of Income

The purpose of the statement of income is to provide important financial information regarding *the results of operations for a stated period of time*. The time period may be one month or longer, but does not exceed one business year. The business year is called the fiscal year. Since the owners of proprietorships or partnerships pay personal income taxes on the net income from their operations, their fiscal years generally begin on the first of January. However, the fiscal year of certain corporate forms of business organization may be any 12 consecutive months.

Since the statement of income reveals the results of operations for a period of time, it is an important measure of the effectiveness and efficiency of management. Understanding how the statement is used to evaluate management is the key to understanding the logic behind the sequence of categories which appears on the statement. The major categories that appear on the statement of income are:

- Revenue
- Cost of Sales
- Operating Expenses
- Fixed Charges
- Net Income (or Loss)

The following sections discuss these categories in some detail and provide a brief explanation of the line items appearing within them. Exhibits 3.1 and 3.2 will be used to point out the differences between statements of income prepared for proprietorships and those prepared for corporations.

Revenue   Revenue results when products and services are sold to guests. The total revenue figure on the statement of income indicates the actual dollar amount that guests have been billed for products and services offered by the hospitality property.

Revenue is *not* income. Revenue appears at the top of the statement of income; net income (or loss) appears at the bottom. Income results when total revenue exceeds total expenses. A loss results when total expenses exceeds total revenue.

Exhibits 3.1 and 3.2 show the total revenue figure for Deb's Steakhouse at $170,000. Note that revenue generated by food sales ($120,000) is listed separately from revenue generated by beverage sales ($50,000). Distinguishing the major sources of revenue allows management to identify the separate contributions of the food operation and the beverage operation to the total gross profit of the establishment.

Exhibit 3.1 Statement of Income for a Proprietorship

Deb's Steakhouse
Statement of Income
For the Year Ended December 31, 19X2

REVENUE
Food Sales ... $120,000
Liquor Sales ... 50,000
  Total Revenue ... $170,000

COST OF SALES
Food ... 42,000
Liquor ... 11,000
  Total Cost of Sales ... 53,000

GROSS PROFIT ... 117,000

OPERATING EXPENSES
Salaries and Wages ... 36,000
Employee Benefits ... 6,900
China, Glassware, and Silverware ... 300
Kitchen Fuel ... 900
Laundry and Dry Cleaning ... 2,100
Credit Card Fees ... 1,500
Operating Supplies ... 5,000
Advertising ... 2,000
Utilities ... 3,800
Repairs and Maintenance ... 1,900
  Total Operating Expenses ... 60,400

INCOME BEFORE FIXED CHARGES ... 56,600

FIXED CHARGES
Rent ... 6,000
Property Taxes ... 1,500
Insurance ... 3,600
Interest Expense ... 3,000
Depreciation ... 5,500
  Total Fixed Charges ... 19,600

NET INCOME ... $ 37,000

Note: The net income figure is transferred to the Statement of Owner's
Equity illustrated in Exhibit 3.3.

Cost of Sales   The cost of sales section of the statement of income shows the cost of merchandise held for resale that is used in the selling process; it does not contain any cost for labor or operating supplies. Since the revenue appearing on the income statement for Deb's Steakhouse resulted from sales of food and beverages to guests, the cost of sales figure ($53,000) represents *the cost of food and beverage merchandise served to guests.*

The cost of sales figure is not calculated simply by computing the

Exhibit 3.2 Statement of Income for a Corporation

Deb's Steakhouse, Inc.
Statement of Income
For the Year Ended December 31, 19X2

REVENUE

Food Sales	$120,000	
Liquor Sales	50,000	
Total Revenue		$170,000

COST OF SALES

Food	42,000	
Liquor	11,000	
Total Cost of Sales		53,000

GROSS PROFIT — 117,000

OPERATING EXPENSES

Salaries and Wages	55,000	
Employee Benefits	7,900	
China, Glassware, and Silverware	300	
Kitchen Fuel	900	
Laundry and Dry Cleaning	2,100	
Credit Card Fees	1,500	
Operating Supplies	5,000	
Advertising	2,000	
Utilities	3,800	
Repairs and Maintenance	1,900	
Total Operating Expenses		80,400

INCOME BEFORE FIXED CHARGES AND INCOME TAXES — 36,600

FIXED CHARGES

Rent	6,000	
Property Taxes	1,500	
Insurance	3,600	
Interest Expense	3,000	
Depreciation	5,500	
Total Fixed Charges		19,600

INCOME BEFORE INCOME TAXES — 17,000

INCOME TAXES — 2,000

NET INCOME — $ 15,000

Note: The net income figure is transferred to the Statement of Retained
Earnings illustrated in Exhibit 3.4.

cost of merchandise issued from storerooms during the accounting
period. All the merchandise that entered the operation during the period
was not necessarily used and served to guests. For example, some food
may be used to prepare free employee meals. This use of food merchan-

dise does not generate revenue; therefore, the cost of merchandise used to prepare employee meals should not be included in the cost of food sales figure. The last section of this chapter presents a detailed explanation of how to calculate cost of sales.

Cost of sales is only one of the many expenses of doing business. The statement of income includes a lengthy section on operating expenses and fixed charges. The question naturally arises: why separate cost of sales from other expenses which must eventually be subtracted from total revenue in order to yield the bottom-line figure for net income? Cost of sales is shown separately from other expenses because operators want to be able to compare the revenue generated by food and beverage sales with the cost of the food and beverage merchandise used to generate that revenue. This is the purpose served by the next line item on the statement of income—gross profit.

Gross Profit

Gross profit is calculated by subtracting cost of sales from net revenue (net sales). Gross profit is sometimes referred to as gross margin or gross margin on sales.

Gross profit is an intermediate income amount from which operating expenses and fixed charges are deducted to arrive at net income. Gross profit must be large enough to cover all of these expenses for the business to earn a net income.

Operating Expenses

The operating expenses section of the statement of income lists expenses which are most directly influenced by operating policy and management efficiency. If the statement of income showed these expenses as a single line item, this would not communicate very much information to the users of the statement. Breaking out each of the significant operating expenses allows management and others to readily identify expense areas which may be excessive and which call for further analysis and possible corrective action. A brief explanation of the line items included under operating expenses on the statements of income for Deb's Steakhouse follows.

Salaries and Wages. This line item includes the regular salaries and wages, extra wages, overtime pay, vacation pay, and any commission or bonus payments to employees. Note that the figure shown as salaries and wages for the corporate form of Deb's Steakhouse is greater than the salaries and wages figure shown for the proprietorship form of Deb's Steakhouse. This difference results from the fact that the owner of a proprietorship cannot be paid a salary or wage.

Employee Benefits. This line item includes the cost of free employee meals, social security taxes (FICA), federal and state unemployment, union and nonunion insurance premiums, state health insurance, union and nonunion pension fund contributions, medical expenses, workers' compensation insurance, and other similar expenses. Expenses related to employee benefits can be significant for restaurant operations. Note that the amount for employee benefits shown for Deb's Steakhouse, Inc., is greater than that shown for Deb's Steakhouse (proprietorship). This difference arises for two reasons: (a) an owner of a proprietorship cannot deduct benefits on his or her behalf, and (b) since wages cannot be paid to an owner, there are no payroll taxes on behalf of the owner.

China, Glassware, and Silverware. These items are generally considered direct service expenses rather than repair and maintenance expenses. Therefore, replacement costs for china, glassware, and silverware appear here as a separate item under Operating Expenses. This line item also includes the depreciation expense for china, glassware, and silverware.

Kitchen Fuel. This line item includes only the cost of fuel used for cooking such as gas, coal, charcoal, briquettes, steam, electricity, or hickory chips.

Laundry and Dry Cleaning. This line item includes the cost of laundering table linens and uniforms; contracting for napkin, towel, and apron service; and cleaning uniforms, wall and window hangings, and floor coverings.

Credit Card Fees. This item includes the amount paid to credit card organizations for central billing and collection of credit card accounts.

Operating Supplies. This item represents supplies that have been used and are not includable as inventory. These supplies include cleaning supplies, paper supplies, guest supplies, and bar supplies. The statements of income for Deb's Steakhouse list operating supplies as a single line item. However, large operations may list the categories of operating supplies separately on the statement of income.

Advertising. Marketing is the more general term used to describe the varied expenses incurred in promoting a restaurant operation to the public. Items listed under marketing vary with the needs and requirements of individual properties. Deb's Steakhouse is a relatively small operation. Its marketing expenses consistently include only advertising costs such as newspaper ads, circulars, and brochures. Therefore, it is more appropriate and informative for that operation to list advertising instead of marketing as the operating expense item on the statement of income. Large restaurant operations, on the other hand, may incur significant marketing expenses in such areas as sales, advertising, and public relations. It would be appropriate for these properties to list the term marketing as a direct expense line item on the statement of income.

Utilities. This line item includes the cost of electric current, fuel, water, ice and refrigeration supplies, waste removal, and engineer's supplies. Note, however, that Utilities does not include fuel used for cooking purposes. The cost of energy used for cooking purposes appears as a separate line item. If electricity or gas is used as kitchen fuel and for heating and lighting, it is necessary to use meter readings or estimate usage in order to isolate kitchen fuel expense.

Repairs and Maintenance. This line item includes the cost of plastering, painting, decorating, repairing dining room furniture and kitchen equipment, plumbing and heating repairs, and other maintenance and repair expenses.

Income Before Fixed Charges and Income Taxes

The figure for income before fixed charges and income taxes is used to measure the success of operations and the effectiveness and efficiency of management. Therefore, this section of the statement of income is extremely important to management. This figure is calculated by subtracting total operating expenses from the gross profit figure.

Note that for a proprietorship form of business organization (Exhibit 3.1) this section of the statement of income reads as "Income Before Fixed Charges." Income taxes are not mentioned because a proprietorship does not pay income taxes—the owner does. A proprietorship's business income is reported on the owner's personal income tax return.

Fixed Charges

The fixed charges section of the statement of income includes rent, property taxes, property insurance, interest expense, and depreciation. Fixed charges are those expenses which are incurred regardless of whether the business is open or closed, and they remain relatively constant even with changes in sales volume.

Income Before Income Taxes

Fixed charges are subtracted from the figure for income before fixed charges and income taxes to arrive at the amount of income before income taxes. As mentioned at the end of Chapter 1, this figure may not be the same figure that appears on the operation's income tax return as taxable income.

Note that the statement of income for a proprietorship form of business organization (Exhibit 3.1) does not include this line item. Again, this is because a business organized as a proprietorship does not pay income taxes—the owner does.

Income Taxes

The income taxes section of the statement of income includes federal and other government taxes that are imposed on business income. Again, note that this line item does not appear on the statement of income for a proprietorship.

Net Income (or Loss)

The bottom line of the statement of income reveals the net income (or loss) of the operation for a stated period. This figure will indicate the overall success of operations for the period of time covered by the statement of income. The amount of net income shown for the corporate form of Deb's Steakhouse differs from that of the proprietorship form of business organization because of the following:

- The owner of a proprietorship cannot be paid a salary or wage; thus there are also no applicable payroll taxes.

- The owner of a proprietorship is not entitled to deductible benefits.

- The owner of a proprietorship pays the income taxes of the business on his or her personal income tax return.

Equity Statements

Chapter 2 discussed some of the differences involved in recording equity transactions for proprietorships, partnerships, and corporations. These differences are reflected in the equity statements which are prepared for each form of business organization. Equity statements reflect changes in equity which occurred during an accounting period. Exhibit 3.3 illustrates a statement of owner's equity prepared for a proprietorship and Exhibit 3.4 illustrates a statement of retained earn-

Exhibit 3.3   Statement of Owner's Equity for a Proprietorship

Deb's Steakhouse
Statement of Owner's Equity
For the Year Ended December 31, 19X2

Deb Barry, Capital--January 1, 19X2	$ 91,000
Add Net Income for the year ended December 31, 19X2	37,000
Total	128,000
Less Withdrawals during the year	30,000
Deb Barry, Capital--December 31, 19X2	$ 98,000

Notes:
1. The net income figure is from the Statement of Income illustrated in Exhibit 3.1.
2. The ending capital amount is transferred to the Balance Sheet illustrated in Exhibit 3.5.

Exhibit 3.4   Statement of Retained Earnings for a Corporation

Deb's Steakhouse, Inc.
Statement of Retained Earnings
For the Year Ended December 31, 19X2

Retained Earnings, January 1, 19X2	$43,000
Add Net Income for the year ended December 31, 19X2	15,000
Total	58,000
Less Dividends Declared during the year	0
Retained Earnings, December 31, 19X2	$58,000

Notes:
1. The net income figure is from the Statement of Income illustrated in Exhibit 3.2.
2. The ending retained earnings amount is transferred to the Balance Sheet illustrated in Exhibit 3.6.

ings prepared for a corporation. The following sections explain the line items which appear on these equity statements.

Statement of Owner's Equity   The statement of owner's equity is prepared for a proprietorship form of business organization. The owner's capital account reflects the owner's residual claims to the assets of the business. The owner's claims are residual because they follow any claims to assets that creditors may have as represented by the liabilities section of the balance sheet.

Exhibit 3.3 illustrates the statement of owner's equity for Deb's Steakhouse. Deb Barry's equity for the period just ended is calculated by adding net income and subtracting withdrawals from the amount of owner's equity shown on the previous statement of owner's equity prepared for the prior period. The net income figure is the same figure that appears on the bottom line of the statement of income in Exhibit 3.1.

Statement of Retained Earnings

The statement of retained earnings is prepared for a corporate form of business organization. *Retained Earnings* is defined as that portion of stockholder's equity which reflects the accumulated net income of the corporation that has not been paid out as dividends to stockholders.

Exhibit 3.4 illustrates the statement of retained earnings for Deb's Steakhouse, Inc. Note that the amount of retained earnings for the period just ended is calculated by adding net income and subtracting dividends declared from the amount of retained earnings shown on the previous statement of retained earnings prepared for the prior period. The net income figure is the same figure that appears on the bottom line of the statement of income in Exhibit 3.2. *Dividends Declared* includes all dividends declared during the current accounting year regardless of whether they are paid or unpaid.

Balance Sheet

The balance sheet provides important information regarding the financial position of the hospitality business by showing the assets, liabilities, and equity *on a given date*. The phrase "on a given date" carries an entirely different meaning than "for a stated period of time." A balance sheet dated December 31, 19X2, shows the financial position of the business *on December 31, 19X2*, not for the month of December or any other period of time.

Understanding how the statement is used to reveal the financial position of a business is the key to understanding the logic behind the sequence of categories which appear on the statement. The major categories that appear on the balance sheet are:

- Assets
- Liabilities
- Equity

Simply stated, assets represent anything a business owns which has commercial or exchange value, liabilities represent the claims of outsiders (such as creditors) to assets, and equity represents the claims of owners to assets. On every balance sheet, the total assets must always agree (that is, balance) with the total of the liabilities and equity sections. Therefore, the very format of the balance sheet reflects the fundamental accounting equation:

$$\text{Assets} = \text{Liabilities} + \text{Equity}$$

Assets and liabilities are arranged on the balance sheet according to their current or noncurrent status. For the present, current items are defined as those assets which are convertible to cash or those liabilities which will require an outlay of cash within 12 months of the balance sheet date. All other items will be classified as noncurrent.

The following sections discuss the assets, liabilities, and equity sections of the proprietorship and corporate balance sheets for Deb's Steakhouse as illustrated by Exhibits 3.5 and 3.6, respectively. A brief explanation of the line items appearing under the basic balance sheet categories will also be provided. The only significant difference between balance sheets prepared for proprietorships and those prepared for corporations is in the equity section.

Current Assets

For the present, current assets are defined as those assets which are convertible to cash within 12 months of the balance sheet date. Items appearing as current assets are usually listed in the order of their liquidity, that is, the ease with which they can be converted to cash.

Cash. Cash consists of cash in house banks, cash in checking and savings accounts, and certificates of deposit.

Accounts Receivable. This line item includes all amounts due from customers carried by the restaurant on open accounts.

Inventories. This line item includes merchandise held for resale, such as food provisions and liquor stock. Inventories also include operating supplies such as guest supplies, office supplies, and cleaning supplies.

Prepaid Expenses. This line item shows the value of prepayments whose benefits will expire within 12 months of the balance sheet date. Prepaid expense items may include prepaid interest, rent, taxes, and licenses.

Property and Equipment

The property and equipment portion of the balance sheet lists noncurrent assets. The major noncurrent assets are land, buildings, and equipment. The costs for Building and for Furniture and Equipment which appear on the balance sheets for Deb's Steakhouse are decreased by amounts shown as *Accumulated Depreciation*.

Depreciation spreads the cost of an asset over the term of its useful life. It is important to stress that this procedure is not an attempt to establish the market values of assets. The cost of the asset minus the amount of its accumulated depreciation leaves the net asset value, or what is sometimes called the "book value." This should not be confused with market value—the value which the asset could bring if sold on the open market.

Accumulated depreciation does not affect the noncurrent asset Land because land does not wear out *in the normal course of business*. Accumulated depreciation also does not affect China, Glassware, and Silver on the balance sheet because amounts for deterioration, breakage, and loss have already been deducted directly from this asset account.

Other Assets

The other assets portion of the balance sheet includes assets which do not apply to line items previously discussed. Security deposits include funds deposited with public utility companies (for instance, telephone, water, electric, and gas companies) and other funds used for similar

Exhibit 3.5 Balance Sheet for a Proprietorship

Deb's Steakhouse
Balance Sheet
December 31, 19X2

ASSETS

CURRENT ASSETS

Cash	$34,000	
Accounts Receivable	4,000	
Inventories	5,000	
Prepaid Expenses	2,000	
Total Current Assets		$ 45,000

PROPERTY AND EQUIPMENT

	Cost	Accumulated Depreciation	
Land	$ 30,000		
Building	60,000	$15,000	
Furniture and Equipment	52,000	25,000	
China, Glassware, Silver	8,000		
Total	150,000	40,000	110,000

OTHER ASSETS

Security Deposits	1,500	
Preopening Expenses	2,500	
Total Other Assets		4,000

TOTAL ASSETS		$159,000

LIABILITIES

CURRENT LIABILITIES

Accounts Payable	$11,000	
Sales Tax Payable	1,000	
Accrued Expenses	9,000	
Current Portion of Long-Term Debt	6,000	
Total Current Liabilities		$ 27,000

LONG-TERM LIABILITIES

Mortgage Payable	40,000	
Less Current Portion of Long-Term Debt	6,000	
Net Long-Term Liabilities		34,000

TOTAL LIABILITIES		61,000

OWNER'S EQUITY

Capital, Deb Barry--December 31, 19X2		98,000
TOTAL LIABILITIES AND OWNER'S EQUITY		$159,000

Exhibit 3.6 Balance Sheet for a Corporation

Deb's Steakhouse, Inc.
Balance Sheet
December 31, 19X2

ASSETS

CURRENT ASSETS

Cash	$34,000	
Accounts Receivable	4,000	
Inventories	5,000	
Prepaid Expenses	2,000	
Total Current Assets		$ 45,000

PROPERTY AND EQUIPMENT

	Cost	Accumulated Depreciation	
Land	$ 30,000		
Building	60,000	$15,000	
Furniture and Equipment	52,000	25,000	
China, Glassware, Silver	8,000		
Total	150,000	40,000	110,000

OTHER ASSETS

Security Deposits	1,500	
Preopening Expenses	2,500	
Total Other Assets		4,000

TOTAL ASSETS	$159,000

LIABILITIES

CURRENT LIABILITIES

Accounts Payable	$11,000	
Sales Tax Payable	1,000	
Accrued Expenses	9,000	
Current Portion of Long-Term Debt	6,000	
Total Current Liabilities		$ 27,000

LONG-TERM LIABILITIES

Mortgage Payable	40,000	
Less Current Portion of Long-Term Debt	6,000	
Net Long-Term Liabilities		34,000

TOTAL LIABILITIES	61,000

STOCKHOLDERS' EQUITY

Common Stock		
Par Value $1,		
Authorized 50,000 shares,		
Issued 25,000 shares	25,000	
Additional Paid-In Capital	15,000	
Total Paid-In Capital		40,000
Retained Earnings, December 31, 19X2		58,000
TOTAL LIABILITIES AND STOCKHOLDERS' EQUITY		$159,000

types of deposits. Preopening expenses include capitalized expenses incurred prior to the opening of the property.

Current Liabilities

Current liabilities are obligations which will require an outlay of cash within 12 months of the balance sheet date. The total current liabilities alerts the restaurant operator to cash requirements of the operation and is often compared with the total figure for current assets.

Accounts Payable. This line item shows the total of unpaid invoices due to creditors from whom the restaurant receives merchandise or services in the ordinary course of business.

Sales Tax Payable. This line item includes all sales taxes collected from customers which are payable to federal or local governmental agencies.

Accrued Expenses. This line item lists the total amount of expenses incurred for the period up to the balance sheet date but which are not payable until after the balance sheet date and have not been shown elsewhere as a current liability.

Current Portion of Long-Term Debt. Since the total figure for current liabilities includes all obligations which will require an outlay of cash within 12 months of the balance sheet date, this line item includes the principal portion of long-term debt which is due within one year of the balance sheet date.

Long-Term Liabilities

A long-term liability (also called long-term debt) is any debt *not* due within 12 months of the balance sheet date. Any portion of long-term debt which is due within 12 months of the balance sheet date is subtracted from the total outstanding obligation and is shown in the current liabilities portion of the balance sheet.

Equity Section

Exhibit 3.5 illustrates the equity section of the balance sheet prepared for a proprietorship. The Owner's Equity line item shows the interests of the sole owner in the assets of Deb's Steakhouse. The figure for Deb Barry's Capital account in Exhibit 3.5 is the same figure that appears as the current balance on the statement of owner's equity in Exhibit 3.3. If the balance sheet were prepared for a partnership, the interests of each partner would be shown as line items under Partners' Equity. Changes in equity accounts of the partners would be shown in a statement of partners' equity whose format would be similar to that of the statement of owner's equity.

Exhibit 3.6 illustrates the equity section of the balance sheet prepared for a corporate form of business organization. *Common Stock* shows the par value, the number of shares authorized, and the number of shares issued. *Additional Paid-In Capital* shows the total amount for cash, property, and other capital contributed by stockholders in excess of the par value of the common stock. *Retained Earnings* includes that portion of net income earned by the corporation which is not distributed as dividends, but is retained in the business. The figure for Retained Earnings in Exhibit 3.6 is the same figure shown at the bottom of the statement of retained earnings in Exhibit 3.4.

Other Basic Financial Statements

In addition to the basic financial statements we have just discussed, properties also prepare a statement of changes in financial position (SCFP) and a statement of cash flow.

The SCFP reports information which is not directly provided by either the balance sheet or the statement of income. It is sometimes referred to as a funds flow statement because it discloses the sources and uses of funds of the business. The SCFP reveals the extent to which the restaurant has provided funds to operations or used funds from operations and summarizes financing and investing activities of the property for the period covered by successive balance sheets. This financial information is useful to managers, investors, and creditors.

The statement of cash flow summarizes the sources of cash and the uses of cash during the period covered by successive balance sheets. This statement identifies items that contribute to the net change in the cash balance between the beginning and the end of an accounting period.

Role of the Independent CPA

The management of a hospitality business is responsible for safeguarding the assets of the business and maintaining a system of internal control which ensures that the financial statements are properly prepared. However, bankers, creditors, and governmental agencies may demand assurances that the information in the financial statements is reliable and presented in conformity with generally accepted accounting principles. In these cases, financial statements prepared by an employee of the hospitality business may not be acceptable, even if that employee is a certified public accountant. External users may require that the financial statements which they receive from a hospitality business involve, in some way, an *independent* certified public accountant.

An independent CPA is a professional who is free from any interest in the hospitality business and free of any obligations in relation to the managers or owner(s). In addition, the work of the independent CPA must conform to the requirements of a number of standards such as:

- Auditing standards of the American Institute of Certified Public Accountants
- Standards for accounting and review services
- Financial accounting standards
- Professional standards
- Generally accepted accounting principles

An example of the degree of conformity expected by AICPA is Rule 201 of the AICPA's *Professional Standards*, which states:

1. Only those engagements shall be undertaken which can be reasonably expected to be completed with professional competence.

2. A member shall exercise due professional care in the performance of an engagement.

3. A member shall adequately plan and supervise an engagement.

4. A member shall obtain sufficient relevant data to afford a reasonable basis for conclusions or recommendations in relation to an engagement.[1]

The role of the independent CPA in relation to the financial statements of a business can vary from offering suggestions on the form or content of the statements to actually drafting (in whole or in part) the statements themselves. External users may want the hospitality business to specify the degree of responsibility that the independent CPA had with respect to the financial statements. In such cases, a written report accompanies the financial statements of the business and identifies the degree of responsibility which the independent CPA acknowledges in regard to the business's financial statements. An independent CPA may attach one of three different kinds of reports to the financial statements of a business: an audit report, a review report, or a compilation report.

Audited Financial Statements

An audit is a comprehensive investigation of the items that appear on the financial statements and in the notes which may accompany the financial statements. After completing an audit, the independent CPA will express *an opinion as to the fairness of the financial statements*; this opinion is called the auditor's report.

Unless the CPA finds it necessary to comment on unusual items or exceptions, the auditor's report usually consists of two paragraphs. The first paragraph describes the scope of the auditor's investigation and examination of the accounting records; the second paragraph states an opinion on the financial statements.

Let's assume that a team of independent CPAs audited the financial statements for Deb's Steakhouse, Inc. Attached to the financial statements we should find an audit report, which may read as follows:

> We have examined the balance sheet of Deb's Steakhouse, Inc. as of December 31, 19X2, and the related statements of income, retained earnings, and the changes in financial position for the year then ended. Our examination was made in accordance with generally accepted auditing standards, and accordingly included such tests of the accounting records and such other auditing procedures as we considered necessary in the circumstances.
>
> In our opinion, the financial statements referred to above present fairly the financial position of Deb's Steakhouse, Inc. at December 31, 19X2, and the results of its operations and the changes in its financial position for the year then ended, in conformity with generally accepted accounting principles applied on a basis consistent with that of the preceding year.

Reviewed Financial Statements

The objective of a review differs significantly from the objective of an audit. The objective of an audit is to express an opinion as to the fairness of the financial statements. The objective of a review is to express *limited assurance* that no material changes to the financial statements are necessary for them to be in conformity with generally accepted accounting principles.

Let's assume that a team of independent CPAs reviewed the financial statements for Deb's Steakhouse, Inc. Attached to the financial statements we should find a review report, which may read as follows:

> We have reviewed the accompanying balance sheet of Deb's Steakhouse, Inc. as of December 31, 19X2, and the related statements of income, retained earnings, and the changes in financial position for the year then ended, in accordance with standards established by the American Institute of Certified Public Accountants. All information included in these financial statements is the representation of the management of Deb's Steakhouse, Inc.
>
> A review consists principally of inquiries of company personnel and analytical procedures applied to financial data. It is substantially less in scope than an examination in accordance with generally accepted auditing standards, the objective of which is the expression of an opinion regarding the financial statements. Accordingly, we do not express such an opinion.
>
> Based on our review, we are not aware of any material modifications that should be made to the accompanying financial statements in order for them to be in conformity with generally accepted accounting principles.

Compiled Financial Statements

When compiling financial statements, a CPA is not required to make inquiries or perform procedures to verify or review information supplied by the business. The CPA only considers whether the financial statements appear to be in appropriate form and free from obvious arithmetical errors, inadequate disclosure, or the misapplication of accounting principles.

Let's assume that a team of independent CPAs compiled the financial statements for Deb's Steakhouse, Inc. Attached to the financial statements we should find a compilation report, which may read as follows:

> The accompanying balance sheet of Deb's Steakhouse, Inc. as of December 31, 19X2, and the related statements of income, retained earnings, and the changes in financial position for the year then ended have been compiled by us.
>
> A compilation report is limited to presenting in the form of financial statements information that is the representation of management. We have not audited or reviewed the accompanying financial statements and, accordingly, do not express an opinion or any other form of assurance on them.

At the end of this chapter, an appendix has been provided to illustrate sample financial statements from an actual hospitality firm. The appendix includes highlights and excerpts from the annual report of Chi-Chi's, Inc. These sample statements are intended to show the high level of detailed information found in such reports.

Calculating Cost of Sales

Understanding the interrelationships among inventory, sales, and cost of sales is the key to understanding how to calculate cost of sales.

Exhibit 3.7 Food Inventory Operating Cycle

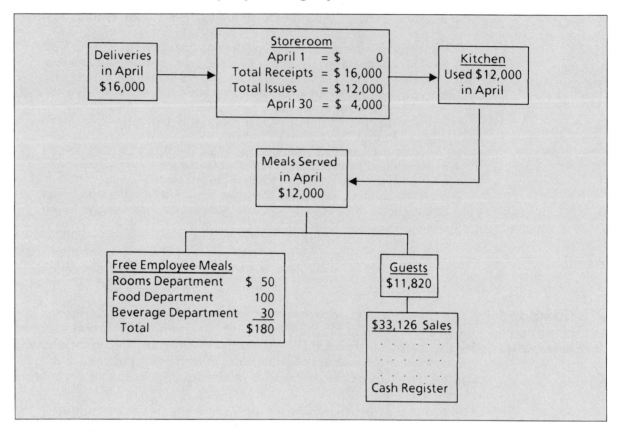

Inventory is an asset account and appears on the balance sheet; Food Inventory represents food merchandise in the storeroom. *Food Sales* is a revenue account and appears on the statement of income; the amount shown as Food Sales represents billings to guests for food products per menu prices. *Cost of Sales* is an expense account and appears on the income statement; Cost of Food Sales represents the cost of food merchandise used to generate revenue from food sales to guests.

Exhibit 3.7 diagrams the activity within a food department and provides the focus of the following discussion on how to calculate cost of food sales. To simplify the discussion, waste, theft, spoilage, and inventories in service areas are ignored. Further, we will assume that all purchased food merchandise is delivered directly to the storeroom and issued later to the kitchen, and that all food issued to the kitchen was prepared and served. Since the use of supplies inventory is charged to a supplies expense account, it is not a factor in calculating cost of sales.

Let's assume that a proprietorship opens a new lodging operation on 4/1/XX. Its beginning inventory at the start of 4/1 is zero because there was no ending inventory on 3/31 to bring forward. Relevant portions of the operation's financial statements for the month ended April 30, 19XX, are shown in Exhibit 3.8.

Food purchases for the month of April were as follows:

4/1:	$ 3,000
4/8:	3,500
4/16:	4,500
4/28:	5,000
	$16,000

The issues from the storeroom to the kitchen throughout the month represented a total cost of $12,000. Since the total food merchandise available for issue was valued at a cost of $16,000 (beginning inventory $0 + purchases $16,000), the ending inventory in the storeroom is $4,000, based on the following calculation:

Ending Inventory = Total Food Merchandise Available for Issue − Food Issued During the Month

Ending Inventory = $16,000 − $12,000

Ending Inventory = $4,000

A physical count of food products in the storeroom should also result in a value of $4,000 (cost) of food merchandise.

If the storeroom issues had a cost of $12,000, then the kitchen used $12,000 worth of food merchandise. Does this mean that the cost of sales is $12,000? *No!* Cost of sales must be related to the cost of merchandise used to generate revenue. In the hospitality industry, some establishments serve free meals to employees who are on duty, mainly for the convenience of the employer. Therefore, not all food used in the kitchen generated revenue through sales of food items to guests.

During the month of April, free meals costing $180 were provided to the following employees:

Rooms Department Employees	$ 50
Food Department Employees	100
Beverage Department Employees	30
	$180

The cost of free employee meals is charged to each department as an operating expense to an account called Employee Meals Expense. Given the previous information, $50 would be charged to the Rooms Department, $100 to the Food Department, and $30 to the Beverage Department. The total cost of all free employee meals is subtracted from cost of sales.

If the cost of food used and served was $12,000 and the cost of free employee meals was $180, then the cost of sales (cost of food sold to guests) is $11,820.

The $11,820 cost of food served to guests generated revenue of $33,126 as billed on guest checks from the menu prices. Therefore, the gross profit made on sales of food products to guests is $21,306 calculated as follows:

Exhibit 3.8 Portions of the Operation's Financial Statements

Hotel Balance Sheet April 30, 19XX	Food Department Income Statement For the month ended 4/30/XX
ASSETS	**REVENUE**
	Food Sales $33,126
CURRENT ASSETS:	**COST OF SALES**
Cash $9,000	Food 11,820
Food Inventory 4,000	**GROSS PROFIT** 21,306
	OPERATING EXPENSES
	Payroll 10,000
	Employee Meals 100
	Other Expenses 8,100
	Total Operating
	Expenses 18,200
	NET INCOME $ 3,106

Food Sales		$33,126
Cost of Sales:		
Food Used Expense	$12,000	
Less Free Employee Meals	180	
Cost of Food Sold		11,820
Gross Profit		$21,306

Notes

1. *AICPA Professional Standards*, Vol. 2, ET §201.02 (New York: American Institute of Certified Public Accountants).

Discussion Questions

1. What is the purpose of the statement of income?

2. What are the basic categories that appear on the statement of income?

3. What is the difference between revenue and net income?

4. What is the difference between gross profit and net income?

5. How is a statement of income prepared for a proprietorship form of business different from a statement of income prepared for a corporation?

6. What is the purpose of the statement of owner's equity and the statement of retained earnings?

7. What is the purpose of the balance sheet?

8. What are the major categories that appear on the balance sheet?

9. What kinds of reports may be submitted by an independent certified public accountant regarding the financial statements of a business?

10. Why is the cost of providing free employee meals not part of the cost of sales figure?

Problems

Problem 3.1
For the month of April, the total cost of the food used by the kitchen was $9,000. Food sales for the month were $29,875.95. The food inventory in the storeroom on April 30 was $3,500. Free employee meals for the month totaled 90 lunches at an average cost of $2.00 each. What is the cost of food sales for the month of April?

Problem 3.2
Given the following information, what is the gross profit?

Payroll	$20,000
China & Glassware	500
Operating Supplies	1,000
Cost of Food Sales	16,700
Utilities	800
Kitchen Fuel	360
Food Sales	50,000

Problem 3.3
Curfew Inn is a proprietorship owned by Susan Plies. For the year ended December 31, 19X2, the net income of the lodging operation was $38,500. During that year, Susan invested $20,000 and withdrew $27,000. The financial records show that the bookkeeping account called *Capital, Susan Plies* had a balance of $12,750 on December 31, 19X1.

Prepare a Statement of Owner's Equity for the year ended December 31, 19X2.

Problem 3.4
For the year ended December 31, 19X9, the net income of National Motels, Inc., was $85,900. The retained earnings account on January 1, 19X9 showed a balance of $62,000. During the year 19X9 the board of directors declared the following dividends to its stockholders:

May 21:	$8,500
November 28:	$8,500

The dividends declared on November 28 have not been paid as of December 31, 19X9. Prepare a Statement of Retained Earnings for the year ended December 31, 19X9.

Problem 3.5
The beginning food inventory on 6/1 was $5,000. Food purchases for the month were $20,000. Food issues from the storeroom to the kitchen were $17,300; all of this food was used and served. Food billings to guests for the month were $50,175. Free employee meals for the month were as follows: $250 to food department employees and $75 to beverage department employees. Payroll costs were $16,000 and other operating expenses were $9,210 for the month.

Problems *(continued)*

a. How much food inventory should be in the storeroom on June 30?

b. What is the cost of food sales for June?

c. What is the food gross profit for June?

d. What is the food department's net income for June?

Problem 3.6
Using the following information, prepare a balance sheet on December 31, 19X7, for the Summer Resort, a proprietorship owned by Stan Robins.

The Statement of Owner's Equity prepared for the year ended December 31, 19X7, shows a total of $97,000. The asset and liability bookkeeping accounts show the following balances on December 31, 19X7:

Accumulated Depreciation on Equipment	$ 5,000
Accounts Receivable	9,000
Cost of Furniture	40,000
Cost of Equipment	10,000
Accumulated Depreciation on Building	20,000
Accumulated Depreciation on Furniture	20,000
Cost of Building	182,000
Cash	16,500
Land	20,000
Accounts Payable	8,000
Accrued Expenses	9,700
Prepaid Expenses	2,500
Wages Payable	4,100
Inventories	3,800

Mortgage Payable is $120,000, of which $15,000 is due currently.

CHI-CHI'S, INC.

Corporate Offices: 10200 Linn Station Road, Louisville, KY 40223

Corporate Profile

Chi-Chi's, Inc. is engaged in the development, operation, and franchising of full-service, family-style Mexican restaurants which serve high quality, moderately-priced Mexican food and alcoholic beverages.

Stock Price Range

The Company's common stock is listed on the NASDAQ's National Market Quotation and the high and low sales prices are reported:

Calendar Year 1984	High-Low	Calendar Year 1985	High-Low	Calendar Year 1986	High-Low
First quarter	$25.13—$16.00	First quarter	$13.63—$10.63	First quarter	$11.50—$7.63
Second quarter	$18.38—$13.25	Second quarter	$12.25—$ 9.38	Second quarter	$11.38—$9.13
Third quarter	$18.75—$12.50	Third quarter	$14.50—$ 9.50	Third quarter	
Fourth quarter	$15.38—$10.00	Fourth quarter	$10.63—$ 8.50	(Through July 15, 1986)	$10.50—$9.38

As of July 14, 1986, the Company's issued and outstanding Common Stock was held by 11,759 holders of record. Information regarding the number of stockholders is based upon holders of record excluding participants in security position listings.

The Company has never paid cash dividends on its Common Stock and does not expect to pay such dividends in the foreseeable future. The management of the Company presently intends to retain all available funds for the development of its business and for use as working capital. Future dividend policy will depend on the Company's earnings, capital requirements, financial condition and other relevant factors.

Table of Contents

Selected Financial Data

The following table summarizes certain selected financial data for the last five fiscal years of the Company.

	Year Ended April 30				
	1986	**1985**	**1984**	**1983**	**1982**
Operating Data:	(Dollars in thousands, except income per share data)				
Sales	$258,766	$192,924	$152,511	$ 94,420	$47,257
Franchise fees and royalties	4,236	5,635	5,467	3,478	2,163
Interest income	5,857	7,177	3,727	3,413	2,206
Other income	410	260	—	—	—
Total revenues	269,269	205,996	161,705	101,311	51,626
Cost of sales	220,083	158,088	115,792	72,642	37,805
Selling, general and administrative expenses	23,554	17,459	13,616	9,577	5,358
Interest expense	6,880	4,553	3,215	4,994	2,786
Provision for the disposition of certain assets	4,800	—	—	—	—
Provision for income taxes	4,897	10,333	12,360	4,993	1,966
Income before extraordinary item	9,055	15,563	16,722	9,105	3,711
Extraordinary item	—	—	—	270	—
Net income	$ 9,055	$ 15,563	$ 16,722	$ 9,375	$ 3,711
Income per share (1):					
Before extraordinary item	$ .34	$ .58	$ .66	$ .40	$ .17
Extraordinary item	—	—	—	.01	—
Net income	$ .34	$ .58	$ .66	$ .41	$ .17
Balance Sheet Data:					
Working capital	$ 70,264	$ 60,570	$ 47,472	$ 24,288	$ 2,339
Total assets	229,435	218,477	147,769	101,927	56,846
Long-term debt including capital lease obligations	70,798	73,961	25,783	45,224	19,920
Shareholders' equity	120,970	111,772	95,291	38,140	19,254

(1)   Adjusted to reflect the three-for-two stock splits effected on June 1, 1981, June 25, 1982, December 17, 1982 and September 27, 1983.

Message to Shareholders

As the new Chairman and Chief Executive Officer, I am very enthusiastic about the future potential of Chi-Chi's. During my career, I have held several executive positions within the industry, including Chairman and Chief Executive Officer of S&A Restaurants (a subsidiary of Pillsbury which owns Steak & Ale and Bennigan's), as well as President and Chief Operating Officer of Chili's, Inc. Based on my experience in the restaurant business, I view the Chi-Chi's concept as a solid foundation on which we can build to improve financial results and to increase our leadership in this segment of the industry.

Fiscal 1986 proved to be a difficult year for Chi-Chi's, as well the restaurant industry as a whole, and the financial results for the year fell short of the intended goal.

A summary of results for the year is as follows:

• Total revenues of $269.3 million compared to $206.0 million reported in Fiscal 1985.

• Net income of $9.1 million compared to $15.6 million reported in Fiscal 1985.

• Earnings per share of $.34 compared to $.58 reported in Fiscal 1985.

• 27 Company-owned restaurants and nine franchised restaurants were opened, bringing the total number of restaurants at year end to 123 Company-owned and 74 franchised.

One of the primary reasons for the decline in earnings was the softness in sales. This impacted not only comparable store volumes, but also resulted in less-than-anticipated sales levels in the new stores. Similar sales declines have been experienced by most restaurant companies during this period, as increased competition and rapid unit expansion have saturated the market.

Store margins declined during the year, reflecting the impact of the decrease in our sales on the fixed components of cost of sales and, reflecting higher labor, occupancy, and pre-opening costs associated with the new stores in the Northeast.

Fiscal 1986 earnings were also significantly impacted by a pretax charge of $5.3 million. This included a $3.8 million reserve resulting from our decision to implement a program to dispose of certain underperforming units, and a $1.5 million write down of assets, primarily related to the planned sale of a corporate aircraft. These decisions reflect our Company's philosophy to dispose of assets that are not generating acceptable returns on investment. We believe that these decisions will ultimately improve profitability and the overall vitality of the concept.

Other improvements to our business are in progress which we believe should provide positive results for the future.

• We have implemented a new advertising campaign to increase Chi-Chi's top-of-mind awareness with the consumer when selecting a destination restaurant. This new campaign was developed by Young and Rubicam of Chicago, after completing an extensive market study to determine what direction our advertising should take. We are very optimistic about this new campaign and are hopeful that it will stimulate sales volumes in all of our restaurants.

• We have begun testing a new lunch menu. This program should provide our customer the opportunity to enjoy the Chi-Chi's experience within the time constraints of a limited lunch hour.

• We continue to enhance our cost control programs, including: more efficient purchasing to improve food and liquor costs; additional in-store programs to reduce operating expenses; and improved recruiting and training to help reduce restaurant management turnover.

During Fiscal 1986, the Company continued to improve the strength of its balance sheet. The current cash position of approximately $70 million provides the financial flexibility to develop restaurants and pursue other opportunities. A current ratio of 3.7 to 1.0 and a debt-to-equity of .90 to 1.0 continue to be among the best in the restaurant industry. Assets increased by approximately 5% to $229.4 million and stockholders equity increased by 8% to $120.9 million.

Management's future philosophy will be one of long-term development for our Company. We plan to focus on the importance of people to our business — our customers, our employees, and of course, our shareholders. The Company already\ has a strong core of profitable restaurants, significant financial strength and a wealth of talented human resources. All these factors should enable us to look forward to future years of continued success and improved financial results.

Everyone at Chi-Chi's looks forward to the challenges ahead and I, in particular, am excited about the prospects of leading our Company in the future.

Sincerely,

Hal W. Smith

Hal W. Smith
Chairman and Chief Executive Officer
July 15, 1986

Management's Discussion and Analysis of Financial Condition and Results of Operations

Results of Operations

Shown for the periods indicated are (i) items in the consolidated statement of income as a percentage of total revenues, (ii) the percentage change in dollar amounts of such items compared to the indicated prior periods.

	Percent of Total Revenues Year Ended April 30			Period to Period Change	
				1986 vs 1985	1985 vs 1984
	1986	1985	1984		
Sales	96.1%	93.7%	94.3%	34.1%	26.5%
Franchise fees and royalties	1.6	2.7	3.4	(24.8)	3.1
Interest income	2.2	3.5	2.3	(18.4)	92.6
Other income	.1	.1	—	57.4	—
Total revenues	100.0	100.0	100.0	30.7	27.4
Cost of sales	81.7	76.8	71.6	39.2	36.5
Selling, general and administrative expenses	8.7	8.4	8.4	34.9	28.2
Interest expense	2.6	2.2	2.0	51.1	41.6
Income before the provision for the disposition of certain assets and income taxes	7.0	12.6	18.0	(27.6)	(11.0)
Provision for the disposition of certain assets	1.8	—	—	—	—
Income before income taxes	5.2	12.6	18.0	(46.1)	(11.0)
Income taxes	1.8	5.0	7.6	(52.6)	(16.4)
Net income	3.4%	7.6%	10.4%	(41.8)	(6.9)

1986 Compared to 1985

Sales increased during the period as a result of the increase in Company-owned operating units from 96 in 1985 to 123 in 1986. Total average unit sales declined 5.2% from the previous year. The primary reasons for this decline were due to the lower volumes from units operating in their trial periods (units' first 17 months of operation) and to the overall softness being experienced in the restaurant industry. Average unit sales for mature units declined only .7% from the previous year.

Franchise fees in 1985 included $725,000 of territory franchise fees which were recorded in income when the respective agreements granting new territory were signed. There were no territory fees included in the 1986 franchise fees. Royalties decreased during the period as a result of the decrease in franchise units from 78 in 1985 to 74

in 1986 and also to the decline in franchise average unit sales. During the fourth quarter of 1986, the Company agreed to a one year abatement of royalty fees for selected franchise units. The impact of this action on the operations of Chi-Chi's, Inc. is expected to be insignificant.

Interest income decreased through the period due to decline in investable funds and a decline in investment rates. Other income results from the sale of excess property.

Cost of sales as a percent of sales for 1986 and 1985 was 85% and 82%, respectively. This increase primarily reflects the impact of the decrease in restaurant sales on the fixed components of cost of sales and, in addition, reflects higher labor, occupancy and pre-opening costs associated with the new stores opened in the Northeast.

Management's Discussion and Analysis of
Financial Condition and Results of Operations — Continued

Selling, general and administrative expenses as a percent of total revenues for 1986 and 1985 were 8.7% and 8.4%, respectively. This increase was due to the overall growth of the Company.

Interest expense increased in 1986 as a result of the issuance of $50,000,000 of 9% convertible subordinated debentures in October 1984.

The provision for the disposition of certain assets results from the Company's plan to dispose of six restaurants and the corporate aircraft.

The Company's effective tax rate was 35.1% in 1986 compared to 39.9% in 1985. The decrease reflects the impact of investment tax and jobs tax credits on a lower pre-tax income.

1985 Compared to 1984

Sales increased during the period as a result of the increase in Company-owned operating units from 69 in 1984 to 96 in 1985. Total average unit sales declined 9.1% from the previous year. Average unit sales for mature units declined only 4.4% from the previous year. The decline in unit sales was due in part to severe weather experienced during the winter and to the strategy of clustering Company units in certain markets to gain additional market share and competitive advantage. While the clustering strategy has contributed to the decline in average unit sales in the short term, the Company believes the strategy is vital for long term stability and will provide growth in total sales and profits.

Franchise fees in 1985 and 1984 included $725,000 and $950,000, respectively, of territory franchise fees which were recorded in income when the respective agreements granting new territory were signed. Royalties increased during the period as a result of the increase in franchise units from 67 in 1984 to 78 in 1985.

Interest income increased through the period due to increased amounts of investments and higher investment rates achieved. Other income results from the sale of excess property.

Cost of sales as a percent of sales for 1985 and 1984 was 82% and 76%, respectively. This increase was due primarily to lower unit sales discussed above and to additional training and implementation costs incurred in the introduction of the new grilled product line.

Selling, general and administrative expenses as a percent of total revenues remained the same in 1985 and 1984.

Interest expense increased in 1985 as a result of the issuance of $50,000,000 of 9% convertible subordinated debentures in October 1984.

The Company's effective tax rate was 39.9% in 1985 compared to 42.5% in 1984. The decrease from 1984 to 1985 reflects an increase in investment tax credits and targeted jobs tax credits available from an increased number of unit openings.

Liquidity and Capital Resources

Chi-Chi's, Inc. working capital has increased from $24,288,000 at the beginning of fiscal 1984 to $70,264,000 at April 30, 1986, an increase of over $45,000,000. The primary sources of working capital during the period has been operations ($70,711,000), borrowings ($25,574,000, net of reductions), sale of stock and exercise of options ($28,778,000), and sale and leasebacks of property and equipment ($49,144,000). Working capital has been used primarily for additions to property and equipment ($127,700,000).

Total borrowings include $50,000,000 of 9% convertible subordinated debentures issued in October 1984.

The Company believes that funds available from its current working capital, operations and future sales and leasebacks of property and equipment will be more than adequate to meet planned capital requirements for the foreseeable future.

Inflation and Changing Prices

Food and labor costs are significant inflationary factors in the Company's operations. Many of the Company's employees are paid hourly rates related to the statutory minimum wage, therefore, increases in the minimum wage would increase the Company's costs. In addition, most of the Company's leases require it to pay percentage rentals based on revenues and to pay taxes, maintenance, insurance, repairs and utility costs. The Company has been able to offset the effects of inflation to date through small price increases, and economies resulting from the purchase of food products in increased quantities due to the growth in the number of Company restaurants.

Information on the effects of changing prices prepared in accordance with the guidelines of the Financial Accounting Standards Board is presented in Note 11 to the Consolidated Financial Statements.

Consolidated Balance Sheet

April 30, 1986 and 1985

ASSETS	1986	1985
Current assets:		
Cash and temporary investments	$ 71,496,667	$ 63,114,969
Notes receivable	3,583,373	354,873
Receivables, trade and other	3,752,269	4,654,844
Inventories	10,235,899	7,601,711
Prepaid expenses	7,206,867	8,090,709
Total current assets	96,275,075	83,817,106
Net property and equipment	118,233,963	126,388,610
Long-term notes receivable	2,391,658	1,009,180
Other assets	12,534,381	7,262,312
	$229,435,077	$218,477,208

LIABILITIES AND SHAREHOLDERS' EQUITY

	1986	1985
Current liabilities:		
Accounts payable	$ 5,545,558	$ 8,413,889
Accrued liabilities	15,592,839	8,746,080
Income taxes payable	412,096	838,488
Deferred income taxes	2,247,738	2,872,127
Current maturities of long-term debt	2,212,782	2,376,483
Total current liabilities	26,011,013	23,247,067
Long-term debt	70,797,693	73,961,055
Deferred income taxes	10,375,751	9,496,929
Other long-term liabilities	1,280,466	—
Shareholders' equity:		
Preferred stock, par value $.25 per share; authorized 250,000 shares, issued — none	—	—
Common stock, par value $.01 per share; authorized 70,000,000 shares, issued 27,029,456 and 27,013,002 shares	270,294	270,130
Additional paid-in capital	65,923,794	65,755,220
Retained earnings	54,776,066	45,746,807
Total shareholders' equity	120,970,154	111,772,157
	$229,435,077	$218,477,208

See accompanying notes.

Consolidated Statement of Income
Years ended April 30, 1986, 1985 and 1984

	1986	1985	1984
Revenues:			
Sales	$258,765,924	$192,923,636	$152,510,921
Franchise fees and royalties	4,236,021	5,635,515	5,467,916
Interest income	5,857,197	7,176,841	3,727,057
Other income	409,682	260,280	—
	269,268,824	205,996,272	161,705,894
Costs and expenses:			
Cost of sales	220,083,090	158,088,584	115,792,474
Selling, general and administrative expenses	23,553,388	17,459,154	13,616,424
Interest expense	6,880,243	4,552,817	3,215,228
	250,516,721	180,100,555	132,624,126
Income before the provision for the disposition of certain assets and income taxes	18,752,103	25,895,717	29,081,768
Provision for the disposition of certain assets	4,800,000	—	—
Income before income taxes	13,952,103	25,895,717	29,081,768
Provision for income taxes	4,897,000	10,333,000	12,360,000
Net income	$ 9,055,103	$ 15,562,717	$ 16,721,768
Net income per share	$.34	$.58	$.66

See accompanying notes.

Consolidated Statement of Shareholders' Equity

Years ended April 30, 1986, 1985 and 1984

	Common Stock Shares	Dollars	Additional Paid-In Capital	Retained Earnings	Total
Balance May 1, 1983	23,916,660	$239,166	$24,407,748	$13,493,466	$ 38,140,380
Exercise and related tax benefits of stock options	516,323	5,163	6,403,869	(1,649)	6,407,383
Sale of common stock	1,050,000	10,500	21,268,903	—	21,279,403
Issuance of shares upon conversion of 10½% subordinated convertible debentures	1,435,100	14,351	12,769,935	(1,147)	12,783,139
Net income	—	—	—	16,721,768	16,721,768
Other	(428)	(4)	(13,170)	(28,348)	(41,522)
Balance April 30, 1984	26,917,655	269,176	64,837,285	30,184,090	95,290,551
Exercise and related tax benefits of stock options	95,134	952	919,437	—	920,389
Net income	—	—	—	15,562,717	15,562,717
Other	213	2	(1,502)	—	(1,500)
Balance April 30, 1985	27,013,002	270,130	65,755,220	45,746,807	111,772,157
Exercise and related tax benefits of stock options	18,117	181	170,210	—	170,391
Net income	—	—	—	9,055,103	9,055,103
Other	(1,663)	(17)	(1,636)	(25,844)	(27,497)
Balance April 30, 1986	27,029,456	$270,294	$65,923,794	$54,776,066	$120,970,154

See accompanying notes.

Consolidated Statement of Changes in Financial Position

Years ended April 30, 1986, 1985 and 1984

	1986	1985	1984
Sources of working capital:			
Operations:			
Net income	$ 9,055,103	$15,562,717	$16,721,768
Items not affecting working capital in the current period:			
Depreciation and amortization	10,320,707	6,459,856	4,589,085
Deferred income taxes	878,822	4,041,208	3,082,056
Working capital provided by operations	20,254,632	26,063,781	24,392,909
Additions to long-term debt	658,437	50,551,678	670,935
Proceeds from sale of common stock and exercise of stock options and related tax benefits	170,391	920,389	27,686,786
Issuance of common stock upon conversion of debentures	—	—	12,783,139
Proceeds from sale and leasebacks	34,533,230	2,497,847	12,113,000
	55,616,690	80,033,695	77,646,769
Uses of working capital:			
Additions to property and equipment	33,738,169	61,231,435	32,728,249
Reduction of long-term debt	3,821,799	2,373,395	20,112,025
Investments in joint venture	2,703,019	—	—
Other	5,659,680	3,330,549	1,622,941
	45,922,667	66,935,379	54,463,215
Increase in working capital	9,694,023	13,098,316	23,183,554
Working capital at beginning of year	60,570,039	47,471,723	24,288,169
Working capital at end of year	$70,264,062	$60,570,039	$47,471,723
Changes in the components of working capital:			
Increase (decrease) in current assets:			
Cash and temporary investments	$ 8,381,698	$10,729,694	$29,516,108
Notes receivable	3,228,500	(2,227,684)	(6,873,959)
Receivables, trade and other	(902,575)	1,991,419	1,580,620
Inventories	2,634,188	2,487,982	2,044,683
Prepaid expenses	(883,842)	2,124,393	1,966,896
	12,457,969	15,105,804	28,234,348
Decrease (increase) in current liabilities:			
Accounts payable	2,868,331	(2,871,398)	514,000
Accrued liabilities	(6,846,759)	(788,059)	(520,373)
Income taxes payable	426,392	2,521,115	(3,033,439)
Deferred income taxes	624,389	(735,669)	(1,273,514)
Current maturities of long-term debt	163,701	(133,477)	(737,468)
	(2,763,946)	(2,007,488)	(5,050,794)
Increase in working capital	$ 9,694,023	$13,098,316	$23,183,554

See accompanying notes.

Notes to Consolidated Financial Statements

1. Summary of significant accounting policies

Basis of presentation — The Company operates in one industry — the sale of food products to the general public through full-service, family-style restaurants operated by the Company and its franchisees. The accompanying consolidated financial statements include the accounts of the Company and its subsidiaries (all wholly-owned).

Inventories — Inventories are stated at the lower of cost (first-in, first-out) or market.

Pre-opening costs — Costs incurred before a restaurant is opened, consisting primarily of employee training costs, are capitalized and amortized over a twelve-month period commencing the date the restaurant opens.

Revenue recognition — Territory franchise fees are recorded in income when the agreement has been finalized. Territory franchise fees amounted to $725,000 and $950,000 in 1985 and 1984, respectively. Individual unit franchise fees are recorded in income when the restaurant is opened. Royalties are recorded in income on the accrual basis. Expenses associated with franchise fees and royalties are charged to expense as incurred.

Property and equipment — Property and equipment is stated at cost less accumulated depreciation and amortization. Depreciation and amortization are provided on the straight-line method over the following estimated useful lives: buildings — principally 30 years; equipment — 3 to 7 years; leasehold improvements — lesser of useful life of assets or term of leases; and buildings and equipment under capital leases — initial lease term.

Income taxes — Investment tax credits are deducted from the federal income tax provision under the flow-through method.

Income per share — Income per share amounts are based on the weighted average number of shares outstanding. The assumed conversion of convertible subordinated debentures and exercise of stock options do not result in material dilution.

Reclassifications — Certain reclassifications have been made in prior year statements to reflect comparability.

2. Disposition of certain assets

The Company's Board of Directors has approved a plan to dispose of six restaurants and to write-down certain assets primarily related to the corporate aircraft. The total amount charged, during the fourth quarter of fiscal 1986, to pretax income was $5,300,000, of which $500,000 is included in cost of sales, and therefore reduced net income per share by $.10.

Notes to Consolidated Financial Statements

3. Business combination

During the third quarter of 1984, the Company acquired all of the capital stock of Chi-Chi's of New England, Inc. (CCNE) in exchange for 418,704 shares of the Company's common stock. This transaction was accounted for as a pooling of interests and, accordingly, the accompanying consolidated financial statements have been restated to include the accounts and operations of the acquired company.

Separate summarized operating results of the combined entities are as follows:

	Year Ended April 30 1984
Revenues:	
Chi-Chi's, Inc.	$155,958,533
CCNE	5,975,444 (A)
Intercompany	(228,083)
Total	$161,705,894
Net income:	
Chi-Chi's, Inc.	$ 15,999,863
CCNE	748,955 (A)
Intercompany	(27,050)
Total	$ 16,721,768

(A) Nine months ended January 31, 1984 (unaudited).

Notes to Consolidated Financial Statements

4. Net property and equipment

Interest capitalized during the construction period totaled approximately $871,000, $1,210,000 and $721,000 for the years ended April 30, 1986, 1985 and 1984, respectively.

Net property and equipment at April 30, 1986 and 1985 consists of the following:

	1986	1985
Owned:		
Land	$ 9,062,652	$ 17,879,832
Buildings	51,372,465	54,780,837
Equipment	50,759,770	36,685,410
Leasehold costs and improvements	20,920,401	6,259,829
Construction in progress	3,157,982	17,535,050
	135,273,270	133,140,958
Less accumulated depreciation and amortization	21,534,122	12,958,539
	113,739,148	120,182,419
Leased under capital leases:		
Buildings	5,313,128	4,714,059
Equipment	1,245,387	3,194,333
	6,558,515	7,908,392
Less accumulated amortization	2,063,700	1,702,201
	4,494,815	6,206,191
Net property and equipment	$118,233,963	$126,388,610

5. Accrued liabilities

Accrued liabilities at April 30, 1986 and 1985 consists of the following:

	1986	1985
Provision for the disposition of certain assets	$ 4,800,000	$ —
Taxes other than income taxes	2,708,535	2,261,686
Insurance	2,644,945	888,916
Compensation	2,636,137	2,874,979
Accrued advertising	1,222,117	1,427,666
Other	1,581,105	1,292,833
	$15,592,839	$8,746,080

Notes to Consolidated Financial Statements

6. Long-term debt

Long-term debt at April 30, 1986 and 1985 consists of the following:

	1986	1985
9% convertible subordinated debentures due October 2009, payable in annual installments of $2,500,000 commencing October 1995 (See A below)	$50,000,000	$50,000,000
Obligations under Industrial Revenue Bonds due in varying amounts to December 1997; at rates ranging from 65% to 77% of the banks' prime rate (8.5% at April 30, 1986) (See B below)	5,204,584	5,679,329
Obligations under Industrial Revenue Bonds due in varying amounts to October 2000; at rates ranging from 9% to 12.625% (See B below)	11,854,666	12,871,367
Notes payable due in monthly installments totaling up to $30,354 through December 1992; plus interest ranging from 8.9% to 17.5%	949,348	1,697,707
Capital lease obligations	4,993,877	6,041,135
Other	8,000	48,000
	73,010,475	76,337,538
Less current maturities	2,212,782	2,376,483
	$70,797,693	$73,961,055

(A) The debentures are convertible into common stock at $17.00 per share. Under certain circumstances, the debentures are redeemable at 108% of the principal amount plus accrued interest and at declining prices thereafter.

(B) Under certain bond agreements, the Company is required to maintain certain financial ratios which include current ratio, fixed charge coverage and debt to equity ratio and maintain a minimum tangible net worth. At April 30, 1986, $11,000,000 of the bonds are secured by bank letters of credit. The fees for the letters of credit are at rates of 1.0% to 1.5% of the outstanding balance.

Exclusive of capital lease commitments, long-term debt maturing during the five years subsequent to April 30, 1986 is as follows: 1987 — $1,879,511; 1988 — $1,727,090; 1989 — $1,829,415; 1990 — $2,094,088; and 1991 — $2,649,224.

At April 30, 1986 owned property and equipment having an aggregate cost of approximately $27,300,000 was pledged as collateral for long-term debt.

Notes to Consolidated Financial Statements

7. Leases

The Company leases certain land, buildings and equipment. Many of these leases contain renewal options. The majority of leases on land and buildings contain contingent rental provisions based on percentages of gross sales. The leases generally obligate the Company for the cost of property taxes, insurance and maintenance.

Rental expense under operating leases for the years ended April 30, 1986, 1985 and 1984 consists of the following:

	1986	1985	1984
Base rentals	$11,536,550	$7,857,470	$5,299,142
Contingent rentals	555,592	559,921	612,801
	$12,092,142	$8,417,391	$5,911,943

Future lease commitments are as follows:

Year ending April 30	Capital Leases	Operating Leases
1987	$ 926,493	$ 14,845,208
1988	884,355	14,604,199
1989	879,336	14,667,282
1990	878,502	14,335,495
1991	762,191	14,223,578
Thereafter	6,803,674	189,027,750
	11,134,551	$261,703,512
Less amount representing interest	6,140,674	
Present value of minimum lease payments	4,993,877	
Less current maturities	333,271	
Long-term debt under capital leases	$ 4,660,606	

8. Capital stock and stock options

In September 1983, the Board of Directors approved a three-for-two stock split which was effected by issuing one additional share of common stock for every two shares held by shareholders of record. All share and per share amounts have been restated for the stock split.

On October 5, 1981, the Company's shareholders approved a Stock Option and Stock Appreciation Rights (SARs) Plan (the Plan). At April 30, 1986, 1,681,576 shares of common stock were reserved under the Plan. An additional 500,000 shares have been approved by the Company's Board of Directors to be reserved under the Plan subject to shareholder approval. Options are granted at the fair market value on the date of the grant. Most options are exercisable in whole or part beginning one year after grant and ending five years after grant. At April 30, 1986 options for 804,934 shares were exercisable. Options covering a maximum of 48,515 shares may be granted under the Plan in the future.

The Company also has made grants under a Stock Option Plan for Non-Employee Directors. At April 30, 1986, 89,000 shares were reserved under this Plan. 44,000 shares were exercisable. Options covering a maximum of 37,500 shares may be granted in the future.

SARs granted under the Plan were exercisable with certain prescribed exceptions and limitations at any time after the first anniversary of their date of grant and, if not exercised before, were deemed automatically exercised on the fifth anniversary of their date of grant. The maximum amount payable upon exercise of SARs increased periodically from $.99 for SARs exercised within 12 months and 55 days after the date of grant, to $5.56 for SARs exercised more than four years and 55 days following the date of grant. A total of 287,408 SARs were granted under the Plan at $4.67 per share. During 1986, 1985 and 1984, respectively, 5,063, 5,062 and 229,190 SARs were exercised. All SARs have been exercised as of April 30, 1986.

Notes to Consolidated Financial Statements

The following is a summary of common stock options outstanding, all of which are issued to current or former officers, key employees and directors:

	Number of Shares	Option Price Per Share
Outstanding, May 1, 1983	970,911	$ 5.30-16.08
Granted during 1984	783,248	17.75-23.50
Exercised during 1984	(516,320)	5.30-15.33
Cancelled during 1984	(70,380)	6.33-23.50
Outstanding, April 30, 1984	1,167,459	5.30-23.50
Granted during 1985	1,016,331	10.13-18.00
Exercised during 1985	(95,772)	6.17-16.75
Cancelled during 1985	(738,922)	6.33-23.50
Outstanding, April 30, 1985	1,349,096	5.30-22.17
Granted during 1986	526,568	9.00-11.25
Exercised during 1986	(18,117)	6.33-12.25
Cancelled during 1986	(218,521)	5.30-20.83
Outstanding, April 30, 1986	1,639,026	6.33-20.83

9. Income taxes

The provision for income taxes consists of the following for the years ended April 30, 1986, 1985 and 1984:

	1986	1985	1984
Current:			
Federal	$3,096,000	$ 4,281,000	$ 4,301,000
State and local	1,348,000	1,012,000	659,000
	4,444,000	5,293,000	4,960,000
Deferred	418,000	4,777,000	4,356,000
Tax effect of stock option transactions	35,000	263,000	3,044,000
	$4,897,000	$10,333,000	$12,360,000

A reconciliation of the provision for income taxes for the years ended April 30, 1986, 1985 and 1984 with the federal statutory rate of 46% is as follows:

	1986	1985	1984
Provision computed at statutory rate	$6,418,000	$11,912,000	$13,378,000
State and local income taxes, net of federal income tax benefit	715,000	904,000	762,000
Investment tax credit	(1,108,000)	(1,572,000)	(1,112,000)
Targeted jobs tax credit, net of federal income tax effect	(797,000)	(692,000)	(278,000)
Tax effect of income taxed to owners of acquired companies	—	—	(332,000)
Other	(331,000)	(219,000)	(58,000)
	$4,897,000	$10,333,000	$12,360,000

Notes to Consolidated Financial Statements

Deferred income taxes arise from timing differences in the recognition of revenues and expenses for tax and accounting purposes. The provision for deferred income taxes for the years ended April 30, 1986, 1985 and 1984 results from the following items:

	1986	1985	1984
Accelerated depreciation	$3,813,000	$3,527,000	$2,523,000
Safe harbor lease	260,000	263,000	266,000
Deferred pre-opening costs	(558,000)	211,000	602,000
Franchise fee deposits	(279,000)	156,000	10,000
Gain on sale and leasebacks	(837,000)	—	(276,000)
Provision for the disposition of certain assets	(2,364,000)	—	—
Other	383,000	620,000	1,231,000
	$ 418,000	$4,777,000	$4,356,000

10. Supplemental quarterly financial data results (unaudited)

The following is a summary of selected quarterly data for the years ended April 30, 1986 and 1985:

	First Quarter	Second Quarter	Third Quarter	Fourth Quarter
1986				
Revenues	$66,614,346	$66,564,666	$67,425,217	$68,664,595
Gross profit	12,590,384	9,368,628	8,579,992	8,143,830
Income before the provision for the disposition of certain assets and income taxes	7,826,396	5,612,518	3,151,317	2,161,872
Provision for the disposition of certain assets	—	—	—	4,800,000
Income (loss) before income taxes	7,826,396	5,612,518	3,151,317	(2,638,128)
Net income (loss)	4,496,396	3,499,518	2,144,317	(1,085,128)
Net income (loss) per share	.17	.13	.08	(.04)
1985				
Revenues	$47,993,307	$49,717,432	$51,749,225	$56,536,308
Gross profit	9,964,379	8,889,783	7,114,708	8,866,182
Income before income taxes	8,470,794	7,384,969	4,209,235	5,830,719
Net income	5,010,794	4,462,969	2,585,235	3,503,719
Net income per share	.19	.17	.10	.13

Notes to Consolidated Financial Statements

11. Impact of Inflation and Changing Prices on Financial Data (Unaudited)

The Company's consolidated financial statements are prepared using the historical cost method in accordance with generally accepted accounting principles. As such statements do not reflect the full impact of inflation, the Financial Accounting Standards Board requires disclosure of restated historical financial data adjusted to reflect the effect of changes in specific prices of the resources employed by the Company. The measurement of the Company's assets using specific prices reflects the current cost of replacing resources rather than the historical costs of acquiring them.

The current cost of property and equipment was determined principally by recent construction costs or purchase prices for like land, building and equipment packages and external cost indices. Depreciation and amortization expense related to these assets was calculated based upon current cost amounts using the same depreciation methods and lives as were used for historical amounts. Due to the rapid turnover of inventories, cost of goods sold in the historical financial statements does not differ significantly from current cost.

The following information for the year ended April 30, 1986 is presented as an estimate of the effect of price changes on the Company:

	As Reported	Current Cost
Net operating revenues	$269,268,824	$269,268,824
Costs and expenses:		
Cost of sales	210,345,236	210,345,236
Depreciation and amortization of property and equipment	10,115,819	10,924,662
Selling, general and administrative expenses, exclusive of depreciation and amortization	23,175,423	23,175,423
Interest expense	6,880,243	6,880,243
	250,516,721	251,325,564
Income before the provision for the disposition of certain assets and income taxes	18,752,103	17,943,260
Provision for disposition of certain assets	4,800,000	4,800,000
Income before income taxes	13,952,103	13,143,260
Provision for income taxes	4,897,000	4,897,000
Net income	$ 9,055,103	$ 8,246,260
Net income per share	$.34	$.31
Effective tax rate	35.1%	37.3%
Unrealized gain from decline in purchasing power of net amounts owed		$ 580,250
Effect of increase in the specific price level over increase in general prices		$ 1,439,803

Notes to Consolidated Financial Statements

At April 30, 1986, the current cost of inventories was $10,235,899 and the current cost of property and equipment, net of accumulated depreciation and amortization, was $127,687,533.

The following is a five-year comparison of historical and current cost data. Current cost data, for all years, is presented in terms of average fiscal year 1986 "purchasing power" dollars.

	1986	1985	1984	1983	1982
Net Revenues:					
Historical cost	$269,268,824	$205,996,272	$161,705,894	$101,311,081	$51,626,324
Current cost	269,268,824	212,200,293	173,331,383	112,179,057	59,826,790
Net Income:					
Historical cost	$ 9,055,103	$ 15,562,717	$ 16,721,768	$ 9,374,952	$ 3,711,297
Current cost	8,246,260	15,492,970	17,610,687	10,274,601	4,217,522
Net income per share:					
Historical cost	$ .34	$ .58	$ .66	$ .41	$ .17
Current cost	$ .31	$ .57	$ .69	$ .45	$ .19
Net Assets at fiscal year-end:					
Historical cost	$120,970,154	$111,772,157	$ 95,290,551	$ 38,140,380	$19,253,885
Current cost	130,182,669	127,142,483	108,065,411	45,898,009	25,377,989
Increase (decrease) in the current cost amounts of inventories and property and equipment, net of inflation	$ 1,439,803	$ 3,457,807	$ (27,479)	$ 704,671	$ 737,529
Unrealized gain from decline in purchasing power of net amounts owed	$ 580,250	$ 461,279	$ 616,324	$ 879,490	$ 719,969
Market price per common share at fiscal year-end	$ 10.13	$ 9.75	$ 17.00	$ 25.00	$ 24.13
Average consumer price index	325.1	314.8	302.8	292.6	278.8
Percentage change in average consumer price index	3.3%	4.0%	3.5%	4.9%	9.1%

Notes to Consolidated Financial Statements

12. Summary of restaurant activity:

	1986	1985	1984
Company owned restaurants:			
In operation; beginning of year	96	69	46
Opened during the year	27	27	23
In operation, end of year	123	96	69
Franchisee owned restaurants:			
In operation, beginning of year	78	67	46
Opened during the year	9	15	24
Closed during the year	(13)	(4)	(3)
In operation, end of year	74	78	67

Accountant's Report

The Board of Directors and Shareholders
Chi-Chi's, Inc.

We have examined the accompanying consolidated balance sheet of Chi-Chi's, Inc. at April 30, 1986 and 1985, and the related consolidated statements of income, shareholders' equity and changes in financial position for each of the three years in the period ended April 30, 1986. Our examinations were made in accordance with generally accepted auditing standards and, accordingly, included such tests of the accounting records and such other auditing procedures as we considered necessary in the circumstances.

In our opinion, the statements mentioned above present fairly the consolidated financial position of Chi-Chi's, Inc. at April 30, 1986 and 1985, and the consolidated results of operations and changes in financial position for each of the three years in the period ended April 30, 1986, in conformity with generally accepted accounting principles applied on a consistent basis during the period.

ARTHUR YOUNG & COMPANY

Louisville, Kentucky
July 3, 1986

4
Chart of Accounts

The previous chapter introduced the major financial statements prepared by businesses in the hospitality industry. Financial statements represent the end result of the financial accounting cycle. This chapter focuses on one of the earliest stages of the accounting process—the organization of the basic bookkeeping system. This system is the foundation for recording financial information which is eventually used to prepare the major financial statements. Questions answered in this chapter include:

1. What do bookkeepers use as a guide when they enter the results of business transactions in accounting records?

2. How are the individual accounts classified in order to facilitate the preparation of major financial statements?

3. What is the logic used to design account numbering systems?

4. How are the various accounts related to the fundamental accounting equation?

5. Are there accepted industry practices that guide businesses in the organization of basic financial information?

This chapter defines the purpose of a chart of accounts and identifies its function in an accounting system. The methodology employed in constructing a chart of accounts is addressed, as well as the sequence of bookkeeping procedures for the five major account classifications. The chapter then discusses and analyzes the relationship of the five major account classifications to the accounting equation. The chapter closes by presenting the three major uniform system of accounts manuals published for specific segments of the hospitality industry.

Purpose of a Chart of Accounts

A chart of accounts is a listing of the titles (names) of all the accounts used by a particular business. It does not show any account balances. The main purpose of a chart of accounts is to serve as a "table of contents" which bookkeepers may use as a guide when they enter the results of business transactions into accounting records. Bookkeepers are generally not allowed to use an account unless it specifically appears on the company's chart of accounts.

The chart of accounts lists the titles of all bookkeeping accounts to be used for recording business transactions. The following sample bookkeeping accounts are typical of almost any business:

- Cash

- Accounts Receivable

- Accounts Payable

- Sales

- Payroll

- Depreciation

The account names on the chart of accounts are listed in a sequence that parallels the order of their appearance on the financial statements and in the general ledger. The *general ledger* contains the accounts in which the results of business transactions are recorded (posted).

Major Account Classifications

For most businesses, the chart of accounts arranges all accounts according to five major classifications. Accounts are classified as either asset, liability, equity, revenue, or expense accounts. Accounts classified as asset, liability, or equity accounts are used to prepare the balance sheet, and are sometimes called the balance sheet accounts. Accounts classified as revenue or expense accounts are used to prepare the statement of income, and are sometimes called the income statement accounts.

The sequence of major account classifications appearing on a chart of accounts is as follows:

- Asset accounts

- Liability accounts

- Equity accounts

- Revenue accounts

- Expense accounts

The following sections explain the particular sequence within which individual accounts of each major account classification are arranged.

Sequence of Asset Accounts. Cash is always listed first, followed by other items according to their liquidity (nearness to becoming cash). Prepaid expenses are included because their prepayment precludes the requirement of using cash in the future. A more elaborate asset section of the chart of accounts for a particular company may include:

- Cash on Hand

- Cash in Bank

- Notes Receivable

- Accounts Receivable
- Food Inventory
- Beverage Inventory
- Supplies Inventory
- Prepaid Rent
- Prepaid Insurance

Next appear the relatively permanent assets which include property and equipment items. These assets are also called fixed assets. In this category, Land is listed first, followed by Buildings. After these two items, any sequence is acceptable for the other "permanent" assets such as vehicles; furniture; computers; cooking equipment; and china, glassware, and silver.

Sequence of Liability Accounts. Liability accounts are listed according to whether the debt is current or noncurrent. Current liabilities appear before long-term liabilities.

Liabilities are normally listed in order of maturity, with those to be met earliest listed first. Thus, Accounts Payable is generally the first liability account. While it is not possible to specify the sequence of liability accounts for all businesses, the following sample listing is provided as an example:

- Accounts Payable
- Income Taxes Payable
- Sales Tax Payable
- Accrued Payroll
- Accrued Payroll Taxes
- Mortgage Payable

Sequence of Equity Accounts. The equity accounts which appear on a chart of accounts will depend on whether the business is organized as a proprietorship, partnership, or corporation.

For proprietorships, the sequence of equity accounts is as follows:

- Capital, (Owner's Name)
- Withdrawals, (Owner's Name)

The sequence of equity accounts for partnerships is similar to that for proprietorships. The major difference is that there are separate Capital and Withdrawal accounts for each partner. For partnerships, the sequence of accounts would appear similar to the following:

- Capital, (Partner A)
- Capital, (Partner B)
- Withdrawals, (Partner A)
- Withdrawals, (Partner B)

For corporations, the sequence of the ordinary equity accounts is as follows:

- Common Stock Issued
- Additional Paid-In Capital
- Retained Earnings

Chapter 5 will discuss other equity accounts which may appear on a chart of accounts for corporations.

Sequence of Revenue and Expense Accounts. A chart of accounts lists revenue accounts before expense accounts. The sequence of individual accounts within these categories will vary from one business to another. For a hotel, Rooms Sales is listed first, followed by Food Sales, Beverage Sales, and other revenue accounts.

For hospitality businesses, the expense account section of the chart of accounts usually lists Cost of Sales accounts first, and Payroll and payroll-related expenses next, followed by the other expenses of doing business. Cost of Sales, Payroll, and payroll-related expenses (such as payroll taxes and employee benefits) are referred to as *prime costs*.

Account Numbering Systems

The use of computers in the recording process requires that each account be assigned an account number. The account number is usually designed so that a significant digit represents one of the major account classifications (asset, liability, equity, revenue, or expense accounts). The digits which follow define the individual account's sequential relationship within that classification.

For example, assume that an accountant has designed a three-digit account numbering system. Since the first major account classification is assets, the number 1 is assigned as the first digit for all asset account numbers. The number series of 1xx will therefore include all asset accounts. Cash is the first account to appear within the sequence of accounts classified as asset accounts. *Therefore*, in a three-digit account numbering system, the account number assigned for the cash account may be 101.

Since liabilities are the second major account classification, the number 2 is assigned as the first digit for all liability accounts. Thus, the number series 2xx will include all liability accounts. Accounts Payable is generally the first account to appear within the sequence of accounts classified as liability accounts. In a three-digit numbering system, the account number assigned for the accounts payable account may be 201.

A business may use any account numbering configuration which meets its particular needs and requirements. The variety of accounts and the design of numbering systems vary from business to business, depending on a company's size and the detail of management information required. Some businesses that use a manual accounting system may also employ an account numbering system.

Exhibit 4.1 illustrates a chart of accounts used by the fictional Hospitality Management Associates, a proprietorship owned by Stephen Roland. For the purposes of our illustration, this example of a chart of accounts is for a hospitality service business—a type of business that sells

Exhibit 4.1   Chart of Accounts for Hospitality Management Associates

HOSPITALITY MANAGEMENT ASSOCIATES
Chart of Accounts

ASSET ACCOUNTS
Cash	101
Accounts Receivable	112
Prepaid Rent	121
Prepaid Insurance	122
Land	141
Building	145
Furniture & Equipment	147
Accumulated Depreciation--Building	155
Accumulated Depreciation--F&E	157

LIABILITY ACCOUNTS
Accounts Payable	201
Accrued Payroll	211
Accrued Payroll Taxes	212
Accrued Interest	217
Mortgage Payable	251

EQUITY ACCOUNTS
Capital, Stephen Roland	301
Withdrawals, Stephen Roland	302

REVENUE ACCOUNTS
Sales	401

EXPENSE ACCOUNTS
Payroll	501
Payroll Taxes	502
Employee Group Insurance	503
Utilities	521
Telephone	522
Advertising	531
Office Supplies	541
Repairs & Maintenance	551
Interest	561
Property Insurance	571
Property Taxes	572
Depreciation	591

professional consulting services and does not sell any inventory. Thus, the business does not have any cost of sales (cost of inventory sold).

The supplementary material at the end of this chapter presents a sample chart of accounts reprinted from the Educational Institute's *Uniform System of Accounts and Expense Dictionary for Small Hotels, Motels, and Motor Hotels.* This sample chart of accounts can be useful to a lodging property in establishing an account numbering system for its operations.

Note that the sample chart of accounts uses a five-digit numbering system. The first two digits identify individual revenue or support centers within a lodging operation. The last three digits represent individual account numbers which are assigned in much the same way as outlined in our discussion of a three-digit account numbering system.

Also, note that the sample chart of accounts breaks down the expense classification of accounts into the categories of Cost of Sales, Payroll, Other Expenses, and Fixed Charges. Remember that the variety of accounts and the design of numbering systems vary from company to company. The sample chart of accounts is designed for a fairly large lodging operation; however, individual owners and managers are encouraged to add or delete accounts to meet the individual needs and requirements of their properties.

The Accounting Equation

The discussion of the balance sheet in Chapter 3 presented *the technical form of the accounting equation* as:

$$Assets = Liabilities + Equity$$

The abbreviated form of the accounting equation is:

$$A = L + E$$

Our discussion of the chart of accounts defined the sequence of major account classifications as follows:

- Asset accounts
- Liability accounts
- Equity accounts
- Revenue accounts
- Expense accounts

At this point, the question naturally arises why revenue and expense accounts are not identified within the accounting equation.

The answer is that during the closing entries process at the end of the accounting period, the revenue and expense accounts are closed to an equity account. The type of equity account depends on the form of business organization. For a proprietorship, the equity account used is the Capital account; for a corporation, the equity account used is Retained Earnings.

The relationship of revenue and expense accounts to asset, liability, and equity accounts is expressed by *the long form of the accounting equation*, which is as follows:

$$Assets = Liabilities + Equity + Revenue - Expenses$$

The accounting equation is not technically stated in this format because the revenue and expense accounts are closed (set to zero) at the end of the business year, their balances having been transferred to the proper equity accounts.

To illustrate both the technical and long forms of the accounting equation, we will use the following dollar amounts as the totals of all the account classifications:

$$
\begin{array}{ll}
\text{Asset accounts total} & \$11,000 \\
\text{Liability accounts total} & 4,000 \\
\text{Equity accounts total} & 2,000 \\
\text{Revenue accounts total} & 20,000 \\
\text{Expense accounts total} & 15,000
\end{array}
$$

Using the long form of the accounting equation produces the following:

$$
\begin{array}{ccccccccc}
\text{Assets} & = & \text{Liabilities} & + & \text{Equity} & + & \text{Revenue} & - & \text{Expenses} \\
11,000 & = & 4,000 & + & 2,000 & + & 20,000 & - & 15,000
\end{array}
$$

The net income is $5,000 (revenue less expenses). Since the revenue and expense accounts are closed at the end of the accounting period and transferred to an equity account, the equity accounts will total $7,000; the revenue accounts will have a zero total, and the expense accounts will also have a zero total. Therefore, at the end of the accounting period, the accounting equation will read:

$$
\begin{array}{ccccc}
\text{A} & = & \text{L} & + & \text{E} \\
11,000 & = & 4,000 & + & 7,000
\end{array}
$$

Uniform System of Accounts

Several major trade associations in the hospitality industry have published manuals defining accounts for various types and sizes of operations. A hospitality business using the uniform system of accounts designed for its segment of the industry may select from the manual those accounts which apply to its operations and ignore those which do not. These manuals may also provide standardized financial statement formats, explanations of individual accounts, and sample bookkeeping documents. A uniform system of accounts serves as a turnkey accounting system because it can be quickly adapted to the needs and requirements of new businesses entering the hospitality industry.

The idea of a uniform system of accounts is not new and is not unique with the hospitality industry. The *Uniform System of Accounts for Hotels* was first published in 1926 by a number of outstanding hoteliers who had the foresight to recognize the value of such a system to the hotel industry. Although there have been several revised editions since the 1926 publication, the fundamental format of the original uniform system has survived as testament to the success of the system in meeting the basic needs of the industry.[1]

Following the lead of the lodging industry, the National Restaurant Association published the *Uniform System of Accounts for Restaurants* in 1930. Its objective was to give restaurant operators a common accounting language and provide a basis upon which to compare the results of their operations. This uniform accounting system has been revised five times and today many restaurant operators find it a valuable accounting handbook.[2]

There are many uniform accounting systems serving the needs of the various segments of the hospitality industry. The *Uniform System of Accounts and Expense Dictionary for Small Hotels, Motels, and Motor Hotels* provides a standardized accounting system for full-service properties (those with extensive food and beverage facilities) and limited-service properties (those which have limited food and beverage facilities or that lease out food and beverage operations).[3]

In addition to the uniform accounting systems for hotels, motels, and restaurants, there are also uniform systems of accounts for clubs, hospitals, condominium operations, and conference centers. The uniform accounting systems for the hospitality industry are continually revised to reflect changes in acceptable accounting procedures and changes in the business environment which may affect hospitality accounting. They now enjoy widespread adoption by the industry and recognition by banks and other financial institutions, as well as the courts.

Advantages of Adopting a Uniform System of Accounts

Hotels, motels, restaurants, and other segments of the hospitality industry benefit from adopting the uniform system of accounts appropriate for their operations. Perhaps the greatest benefit provided is that the uniformity of account definitions provides a common language with which managers from different properties may discuss the results of their operations. This common language permits useful comparisons among properties of the same size and service level. When managers and executives from businesses using the same uniform system of accounts gather to talk shop, compare properties, and evaluate operations, they know that they are all speaking the same language.

Another benefit of a uniform accounting system is that regional and national statistics can be gathered and the industry can be alerted to threats and/or opportunities of developing trends. Industry statistical reports also serve as general standards by which to compare the results of individual operations. Exhibit 4.2, Comparative Results of Operations, provides statistics gathered by the national accounting firm of Pannell Kerr Forster published in *Trends—USA*. These statistics reveal the percentage distribution of revenue and expenses for the average hotel or motel. Industry averages such as these are meant to be used only as guidelines for general comparative purposes. A significant variance between the results of a particular operation and the industry average may be due to circumstances which are unique to that operation or locality. If this is the case, there may not be cause for alarm or any need for action.

Other kinds of industry reports, such as the monthly occupancy rates illustrated in Exhibit 1.5 in Chapter 1, also provide managers with tools by which to compare the performance of their operations against the performance of similar operations within their region. Exhibit 4.3 lists a number of important sources of statistical information regarding the major segments of the hospitality industry.

Exhibit 4.2 Comparative Results of Operations

Revenues:	1985	1984
Rooms	62.0%	61.5%
Food--Including Other Income	23.4	23.2
Beverages	7.8	8.3
Telephone	2.3	2.4
Other Operated Departments	2.4	2.4
Rentals and Other Income	2.1	2.2
Total Revenues	100.0%	100.0%

Departmental Costs and Expenses:		
Rooms	17.1%	16.5%
Food and Beverages	25.4	25.7
Telephone	2.4	2.6
Other Operated Expenses	1.7	1.8
Total Costs and Expenses	46.6%	46.6%
Total Operated Departmental Income	53.4%	53.4%

Undistributed Operating Expenses:		
Administrative and General	8.9%	8.3
Management Fees*	2.4	2.4
Marketing and Guest Entertainment*	5.7	5.3
Property Operation and Maintenance	5.7	5.6
Energy Costs	5.2	5.2
Other Unallocated Operated Departments*	.3	.4
Total Undistributed Expenses	28.2%	27.2%
Income Before Fixed Charges	25.2%	26.2%

Property Taxes and Insurance:		
Property Taxes and Other Municipal Charges	2.7%	2.5%
Insurance on Building and Contents	.5	.3
Total Property Taxes and Insurance	3.2%	2.8%
Income Before Other Fixed Charges**	22.0%	23.4%
Percentage of Occupancy	66.9%	70.0%
Average Daily Rate per Occupied Room	$62.60	$58.40
Average Daily Room Rate per Guest	$43.43	$40.71
Percentage of Double Occupancy	44.1%	43.5%
Average Size (Rooms)	246	247

Rooms Department:	1985	1984
Rooms Net Revenue	100.0%	100.0%

Departmental Expenses:		
Salaries and Wages Including Vacation	13.0%	13.3%
Payroll Taxes and Employee Benefits	3.8	3.8
Subtotal	16.8%	17.1%
Laundry, Linen, and Guest Supplies	3.0	3.1
Commissions and Reservation Expenses	2.8	2.7
All Other Expenses	3.9	3.0
Total Rooms Expense	26.5%	25.9%
Rooms Departmental Income	73.5%	74.1%

Food and Beverage Department:		
Food Net Revenue	100.0%	100.0%
Cost of Food Consumed	32.8%	34.6%
Less: Cost of Employees Meals	2.4	2.4
Net Cost of Food Sales	30.4%	32.2%
Food Gross Profit	69.6%	67.8%
Beverage Net Revenue	100.0%	100.0%
Cost of Beverage Sales	20.9	21.3
Beverage Gross Profit	79.1%	78.7%
Food and Beverage Revenue	100.0%	100.0%
Net Cost of Food and Beverage Sales	27.8%	29.0%
Gross Profit on Combined Sales	72.2%	71.0%
Public Room Rentals	1.9	2.1
Other Income	2.1	1.9
Gross Profit and Other Income	76.2%	75.0%

Departmental Expenses:		
Salaries and Wages Including Vacation	30.0%	30.8%
Payroll Taxes and Employee Benefits	9.3	9.4
Subtotal	39.3%	40.2%
Laundry and Dry Cleaning	.9	.9
China, Glassware, Silver and Linen	1.6	1.7
Contract Cleaning	.4	.4
All Other Expenses	9.2	8.5
Total Food and Beverage Expenses	51.4%	51.7%
Food and Beverage Departmental Income	24.8%	23.3%

*Averages based on total groups although not all establishments reported data.

**Income before deducting Depreciation, Rent, Interest, Amortization, and Income Taxes.

NOTE: Payroll Taxes and Employee Benefits distributed to each department.

Source: Pannell Kerr Forster, *Trends in the Hotel Industry*, USA Edition, 1986, Figure No. 5, p. 32.

Exhibit 4.3 Major Hospitality Statistical Publications

Publication	Industry Segment	Firm
Trends--Worldwide	Lodging	Pannell Kerr Forster
Trends--USA	Lodging	Pannell Kerr Forster
Clubs in Town and Country	Clubs	Pannell Kerr Forster
Worldwide Lodging Industry	Lodging	Laventhol & Horwath
U. S. Lodging Industry	Lodging	Laventhol & Horwath
Restaurant Industry Operations Report	Restaurant	National Restaurant Association and Laventhol & Horwath

The Expense Dictionary

The Expense Dictionary is published by the Educational Institute as part of its uniform system of accounts for small hotels, motels, and motor hotels. The dictionary is designed to help hotel controllers classify the numerous expense items they encounter in their daily work. It also serves as a ready reference for executives, managers, and purchasing agents, showing them to which account or expense group the accounting department will charge each expense item.

The Expense Dictionary has been recently revised under the direction of the Committee on Financial Management of the American Hotel & Motel Association. The revision was undertaken to ensure that the expense distribution shown in the dictionary conforms to the changes reflected in the new uniform system of accounts. Exhibit 4.4 explains how to read the expense dictionary and includes a sample page reproduced from the dictionary.

The specific changes in expense distribution were necessitated by the increased number of limited-service properties, the increasing importance of the marketing function in the industry, and the recognition of the need for separately identifying charges associated with data processing, human resources, and transportation. The revised dictionary also includes the most recent changes in accounting principles and terminology, in conformity with the pronouncements of various accounting boards as well as industry practice.

Notes

1. *Uniform System of Accounts for Hotels*, 8th rev. ed. (New York, N.Y.: Hotel Association of New York City, 1986).

Exhibit 4.4   Portions of the Expense Dictionary

How to Read the Expense Dictionary

GUIDE TO ABBREVIATIONS

Abbreviation	Department/Function/Item
A&G	Administrative and General
Adv.	Advertising and Merchandising
China	China, Glassware, Silver, and Linen
Depr. & Amort.	Depreciation and Amortization
Elec. & Mech.	Electrical and Mechanical Equipment
F&B	Food and Beverage
Mdse.	Merchandise
Misc.	Miscellaneous
Mktg.	Marketing
POM	Property Operation and Maintenance
POM & EC	Property Operation, Maintenance and Energy Costs
Prtg. & Stat.	Printing and Stationery
PTEB	Payroll Taxes and Employee Benefits
R&M	Repair and Maintenance
T&E	Travel and Entertainment
Trans.	Transportation

The Expense Dictionary is divided into three columns. Column I lists expense items alphabetically. Column II identifies the accounts to which the expense items would be charged in a limited-service property. Column III identifies the accounts to which the expense items would be charged in a full-service property. Items purchased for direct sale in any department are not included, since their distribution is obviously direct to the cost of sales of the department concerned.

Columns II and III list expense accounts in a number of ways. The following is a short explanation of the various forms these listings can take.

If a single word or phrase is listed, it is the account. For example, the limited-service entry for Chemicals (Water Treatment) is Swimming Pool Expense. There is no further breakdown.

If a department, operational function, or cost center is followed by a dash, the entry following the dash is the account charged within that department, operational function, or cost center. For example, the limited-service entry for Bath Mats is Rooms—Linen.

Some expenses are broken down even further. The full-service entry for Advertising—Directories is Mktg.—Adv.—Print. Marketing is the department; advertising and merchandising is the function within the department, and print is the account.

If more than one department or cost center can charge a particular expense item to accounts with the same name, the departments or cost centers are separated by semicolons. For example, the full-service entry for Acids—Cleaning is Rooms; F&B—Cleaning Supplies.

If the same item is charged by different departments or cost centers to different accounts, departments and accounts are listed consecutively and separated by semicolons. For example, the full-service entry for Adding Machine—Tapes is F&B—Prtg. & Stat.; A&G—Operating Supplies.

When one account is followed by another account listed in parentheses, the first is more specific than the second. If your property does not use the more specific breakdown, use the more general account listed in the parentheses. For example, the full-service entry for Athletic Equipment for Employees is Human Resources—Employee Relations (A&G—Human Resources).

Sometimes, one department, operational function, or cost center can charge a particular expense item to more than one account, depending on how the item is used. In this case, the accounts following the dash are separated by semicolons. For example, the limited-service entry for Airport Transportation—Not Chargeable to Guest is General—T&E; Mktg. The full-service entry for Metal Parts is POM—Elec. & Mech; Building Supplies; etc.

Expense Dictionary

Items	Limited-Service Operation	Full-Service Operation
	A	
Accountants' Fees	General—Professional Fees	A&G—Professional Fees
Acids—Cleaning	Rooms—Cleaning Supplies	Rooms; F&B—Cleaning Supplies
Acids—Laundry	POM&EC—R&M	House Laundry—Laundry Supplies
Adding Machine—Service		POM—Elec. & Mech.
Adding Machine—Tapes	General—Operating Supplies	F&B—Prtg. & Stat.; A&G—Operating Supplies
Addressing Machine Supplies	General—Mktg.	Mktg.—Misc. Mktg. Expenses
Adhesive Tape	POM&EC—Operating Supplies	POM—Other
Adhesive Tape	General—Human Resources	Human Resources—Medical Expenses (A&G—Human Resources)
Advertising Agency Fees	General—Mktg.	Mktg.—Fees & Commissions—Agency Fees
Advertising—Direct Mail	General—Mktg.	Mktg.—Adv.—Direct Mail
Advertising—Directories	General—Mktg.	Mktg.—Adv.—Print
Advertising—Due Bills for Room, etc.	General—Mktg.	Mktg.—Adv.—Other
Advertising—Labels	General—Mktg.	Mktg.—Adv.—Other
Advertising—Novelties	General—Mktg.	Mktg.—Adv.—Other
Advertising—Outdoor	General—Mktg.	Mktg.—Adv.—Outdoor
Advertising—Publications	General—Mktg.	Mktg.—Adv.—Print
Advertising—Radio & TV	General—Mktg.	Mktg.—Adv.—Radio & TV
Advertising—Transportation	POM&EC—R&M	Mktg.—Adv.—Outdoor
Air-Cooling Systems Repairs	POM&EC—R&M	POM—Elec. & Mech.
Airport Transportation—Not Chargeable to Guest	General—T&E; Mktg.	A&G—T&E; Mktg.—Sales—Other Expenses
Alarm Service—Fire or Burglar	General—Security	A&G—Other
Alcohol—Cleaning	Rooms—Cleaning Supplies	Rooms; F&B—Cleaning Supplies
Alcohol—Cooking Fuel		F&B—Kitchen Fuel
Alcohol—Painting	POM&EC—R&M	POM—Furniture, Fixtures, Equip. & Decor
Alkalies (Water Softeners)	POM&EC—Engineering Supplies	POM—Engineering Supplies
Aluminum Trays		F&B—Other Operating Supplies
Ammonia—Cleaning	Rooms—Cleaning Supplies	Rooms; F&B—Cleaning Supplies
Ammonia—Refrigerant	POM&EC—Engineering Supplies	POM—Elec. & Mech.
Ammonia Water—Cleaning	Rooms—Cleaning Supplies	Rooms; F&B—Cleaning Supplies

Source: *Uniform System of Accounts and Expense Dictionary for Small Hotels, Motels, and Motor Hotels*, 4th ed. (East Lansing, Mich.: Educational Institute of the American Hotel & Motel Association, 1987), pp. 140-141.

2. *Uniform System of Accounts for Restaurants*, 5th rev. ed. (Washington, D.C.: National Restaurant Association, 1983).

3. *Uniform System of Accounts and Expense Dictionary for Small Hotels, Motels, and Motor Hotels*, 4th rev. ed. (East Lansing, Mich.: Educational Institute of the American Hotel & Motel Association, 1987).

Discussion Questions

1. What is the purpose of a chart of accounts?

2. What are the major account classifications used in a chart of accounts?

3. What major account classifications are used to prepare the balance sheet?

4. What major account classifications are used to prepare the statement of income?

5. How is the technical form of the accounting equation expressed?

6. How is the long form of the accounting equation expressed?

7. Why does the technical form of the accounting equation *not* show revenue or expense accounts?

8. What are the advantages of using a uniform system of accounts?

Problems

Problem 4.1
Assume a company uses a three-digit account numbering system and the left-most digit represents each account's major classification. Assign the left-most digit to the following accounts assuming that the major classifications are sequentially assigned digits of 1 for Assets, 2 for Liabilities, 3 for Equity, 4 for Revenue, and 5 for Expenses.

Accounts Payable	__25
Food Sales	__11
Cash	__05
Notes Payable	__26
Payroll Expense	__02
Land	__61
Retained Earnings	__01

Problem 4.2
Restate the following in terms of the long form of the accounting equation.

Food Sales	$75,000	Payroll Expense	$20,000
Cash	3,000	Accounts Receivable	1,500
Accounts Payable	2,800	Retained Earnings	6,975
Other Assets	65,000	Accrued Payroll	725
Other Liabilities	1,000	Mortgage Payable	45,000
Other Expenses	42,000		

Problem 4.3
Restate the information presented in Problem 4.2 in terms of the technical form of the accounting equation.

Problem 4.4
Restate the following in terms of the long form of the accounting equation.

Asset accounts total	$26,000
Liability accounts total	17,000
Equity	?
Revenue accounts total	55,000
Expense accounts total	49,000

Problem 4.5
Restate the information presented in Problem 4.4 in terms of the technical form of the accounting equation.

5
Asset, Liability, and Equity Accounts

The asset, liability, and equity accounts presented in this chapter are referred to as balance sheet accounts because they are used in the preparation of the balance sheet statement. Many different balance sheet accounts are found in the hospitality industry. The types of accounts used depend on the nature of the business, the assets owned, and the financing structure involving creditors and stockholders.

This chapter will identify and define these accounts in order to provide answers to such questions as:

1. What determines whether a credit card transaction is treated as cash or an account receivable?

2. What is the difference between marketable securities and investments?

3. Why are banquet deposits and room deposits treated as liabilities?

4. How is a long-term debt allocated to its current and noncurrent portions?

5. How is Stockholders' Equity presented on the balance sheet?

This chapter presents the bookkeeping accounts contained within the asset, liability, and equity classifications. Many individual accounts within each major account classification are thoroughly analyzed and discussed. The chapter concludes by discussing an example of a complex equity section for a corporation.

Asset Classification

Assets are items owned by the business which have a commercial or exchange value and are expected to provide a future use or benefit to the business. Ownership in this case refers to possession of legal title and, thus, applies to assets purchased on credit or financed by borrowings, in addition to those assets purchased with cash. Assets include cash, investments, inventory, other specific property, advance payments made by the company, and claims against others.

Assets are further divided into the following major categories, also called subclassifications:

- Current Assets
- Investments
- Property and Equipment
- Other Assets

The following sections define each of these categories and discuss individual accounts in some detail.

Current Asset Accounts

As discussed in Chapter 3, assets and liabilities are arranged on the balance sheet according to their current or noncurrent status. Current assets consist of cash or assets which are convertible to cash within 12 months of the balance sheet date. To be considered a current asset, an asset must be available without restriction for use in payment of current liabilities.

Among the major categories of current assets are the following accounts, listed here in order of liquidity:

- Cash
- Marketable Securities
- Accounts Receivable
- Inventories
- Prepaid Expenses

Items such as marketable securities, accounts receivable, and inventory are liquid assets because of the ease with which they may be converted to cash. Current assets also include prepaid expenses because these items provide a future benefit to be realized within 12 months of the balance sheet date.

The following are definitions for some current asset accounts found in most businesses.

Cash To be included as Cash on the balance sheet, items should be freely available for use. Cash includes cash on hand (change funds and petty cash funds) and cash in the forms of *demand deposits* and *time deposits*. In layman's terms, demand deposits are checking accounts, and time deposits are savings accounts and certificates of deposit. Separate bookkeeping accounts should be maintained for each of the cash items. Rather than show each of these items separately on the balance sheet, they may be combined into a single amount for purposes of financial reporting.

There may be certain time restraints on the immediate withdrawal of cash from time deposits or interest penalties if withdrawals are made before a predetermined date. However, these deposits are usually considered readily available for use as cash.

Any cash that is restricted for current use must be disclosed as such in the financial statements and a determination made whether the cash is to show under current assets or noncurrent assets. Two examples of restricted cash funds are *compensating balances* and *special-purpose funds*.

A compensating balance usually takes the form of a minimum amount that must be maintained in a checking account in connection with a borrowing arrangement with a bank. These compensating balances may be includable under current assets if the arrangement is short-term. Compensating balances required by long-term borrowing arrangements should be included under noncurrent assets, preferably Investments.

Special-purpose funds may be deposited in a special bank account and set aside by management for a specific purpose, such as acquisition of property or equipment. Cash that is earmarked, either voluntarily or by contract, for a special purpose relating to long-term needs should be included under noncurrent assets, preferably Investments.

During the daily operations of a hospitality business, payments by guests may be in the form of cash, personal checks, travelers checks, and credit card vouchers. Accounting systems should be devised in such a way as to distinguish between cash and noncash items. Cash, personal checks, and travelers checks are obviously cash items since they may be readily deposited in the firm's checking account.

Most hospitality firms accept credit cards because they offer increased sales opportunities. In addition, the collection risk is passed on to the credit card company. When a guest uses a credit card, he or she signs a multi-part form. This form is usually composed of a credit card draft, a copy for the business records, and a copy for the guest. This draft is the means by which the hospitality business receives payment.

Certain credit card drafts may be treated as cash transactions if arrangements have been made with a bank to accept them as part of the daily cash deposit. This arrangement is typical for credit cards such as VISA and MasterCard, which are referred to as *bankcards*. The nonbank credit cards, such as American Express, are explained when Accounts Receivable is discussed.

The hospitality firm submits these bankcard drafts along with the daily cash receipts to the bank. The bank increases the firm's checking account; the service fee is usually deducted only once per month. The treatment of credit card fees (credit card commissions) is discussed in *Understanding Hospitality Accounting II* because they are generally not considered in the day-to-day recording of cash.

Marketable Securities

The term "marketable securities" refers primarily to stocks and bonds of large corporations and U.S. government bonds. Securities are included in this category only if the following conditions are met:

1. the securities are readily marketable, *and*

2. management intends to convert them into cash should the need arise.

These securities are considered as liquid as cash, since they may be quickly sold on securities exchanges. Most companies monitor their cash balances and invest excess cash in these securities to earn interest or dividends. Investing in stocks of large corporations also provides the potential of making a gain when the stock is sold at a price higher than its purchase cost.

Although marketable securities are generally classified as current assets, they could instead be classified under the noncurrent asset account called Investments *if* management definitely intends to hold them for more than 12 months from the balance sheet date.

Accounts Receivable

Receivables are the amounts that a business expects to collect at some future date. The most common receivable is Accounts Receivable, which represents the amounts owed to a firm by its guests. It is not unusual for a hospitality business to sell goods or services to guests for the guest's verbal or implied promise to pay at a later date. For example, a guest who enjoys a meal may merely sign the guest check and submit payment only upon receipt of a monthly statement. This type of transaction represents a sale on open account; part of the transaction is recorded as a sale, but instead of an entry to Cash, an entry is recorded as Accounts Receivable.

As discussed previously, nonbank credit cards are not treated as cash. The nonbank credit card drafts must be sent to the credit card company for payment; therefore, these drafts are recorded as Accounts Receivable when they are received in the day-to-day operations. The more common nonbank credit cards are American Express, Diners Club, and Carte Blanche. An American Express draft is shown in Exhibit 5.1.

A hospitality business may issue its own credit cards (usually referred to as in-house credit cards) to the public. Any transactions on these cards are included in Accounts Receivable because the firm directly invoices and collects from the customer.

There may be instances when a hospitality firm might require someone who owes it money to sign a promissory note. It is unlikely that this form of credit would be required of a guest. Its use might arise when the hospitality firm sells property or equipment and, in effect, provides the financing.

A promissory note (see Exhibit 5.2) is a written promise to pay a definite sum of money at some future date. When a promissory note is made payable to the hospitality company, it is called the *payee* of the note; in other words, the hospitality company will receive payment. Promissory notes have two characteristics not normally associated with accounts receivable. First, they are negotiable instruments because these documents are legally transferable among parties by endorsement. Second, these notes generally involve the payment of interest in addition to the principal (amount of loan).

Notes receivable which are collectible within one year of the balance sheet date can be included under current assets. Long-term notes receivable should be included with the noncurrent assets under Investments.

Inventories

This current asset account includes: stocks of food and beverage merchandise held for resale; stocks of operating supplies such as guest supplies, office supplies, cleaning supplies, and engineering supplies;

Exhibit 5.1 Sample American Express Draft

Source: American Express Company

and other supplies held for future use. Inventories are recorded in different bookkeeping accounts as follows:

- Food Inventory
- Beverage Inventory (Liquor Inventory)
- Gift Shop Inventory
- Operating Supplies
- Cleaning Supplies
- Office Supplies
- Restaurant Supplies

Supplies of china, glassware, and silver are not current assets; these items are not intended to be consumed in the short term. They are longer-lived assets and properly belong in the Property and Equipment category.

Prepaid Expenses

Prepaid expenses are expenditures, usually recurring, that produce a measurable benefit which will affect more than one accounting period, but no more than 12 months. Examples of prepaid expenses include prepaid rent (excluding security deposits) and prepaid insurance premiums, both of which are paid in advance and benefit future accounting periods.

Exhibit 5.2 Explanation of a Promissory Note Form

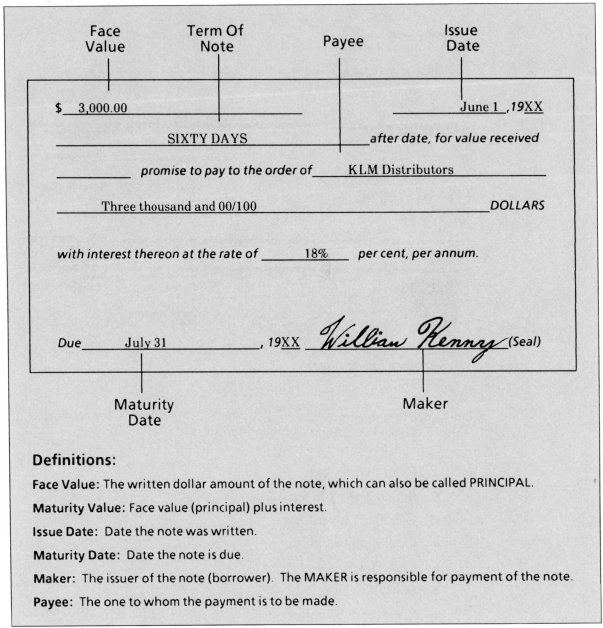

Definitions:

Face Value: The written dollar amount of the note, which can also be called PRINCIPAL.

Maturity Value: Face value (principal) plus interest.

Issue Date: Date the note was written.

Maturity Date: Date the note is due.

Maker: The issuer of the note (borrower). The MAKER is responsible for payment of the note.

Payee: The one to whom the payment is to be made.

Source: Raymond Cote, *Business Math Concepts* (Providence, R.I.: P.A.R. Incorporated, 1985), p. 54.

Prepaid expenses are commonly shown in separate accounts such as the following:

- Prepaid Rent
- Prepaid Insurance
- Prepaid Interest
- Prepaid Service Contracts

Technically, prepaid expenses are unexpired costs that will benefit future periods but are expected to expire within a relatively short period, usually within 12 months of the current accounting period.

For example, payment of the current month's rent on the first of the month or after is *not* a prepaid expense because it is for the current month of the accounting period. However, if the rent for July is paid in June, the payment of the July rent is recorded as prepaid rent in June. (Chapter 11 discusses the use of adjusting entries regarding the separation of prepaid rent and rent expense.)

Noncurrent Asset Accounts

As previously mentioned, assets are arranged on the balance sheet according to their current or noncurrent status. Current assets are those assets which are convertible to cash within 12 months of the balance sheet date. By contrast, noncurrent assets are those assets which are *not* to be converted to cash within 12 months of the balance sheet date.

There are three major categories of noncurrent assets:

- Investments
- Property and Equipment
- Other Assets

Items in the Property and Equipment category are also known as fixed assets.

The following sections discuss these three categories in more detail, providing definitions for some noncurrent asset accounts found in most businesses.

Investments

Like marketable securities, investments may include stocks and bonds of large corporations and U.S. government bonds. However, marketable securities are classified as current assets, while investments are classified as noncurrent assets. Since both marketable securities and investments may involve the purchase of securities, what distinguishes these two categories of assets?

For a particular security to be classified as a current asset, it must be characterized by *all* of the following conditions:

- It is *temporary* in nature.
- A *ready market* exists for its sale.
- Management *intends* to sell it should the need arise.

Unless all of these conditions exist, the stocks or bonds do not fit the definition of a current asset (specifically, a marketable security). Stocks or bonds failing to meet any or all of these conditions must be included under noncurrent assets and recorded as Investments.

As discussed previously, other items that may appear under Investments are cash restricted for use in connection with long-term borrowing arrangements and long-term notes receivable.

Property and Equipment

The noncurrent asset category of Property and Equipment includes those assets of a relatively permanent nature that are tangible (possess physical substance) and are used in the business operation to generate sales. These long-lived assets are also referred to as plant assets or fixed assets.

Property and Equipment accounts include such noncurrent assets as land, buildings, furniture, fixtures, vehicles, ovens, dishwashing machines, and other similar long-lived assets (assets with a life expectancy of more than one year).

China, glassware, silver, linen, and uniforms are also included in Property and Equipment; they are *not* included in Inventories or Prepaid Expenses (both current asset categories). China, glassware, silver, linen, and uniforms are classified as noncurrent assets because their life expectancy is more than one year. Accounting for usage, breakage, and disappearance of these items is explained in *Understanding Hospitality Accounting II*.

The detail required in accounting for fixed assets varies from business to business; however, Land and Buildings are always separate accounts. A typical list of fixed asset accounts might be as follows:

- Land
- Buildings
- Furniture and Equipment
- Transportation Equipment
- China, Glassware, Silver, Linen, and Uniforms

Depreciation is a method to allocate the cost of fixed, tangible assets (except land) over their estimated useful life. The cumulative amount of these allocations is represented in a contra-asset account called Accumulated Depreciation for most of these depreciable assets. Depreciation is discussed in greater detail in the next chapter.

Other Assets

The category Other Assets is for noncurrent assets that cannot be included in the specific groupings given previously. These include initial franchise costs and intangible assets. Intangible assets are long-lived assets having no physical substance, whose ownership provides certain rights and privileges.

As time expires, the cost of certain long-term assets is allocated on a pro-rata (proportional) basis to the operating expenses of the business. This is accomplished through *amortization*—a procedure similar to straight-line depreciation.

The following discussion defines some of the more common accounts classified as Other Assets.

Security Deposits. Security deposits include funds deposited to secure occupancy or utility services (such as telephone, water, electricity, and gas), and any similar types of deposits.

Preopening Expenses. This account includes expenditures incurred in investigating potential business opportunities and getting a new business ready prior to its initial opening for operation.

Organization Costs. Organization costs refer to the costs involved in the legal formation of the business. While they are generally associated with forming a corporation, they may be recorded for a partnership if significant.

Forming a corporation is more costly than forming a proprietorship or a partnership. In addition to state incorporation fees, there are attorneys' fees, printing of stock certificates, fees and expenses paid to the organizers (promoters) of the business, and a variety of other expenditures incurred in organizing the business.

Trademarks and Tradenames. The federal government provides legal protection for trademarks and tradenames if they are registered with the U.S. Patent Office. Material costs associated with their purchase are recorded as Trademarks and Tradenames, a noncurrent asset account.

Franchise Right. Franchising involves a long-term contract wherein the franchiser agrees to lend its name, goodwill, and back-up support to the franchisee. For these benefits, the franchisee agrees to maintain required quality standards and follow certain operating procedures. In addition, the franchisee pays the franchiser in the form of initial costs and annual fees.

An account called Franchise Right may be used to record the initial franchise cost, if material. Annual payments under a franchise agreement should be "expensed" by recording these expenditures to an expense account such as Franchise Fees Expense or Royalties Expense.

Goodwill. Basically, goodwill can be defined as the premium paid in a purchase agreement that reflects the capacity or potential of a business to earn above-normal profits. Goodwill is not recorded as an asset unless it was separately purchased. To avoid any complications with the IRS, goodwill should be separately accounted for when it is part of the cost of purchasing a business.

Liability Classification

Liabilities are the debts of the business (what the business owes its creditors). Liabilities represent the claims of creditors on the assets of a business and are sometimes referred to as *creditors' equities*.

Liabilities are further divided into the following categories or sub-classifications:

- Current Liabilities
- Long-Term Liabilities

Current liabilities are those liabilities which require settlement within 12 months of the balance sheet date. Debts not requiring settlement until later than 12 months of such date are classified as long-term liabilities (also referred to as long-term debts).

Current Liability Accounts

Chapter 3 stated that current liabilities are obligations which will require an outlay of cash within 12 months of the balance sheet date.

While this statement is accurate, it can be refined still further to give a more precise, technical definition: *current liabilities are those liabilities expected to be satisfied by the use of a current asset or to be replaced by another current liability within 12 months of the balance sheet date.*

The reason for this refinement is that a creditor may accept inventory, assignment of accounts receivable, or some other current asset instead of cash as terms for settling a debt. Also, financing agreements may allow for settlement of debt by a new financing agreement when the debt is due. For example, when a 90-day note is due, the borrower may execute a new 90-day note to replace the previous promissory note instead of settling the debt with cash. This is a common financing arrangement between banks and their preferred customers.

The following sections discuss some common current liability accounts.

Notes Payable

A note payable is a written promise (promissory note) by the business to pay a creditor or lender at some future date. A note payable can be either a current liability or a long-term liability, depending on whether it is expected to be paid within 12 months of the balance sheet date. A note requiring payment in cash within 12 months of the balance sheet date is a current liability. Notes payable are discussed in more detail in the section on long-term liabilities.

Accounts Payable

Accounts payable result from verbal or implied promises to pay at some short-term future date. Such transactions usually arise when food, beverages, supplies, services, or utilities are purchased from vendors (also called suppliers or purveyors) *on credit*. Accounts payable are sometimes referred to as trade payables.

Sales Tax Payable

Taxes on retail sales are levied by many states and some cities. Usually the sales tax is imposed on the consumer; however, it is the seller who must collect the tax from the buyer, file the appropriate sales tax return, and remit the sales tax collected. Essentially, the seller acts as a collection agent for the taxing authority. Thus, sales taxes collected are a liability and are excluded from revenue (sales).

Income Taxes Payable

This account generally applies only to corporations as previously discussed. The federal government, most states, and some municipalities impose taxes on the taxable income of a corporation. A corporation might have three accounts as follows:

- Federal Income Tax Payable
- State Income Tax Payable
- Municipal Income Tax Payable

Accrued Expenses

These items represent unrecorded expenses which, at the end of an accounting period, have been incurred but not yet paid. These unpaid expenses often require estimates, which may be computed by reference to historical data or by prescribed analytical procedures. The accrual of expenses is performed to comply with the matching principle—that is, to record expenses to the period in which they are incurred. Some examples are as follows:

- Accrued Payroll
- Accrued Payroll Taxes
- Accrued Property Taxes
- Accrued Interest Expense

Advance Deposits

Advance deposits include amounts paid to the business for goods and/or services it has not yet provided. Examples of advance deposits are banquet deposits and room deposits received from customers for whom no services have yet been provided. The cash received is not revenue (sales) because it has not been earned; thus, an advance deposit represents a liability until the service is performed.

The use of a Banquet Deposits account or a Deposits and Credit Balances account depends on the accounting system used by the hotel or restaurant. Some properties directly credit Accounts Receivable when a customer makes an advance deposit, ignoring the use of a deposits account. This alternate procedure is acceptable; however, when financial statements are prepared, the accountant makes a worksheet entry transferring any credit balances in Accounts Receivable to a liability account called Deposits and Credit Balances or Unearned Revenue for financial reporting purposes.

The rationale behind this transfer is that accounts receivable are defined as money due the company from others. Any credit balances in Accounts Receivable represent obligations on the part of the company and, thus, are more properly classified as liabilities.

Some hotels maintain a separate ledger called the advance deposits ledger to record customer deposits. In preparing financial statements, this ledger is included in the amount shown in Deposits and Credit Balances (or Unearned Revenue).

Other Current Liabilities

Other current liability accounts may exist for various short-term obligations such as unclaimed wages; deposits from employees for keys, badges, and lockers; and other current liabilities which do not apply to categories previously discussed.

Long-Term Liability Accounts

Long-term liabilities include those liabilities which do not meet the parameters defined for current liabilities. A general definition is that long-term liabilities are any debts *not* due within 12 months of the balance sheet date.

The following sections discuss some common long-term liability accounts.

Notes Payable

This account includes those notes payable which cannot be classified as current liabilities; for example, a note due two years from the balance sheet date.

Notes payable are a common financing arrangement in the borrowing of cash and the purchase of equipment, vehicles, and similar assets. When real estate is involved, the obligation is treated as a Mortgage Payable.

A note is signed by the company (or person) who is making the promise to pay, referred to as the *maker*. The bank (or other organization or person) to whom the note is made payable is called the *payee*. Exhibit 5.2 explains the various parts of a promissory note. When a hospitality business secures financing through the execution of a promissory note, it becomes the maker.

A note payable may require one lump-sum payment on the due date or it may require installment payments throughout the life of the note. Even though the note contains a provision for interest in addition to the principal, the interest is not recorded as part of the note payable amount. Any unpaid interest currently due is separately recorded as Interest Payable (or Accrued Interest), a liability account.

Long-term notes payable that require installment payments usually require special treatment for presentation on the balance sheet. Any installment payments that are due within 12 months of the balance sheet date must be removed from the amount shown as long-term debt and reclassified as a current liability, usually called Current Portion of Long-Term Debt. This reclassification procedure is thoroughly explained in the following discussion of Mortgage Payable.

Mortgage Payable

This account is used to record long-term liabilities arising from the purchase of realty (land and/or buildings).

As pointed out in Chapter 4, the sequence of accounts in the chart of accounts and the general ledger is generally arranged to simplify the preparation of financial statements. However, long-term liabilities usually require a special procedure in order to properly present them on the balance sheet.

For example, assume that on April 30, real estate was purchased for $150,000 as follows:

Purchase Cost	$150,000
Cash Paid Out	30,000
Balance Financed with a Ten-Year Mortgage	$120,000

The $120,000 is recorded in a long-term liability account called Mortgage Payable. Assume that the terms of the mortgage call for monthly payments of $1,000 on the principal plus an additional amount for the interest charge. Payments are to start May 30 and are due on the 30th of each month thereafter.

Over the next 12 months, the mortgage requires monthly payments totaling $12,000. Therefore, part of the mortgage represents a liability that must be satisfied by the use of a current asset (cash). *This fits the definition of a current liability.*

Since the Mortgage Payable account is a combination of both current and long-term debt, it is not usable "as is" for preparing financial statements. Until the tenth and final year of the mortgage, there will always be 12 months of current debt ($12,000) and a balance of long-term debt. At the beginning of the tenth year, all of the mortgage payments will be current debt.

This concept may be illustrated by taking our example one step

Exhibit 5.3 Allocating Mortgage Payable on the Balance Sheet: First Month

<u>Balance Sheet as of April 30, 19X2</u>

CURRENT LIABILITIES		
Accounts Payable	$ 7,500	
Accrued Payroll	2,500	
Current Portion of Long-Term Debt	<u>12,000</u>	
Total Current Liabilities		$ 22,000
LONG-TERM LIABILITIES		
Mortgage Payable	120,000	
Less Current Portion of Long-Term Debt	<u>12,000</u>	
Total Long-Term Liabilities		108,000

further. Using the previous facts ($120,000 mortgage liability created on April 30 with monthly payments of $1,000), assume that a balance sheet is to be prepared as of April 30.

The accounting records show that the unpaid balance in the first month for the Mortgage Payable account is $120,000. Of this total, $12,000 ($1,000 for each of 12 months) is currently due, requiring an outlay of cash within 12 months of the balance sheet date. The balance of the mortgage is considered long-term.

Since the Mortgage Payable account contains both current and long-term debt, a manual allocation is necessary on the balance sheet to properly present this financial information. The liability section of the Balance Sheet as of April 30 is presented in Exhibit 5.3.

Next month's balance sheet requires similar treatment. Since a mortgage payment of $1,000 (plus interest) was paid on May 30, the mortgage balance as of May 31 is now reduced to $119,000 as reflected in the Mortgage Payable account. To simplify the example, assume that the Accounts Payable and Accrued Payroll accounts coincidentally show the same amounts as last month. The liability section for the Balance Sheet as of May 31 is presented in Exhibit 5.4.

Notice that the amount paid for the interest charge does not figure into the calculation of liabilities. The payment of interest is recorded as Interest Expense, an expense account. Interest Expense appears as a line item on the statement of income. The expense classification of accounts is discussed in the next chapter.

Equity Classification

The equity accounts represent the claims of the owner(s) on the assets of the business. By contrast, the liability accounts represent creditors' claims on the assets. Taken together, these accounts support the fundamental accounting equation:

$$Assets = Liabilities + Equity$$

Exhibit 5.4 Allocating Mortgage Payable on the Balance Sheet: Second Month

Balance Sheet as of May 31, 19X2

CURRENT LIABILITIES		
Accounts Payable	$ 7,500	
Accrued Payroll	2,500	
Current Portion of Long-Term Debt	12,000	
Total Current Liabilities		$ 22,000
LONG-TERM LIABILITIES		
Mortgage Payable	119,000	
Less Current Portion of Long-Term Debt	12,000	
Total Long-Term Liabilities		107,000

This equation can be restated as:

Assets = Claims of Creditors + Claims of Owners

The equity of the owner is a *residual claim* on the assets because the claims of the creditors have legal priority. The kind of equity accounts a business uses depends upon whether it is organized as a proprietorship, partnership, or corporation.

Proprietorship Equity Accounts

For a proprietorship, the equity section of the balance sheet is called Owner's Equity and is composed of the following accounts:

- Capital, (owner's name)

- Withdrawals, (owner's name)

For a partnership, the equity section of the balance sheet is called Partners' Equity. The accounts composing this section are identical to those for a proprietorship except that separate Capital and Withdrawals accounts are set up for each partner.

Capital   The Capital account contains *investments* made by the owner in the business, plus the *net income* from operations of the business, less any *net loss* from operations of the business, less *withdrawals* of assets from the business by the owner for personal use.

Amounts for net income (or loss) and withdrawals are transferred to the Capital account by a process called closing journal entries, which is performed at the end of the accounting year. This process is explained in Chapter 12.

The Capital account is a *cumulative account*; it contains the net amount of owner's investments, net income (or loss), and withdrawals from the start of the business to the present.

The owner's investment of resources in the business may be cash, inventory, equipment, or other specific property. However, the owner cannot assign a value for personal services and record them as an investment.

Withdrawals

Withdrawals is a temporary account used to record personal withdrawal of business assets by the owner. These assets are usually cash, but may include inventory, equipment, or some other business asset. The Withdrawals account is sometimes called a drawings account; the terms are interchangeable.

At the end of each accounting year, the Withdrawals account is closed, its balance having been transferred to the Capital account which is reduced by that amount. Since the effect of the Withdrawals account is to reduce or offset the Capital account, the Withdrawals account is referred to as a *contra-equity account*.

Corporation Equity Accounts

The equity section of a corporation is called Stockholders' Equity or Shareholders' Equity; the terms are interchangeable. The ordinary equity accounts are as follows:

- Common Stock Issued
- Additional Paid-In Capital
- Retained Earnings

The three accounts just listed are considered typical equity accounts, and are discussed in some detail in this section.

The equity accounts used by a corporation depend on the various equity transactions that have occurred and the particular classes of stock issued. Some corporations have simple equity structures while others may have more complex structures. In addition to the typical accounts discussed in this section, other corporation equity accounts include Capital Stock, Treasury Stock, and Donated Capital, which are discussed in later sections.

Common Stock Issued. This account represents the common stock issued at par value. As discussed in Chapter 2, par value is an arbitrarily selected amount that is referred to as legal value. Par is not indicative of the price or market value of the stock, but rather may be set at any amount (subject to approval by the state division of corporations at the time the articles of incorporation are filed).

Additional Paid-In Capital. When stock is sold above its stated par value, the stock has been issued at a premium. The account Additional Paid-In Capital represents the premium paid on stock issued. The premium is the amount in excess of par value that the stockholders paid for the stock.

For instance, assume that a stock with a par value of $5 is sold for $7 per share. The premium paid per share of stock is $2. If 10,000 shares were sold, the account Additional Paid-In Capital would be increased by $20,000.

Retained Earnings. This account includes the net income of the business since inception, reduced by any net losses of the business and dividends declared since inception.

The net income (or loss) is transferred to the retained earnings account by the process of closing journal entries performed at the end of the accounting year.

A corporation may distribute additional shares of its stock as dividends, referred to as *stock dividends*. This distribution most frequently involves the issuance of common shares to existing common stockholders in proportion to their present ownership in the company. A stock dividend causes no change in assets or equity, and, therefore, is not recorded as a business transaction.

Various reasons may support the issuance of stock dividends. First, issuing stock dividends conserves cash, which can then be used for new ventures such as expansion. Second, stock dividends are not income to the stockholders and therefore not subject to income taxes until the shares are sold. Third, a stock dividend increases the ownership base, which may lead to a decrease in market value per share. The decreased price may ultimately increase the attractiveness of the stock to potential investors.

To illustrate, assume that a corporation with 1,000 shares of stock is owned as follows:

	Shares	Ownership %
Stockholder A:	500	50%
Stockholder B:	500	50%
Total	1,000	100%

Suppose the corporation declares a stock dividend of 20% and issues 200 additional shares: 100 to Stockholder A and 100 to Stockholder B.

	Shares	Ownership %
Stockholder A:	600	50%
Stockholder B:	600	50%
Total	1,200	100%

Even though the stockholders now hold more shares, their ownership interests remain unchanged.

Capital Stock   As a means of selling ownership interests, corporations may issue various classes of common stock and preferred stock (referred to collectively as capital stock). Common stockholders have a residual claim to assets after all claims of creditors and other stockholders have been satisfied.

Preferred stock receives its name because it has priority over common stock regarding assets and dividends. Preferred stock may be cumulative; this means that any dividends in arrears must be paid to the preferred stockholders before any current dividends can be paid to the common stockholders.

Many preferred stock issues are *callable*. That is, the issuing corporation retains the right to reacquire (call) the stock at a preset price. To make this feature acceptable to investors, the call price is usually set slightly higher than the original issue price. However, the call feature frequently limits the value of the stock in the marketplace.

The issuance of callable preferred stock may be viewed as an alternative to financing. The stock can be issued when interest rates for borrowing are high; when these rates drop, it can be called and replaced with cheaper financing.

Separate bookkeeping accounts are established for each type of stock. The accounting treatment for preferred stock is similar to that for common stock. Preferred stock generally has a par value, and any amount paid in excess of par is recorded as Additional Paid-In Capital.

Donated Capital

Sometimes, corporations receive assets (such as land) as gifts from states, cities, or benefactors to increase local employment or encourage business activity in a locality. In such cases, the appropriate asset account would be increased and the equity account Donated Capital would be increased accordingly.

Treasury Stock

A corporation may reacquire shares of its previously issued stock to reduce the number of outstanding and issued shares. This is sometimes done to increase the figure computed for earnings per share, which some regard as an investment guideline. Another reason may be simply to reduce outside ownership.

When stock is reacquired, it is called treasury stock. Treasury stock is no longer considered issued *and outstanding*; therefore, it does not pay any dividends and is not associated with voting privileges. However, it may later be sold again.

The cost method is generally used to record the purchase of treasury stock. Under this method, the account Common Stock Issued is not affected; rather, a contra-equity account called Treasury Stock is used.

For example, assume that a corporation reacquires 5,000 shares of its $1 par value common stock for a cost of $17,000. The business transaction is recorded as follows:

- The Treasury Stock account is increased by $17,000.
- The Cash account is decreased by $17,000.

Stockholders' Equity on the Balance Sheet

A corporation may present an extensive equity section on its balance sheet depending upon the types of equity transactions it carries out. As an example, the equity section of a balance sheet for a particular corporation may appear as in Exhibit 5.5. The section entitled Stockholders' Equity includes the sale of both common and preferred stock, contributions of additional paid-in capital and donated capital, and the deduction of treasury stock reacquired by the corporation.

Throughout this chapter, the composition of the balance sheet has been reduced to its most basic elements. This process provides a clear understanding of the specific accounts and categories which make up this financial statement. Exhibit 5.6 is a list of the basic balance sheet accounts which should be examined before studying debits and credits in Chapter 8.

Exhibit 5.5   Equity Section of a Corporate Balance Sheet

STOCKHOLDERS' EQUITY

Paid-In Capital:

Preferred Stock, 9% dividends, $100 par, cumulative, callable, 600 shares authorized and issued	$ 60,000
Common Stock, $1 par, 200,000 shares authorized, 50,000 shares issued, treasury stock 5,000 shares which are deducted below	50,000
Additional Paid-In Capital	70,000
Total Paid-In Capital	$180,000
Donated Capital	30,000
Retained Earnings	65,000
Total	$275,000
Deduct: Common Treasury Stock at Cost	17,000
Total Stockholders' Equity	$258,000

Exhibit 5.6   Balance Sheet Accounts

ASSET ACCOUNTS

Cash	Prepaid Expenses:
Marketable Securities	Prepaid Rent
Accounts Receivable	Prepaid Insurance
Food Inventory	Land, Buildings, Furniture, Equipment
Beverage Inventory	China, Glassware, Silver
Office Supplies Inventory	Organization Costs
Operating Supplies Inventory	Security Deposits
Cleaning Supplies Inventory	Preopening Expenses

LIABILITY ACCOUNTS

Accounts Payable	Other Payables
Sales Tax Payable	Accrued Expenses:
Notes Payable	Accrued Payroll
Mortgage Payable	Accrued Payroll Taxes
Income Taxes Payable	Other Accrued Expenses

EQUITY ACCOUNTS

For Corporations:	For Proprietorships:
Common Stock Issued	Capital, (owner's name)
Additional Paid-In Capital	Withdrawals, (owner's name)
Retained Earnings	

Discussion Questions

1. How are the following classifications of bookkeeping accounts defined?

   a. Asset

   b. Liability

   c. Equity

2. How are the following categories defined?

   a. Current Asset

   b. Property and Equipment

   c. Other Assets

   d. Current Liability

3. What are the definitions of the following current asset accounts?

   a. Cash

   b. Marketable Securities

   c. Accounts Receivable

   d. Inventories

   e. Prepaid Expenses

4. Why is a 20-year mortgage requiring monthly payments allocated as part current liability and part noncurrent liability on the balance sheet?

5. What are the equity accounts for a proprietorship?

6. What are the equity accounts for a corporation?

Problems

Problem 5.1

On June 30, 19X7, real estate was purchased with a 15-year mortgage of $270,000. The terms of the mortgage were monthly payments of $1,500 on the principal and 12% interest on the unpaid balance, with payments beginning July 30 and due on the 30th of the month thereafter.

a. Show how the mortgage would be presented on the balance sheet for June 30, 19X7.

b. Show how the mortgage would be presented on the balance sheet for July 31, 19X7.

c. Show how the mortgage would be presented on the balance sheet for June 30, 19X8.

Problem 5.2

A corporation has 750,000 shares of authorized common stock at 10¢ par value. On three separate occasions, it has issued the following shares of common stock:

100,000 shares for $700,000

200,000 shares for $1,300,000

150,000 shares for $900,000

The corporation has since repurchased 50,000 shares for a total of $400,000. It had originally issued this stock for $7 per share.

The retained earnings for the year ended June 30, 19X8, were $425,000. The corporation's net income for the year ended June 30, 19X9, was $250,000. Dividends declared during the year 19X9 were $75,000. As of June 30, 19X9, $25,000 of the dividends have not been paid.

Prepare the Stockholders' Equity section for the balance sheet as of June 30, 19X9.

6

Revenue and Expense Accounts

The revenue and expense accounts presented in this chapter are called income statement accounts because they are used in the preparation of the statement of income. The types of income statement accounts used by a hospitality business depend on many different factors, including the size of the business, the nature of its activities, and the amount of detailed information that its managers require.

In Chapter 2, we classified departments as either revenue centers or support centers. Revenue centers include Rooms, Food and Beverage, Telephone, and other revenue-producing departments. Support centers include Administrative and General, Marketing, Property Operation and Maintenance, and other departments which provide supporting services to revenue centers. Individual revenue and expense accounts are established on a departmental basis according to the specific information needed by management. Of course, revenue accounts only apply to revenue centers.

This chapter contributes to a basic understanding of income statement accounts by providing answers to such questions as:

1. When should a sale be recognized and recorded?

2. How do accounting systems treat sales taxes, credit card transactions, and employee tips?

3. How does accounting for cost of sales vary with the type of inventory system used?

4. How are direct purchases, storeroom purchases, and employee meals defined and treated?

5. What is the difference between depreciation and accumulated depreciation?

This chapter presents many of the major accounts contained in the revenue and expense classifications. Cost of sales is intensively analyzed for both the perpetual inventory system and the periodic inventory system in order to stress the role of inventories in an accounting information system. This chapter also discusses special hospitality treatment of storeroom purchases, direct purchases, employee meals, and inventories in service areas. Other topics of discussion include expense accounts for operating expenses, depreciation, and income taxes.

Revenue Classification

The revenue classification comprises a number of accounts used to record the sales of goods and services by revenue centers. It may be helpful at this time to review some important points about the topic of revenue.

Revenue represents the amounts billed to guests for the sales of goods and/or services. The total revenue figure on the statement of income indicates the sum of such billings for a given period of time. It is important to remember that revenue is *not* income; income is the result of total revenue exceeding total expenses.

A sale is recognized and recorded in the accounting records at the time services are rendered or when products are delivered and accepted. Thus, the time to recognize revenue is at the point of sale, regardless of whether the customer pays cash or uses a charge account. This treatment conforms with the *realization principle*, which states that revenue resulting from business transactions should be recorded only when a sale has been made *and* earned. All business transactions must be recorded in the accounting records.

In Chapter 1, we learned that a business transaction is defined as *the exchange of goods, property, or services for cash or a promise to pay*. Accordingly, a sales transaction may involve a receipt of cash or a promise to be paid at some future date. For purposes of this text, transactions involving bank credit cards such as VISA and MasterCard are treated as cash, since arrangements can be made with banks to deposit the credit card drafts in the checking account of a business. Transactions involving credit cards for which such arrangements cannot be made are treated as accounts receivable.

Sales do not include amounts charged for sales taxes since these amounts actually represent a liability rather than revenue. A hospitality business must account for taxes collected from customers and remit these collections to the taxing authority.

For example, assume a guest enjoys dinner at a fine dining establishment and pays $25 for the dinner plus a 6% sales tax (imposed by the state). Suppose the guest pays the tab with cash, which, for our purposes, could also be personal check, travelers check, VISA, or MasterCard. This business transaction creates the following events:

1. The Food Sales account (a revenue account) is increased by $25.00.

2. The Sales Tax Payable account (a liability account) is increased by $1.50 ($25.00 x 6%).

3. The Cash account (an asset account) is increased by $26.50.

If the guest had instead used American Express, Carte Blanche, Diners Club, an in-house credit card, or an open charge account, this business transaction would have created similar events. However, rather than increasing the Cash account, this transaction would have increased the current asset account called Accounts Receivable.

Guests may include service gratuities (tips for servers) on the credit card drafts. However, any tips entered on credit card drafts are excluded from revenue since these amounts belong to employees, not the hospitality company. To facilitate accounting for these tips, hospitality firms often pay the tips to employees at the end of each shift, and then wait for collection from the credit card company.

As presented in Chapter 2, a hospitality establishment may be composed of several separate facilities working simultaneously under the same roof. Such establishments use individual revenue accounts for each of their revenue centers (revenue-producing departments). A small lodging operation may have the following revenue accounts:

- Room Sales
- Food Sales
- Beverage Sales
- Telephone Sales

A more detailed explanation of these accounts and comprehensive coverage of hotel sales are found in *Understanding Hospitality Accounting II*.

Expense Classification

The expense classification includes those accounts that represent: day-to-day expenses incurred in operating the business; expired costs of assets charged to expense by depreciation; and costs of assets (such as inventory) that are consumed in operating the business.

For purposes of discussion, expenses have been grouped into the following topical categories:

- Cost of Sales
- Operating Expenses
- Depreciation
- Income Taxes Expense

Cost of Sales

Cost of sales represents the cost of inventory products used in the selling process, and, therefore, applies only to revenue-producing centers. In relation to cost of sales, the term "inventory products" includes food and beverages, but excludes supplies. The usage of supplies inventory is not charged to cost of sales (also referred to as cost of goods sold); supplies are charged to a supplies expense account listed under Operating Expenses on the statement of income.

Exhibit 6.1   Recording of Purchases

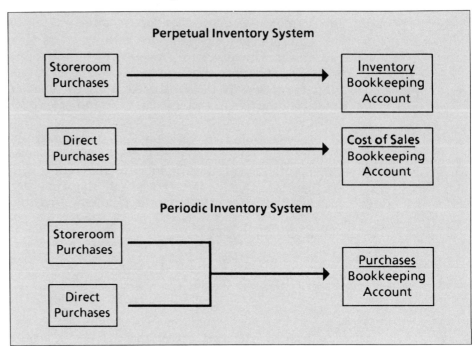

Separate accounting is performed for cost of beverage sales and cost of food sales. Cost of beverage sales is the cost of liquor and mixes used to generate sales. Cost of food sales is the cost of food used in the preparation process for resale to guests. The *net food cost* (that is, cost of food sales) does not include meals provided to employees.

Unlike the food and beverage department, the rooms department does not have any cost of sales. Rooms are not consumed, nor do they involve a sale of inventory; it is room occupancy which is sold. Expenses associated with the upkeep of rooms (for instance, guest supplies, cleaning supplies, and housekeeping labor) are recorded in various operating expense accounts, rather than a cost of sales account.

Inventory Systems

Cost of sales is universal to all accounting systems involving the sale of inventory products. However, the specific procedures used to record cost of sales depend on the type of inventory system employed by a given operation.

One of two systems may be used to account for inventory products: the *perpetual inventory system* or the *periodic inventory system*. Both systems are similar with respect to the storage of inventory items; food and beverages are usually kept in a storeroom (also called a stockroom) until required.

In a number of other respects, however, these two systems differ a

Exhibit 6.2 Sample Perpetual Inventory Form

		|	INVENTORY LEDGER CARD							

No. _____ Description _____

		PURCHASES			ISSUES			BALANCE ON HAND		
Date	Ref.	Units	Unit Cost	Total	Units	Unit Cost	Total	Units	Unit Cost	Total

great deal. Exhibit 6.1 summarizes the recording procedures applicable to each system of inventory accounting.

First, storeroom purchases are treated differently under each of these inventory systems. In a *perpetual* inventory system, all storeroom purchases of food and beverages are recorded in an asset account called *Inventory*. In a *periodic* inventory system, storeroom purchases are recorded in an expense account called *Purchases*.

Second, each of these inventory systems is unique in its treatment of direct purchases and issues. Direct purchases are food products purchased for immediate use and consequently delivered directly to the kitchen. Issues involve the release of food and/or beverages from the storeroom to authorized individuals through an internal requisition process.

Third, the level of recordkeeping required for each type of inventory system varies significantly. This bears heavily on the amount of information readily available and the relative costs of maintaining the system.

Perpetual Inventory System

Under a perpetual inventory system, the storeroom clerk or inventory control clerk maintains a recordkeeping system by which receipts and issues are recorded as they occur. Exhibit 6.2 presents one type of perpetual inventory form used for recording changes in inventory level resulting from these activities.

To appreciate the accounting procedures used in a perpetual inventory system, one must first understand the functions of the storeroom and the accounting department as depicted by the flowchart in Exhibit 6.3.

Refer to the top half of this exhibit, to the section entitled "Purchases." As food is received at the storeroom, the storeroom clerk records the receipt on the perpetual inventory card and *increases* the inventory amount shown on this card. The receiving documents are then forwarded to the accounting department.

The accounting department matches these receiving documents with the corresponding vendor invoices. The bookkeeper records an *increase* to an account called Inventory for the purchase cost of the items received.

Now refer to the bottom half of Exhibit 6.3, to the section entitled "Issues." When food is issued from the storeroom, the storeroom clerk records the issue and *decreases* the quantity on the perpetual inventory card. Information regarding issues is forwarded to the accounting department, where it is summarized on a worksheet. This summarizing procedure may be performed daily or on some other regular basis. The bookkeeping entry is usually made at the end of the month for the total cost of issues from the storeroom.

In the accounting department, the asset account Inventory is *decreased* by the cost of the issues, and this amount (sometimes called "food used" expense) is recorded in an expense account called Cost of Food Sales. This account is later adjusted to remove the cost of employee meals. It is only after this adjustment that the Cost of Food Sales account represents cost of food sold to guests (net food cost). The expenses of employee meals are transferred to the proper departments as part of the employees' fringe benefit package.

Exhibit 6.4 represents how purchasing and issuing activities affect accounting records under a perpetual inventory system. In this example, we assume that the accounting records and the storeroom show an inventory on May 31 of $3,800. This same amount would carry over as the beginning inventory on June 1. Suppose food purchases for the month of June were as follows:

6/1:	$ 2,200
6/9:	3,500
6/18:	3,500
6/29:	3,000
Total	$12,200

Therefore, total food products available for issue would equal $16,000, as shown by the following calculation:

$$\begin{array}{ccc} \text{Total Food Products} & = & \text{Beginning} + \text{Deliveries} \\ \text{Available for Issue} & & \text{Inventory} \quad \text{in June} \end{array}$$

$$\begin{array}{ccc} \text{Total Food Products} & = & \$3,800 + \$12,200 \\ \text{Available for Issue} & & \end{array}$$

$$\begin{array}{ccc} \text{Total Food Products} & = & \$16,000 \\ \text{Available for Issue} & & \end{array}$$

Exhibit 6.3 Operations Flowchart for a Perpetual Inventory System

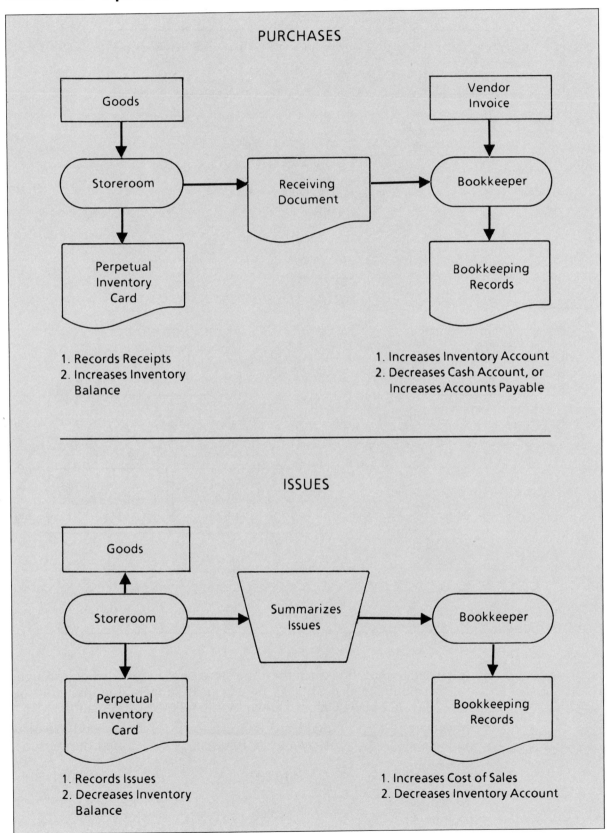

PURCHASES

Goods → Storeroom → Receiving Document → Bookkeeper ← Vendor Invoice

Storeroom → Perpetual Inventory Card

1. Records Receipts
2. Increases Inventory Balance

Bookkeeper → Bookkeeping Records

1. Increases Inventory Account
2. Decreases Cash Account, or Increases Accounts Payable

ISSUES

Goods ← Storeroom → Summarizes Issues → Bookkeeper

Storeroom → Perpetual Inventory Card

1. Records Issues
2. Decreases Inventory Balance

Bookkeeper → Bookkeeping Records

1. Increases Cost of Sales
2. Decreases Inventory Account

Exhibit 6.4   Perpetual Inventory Accounting Process

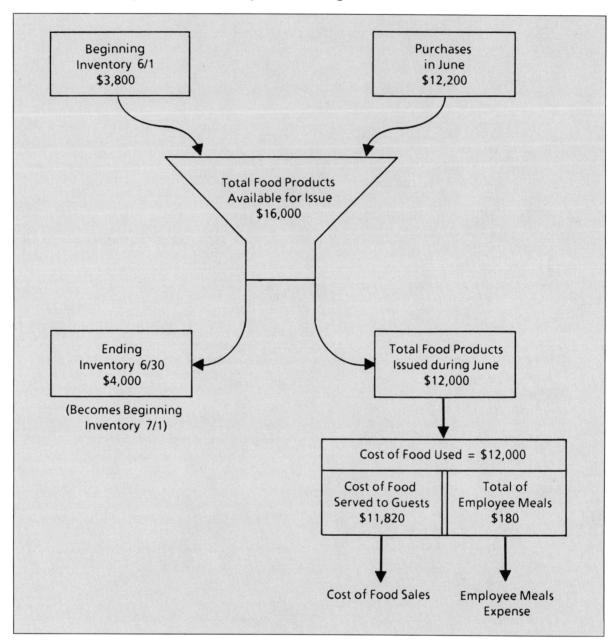

Assume that the issues from the storeroom to the kitchen throughout the month totaled $12,000. Based on these facts, the inventory on June 30 would be $4,000, as shown by the following calculation:

Inventory on June 30	=	Total Food Products Available for Issue	−	Total Food Products Issued during June
Inventory on June 30	=	$16,000	−	$12,000
Inventory on June 30	=	$4,000		

A physical count of the storeroom should verify a $4,000 food inventory (at cost).

The bookkeeping accounts for the month of June would show the following transaction results:

- A balance forward (starting balance) in the Inventory account as of 6/1: $3,800.

- An increase to the Inventory account: $12,200 (Purchases).

- Decreases to cash and/or increases to Accounts Payable totaling $12,200.

- A decrease to the Inventory account: $12,000 (Issues).

- An increase to the Cost of Food Sales account: $12,000 (Issues).

- An ending balance in the Inventory account as of 6/30: $4,000.

Suppose that during the month of June, employee meals (provided at cost) totaled $180, distributed according to the following pattern:

Rooms Department Employees	$ 50
Food Department Employees	100
Beverage Department Employees	30
Total Employee Meals	$180

Accounting for these employee meals would require the following bookkeeping entry:

- *Decrease* Cost of Food Sales Account: $180

- *Increase* Rooms Department Employee Meals Expense: $50

- *Increase* Food Department Employee Meals Expense: $100

- *Increase* Beverage Department Employee Meals Expense: $30

Thus, the Cost of Food Sales account would be adjusted from an amount which showed total food used (issues of $12,000) to an amount now reflecting the cost of food sold ($11,820), as illustrated by the following calculation:

Cost of Food Sales (adjusted)	=	Cost of Food Sales (issues)	−	Total Employee Meals
Cost of Food Sales (adjusted)	=	$12,000	−	$180
Cost of Food Sales (adjusted)	=	$11,820		

Direct Purchases under a Perpetual Inventory System. Daily deliveries may consist of perishable food supplies purchased for immediate use and consequently delivered directly to the kitchen. These purchases are called direct purchases because they bypass the storeroom.

Under a perpetual inventory system, direct purchases are treated differently from storeroom purchases. *Direct purchases* are recorded directly in the *Cost of Sales* account, while *storeroom purchases* are recorded in the *Inventory* account. Refer to Exhibit 6.1 for a summary of this bookkeeping treatment.

A major advantage of the perpetual inventory system is increased internal control; it allows the confirmation of inventory levels on a day-to-day basis. However, operational cost is a disadvantage of the perpetual inventory system, whose increased paperwork requires additional staff hours. For this reason, most small food operations do not use a perpetual inventory system.

Periodic Inventory System

As an alternative to a perpetual inventory system, some businesses may use a periodic inventory system. Unlike the system just discussed, the periodic inventory system does not use any formal methods for tracking inventory levels. All purchases of inventory products are recorded in a bookkeeping account called *Purchases*. Each type of inventory has a separate purchases account; for example, Food Purchases, Beverage Purchases, and, if applicable, Gift Shop Purchases.

One major advantage of the periodic inventory system is that it does not incur the heavy costs associated with maintaining a perpetual inventory system. In a periodic inventory system, goods received by the storeroom and issued from the storeroom to the kitchen throughout the month are *not* recorded on inventory cards. Thus, the periodic inventory system offers day-to-day simplicity compared to a perpetual inventory system.

A major disadvantage of the periodic inventory system is that inventory levels and issues for the period are not readily available at any time. Since records of inventory levels are not kept on an ongoing basis, financial statements may be more difficult to prepare for a business using this system. Whenever the business prepares its monthly financial statements, the inventory must be physically counted and priced at cost, or estimated using a procedure such as the gross profit method. Details about this method are discussed in *Understanding Hospitality Accounting II*.

After inventory is determined through either estimation or physical count, cost of food sales (also called cost of food sold) under the periodic inventory system may be determined by the following procedure:

	Beginning Food Inventory
Plus:	Food Purchases
Result:	Cost of Food Available for Sale
Minus:	Ending Food Inventory
Result:	Cost of Food Used
Minus:	Employee Meals (at cost)
Result:	Cost of Food Sold

Exhibit 6.5 Periodic Inventory Accounting Process

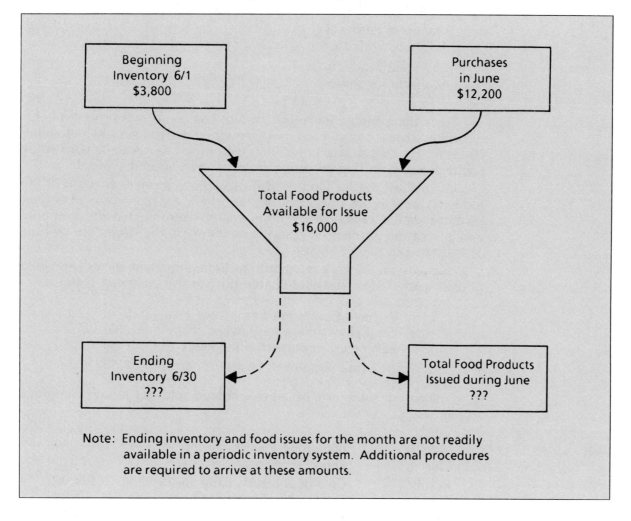

Note: Ending inventory and food issues for the month are not readily available in a periodic inventory system. Additional procedures are required to arrive at these amounts.

Exhibit 6.5 represents how purchasing, inventory levels, and employee meals affect accounting records under a periodic inventory system. As in the previous example, we assume that the accounting records and the storeroom show an inventory on May 31 of $3,800. This same amount would carry over as the beginning inventory on June 1. Suppose food purchases for the month of June were as follows:

6/1:	$ 2,200
6/9:	3,500
6/18:	3,500
6/29:	3,000
Total	$12,200 (Recorded in the Purchases account)

Therefore, total food products available for issue during the month of June would equal $16,000, as shown by the following calculation:

Total Food Products Available for Issue	=	Beginning Inventory	+	Purchases
Total Food Products Available for Issue	=	$3,800	+	$12,200
Total Food Products Available for Issue	=	$16,000		

Since the periodic inventory system has no formal procedures for recording issues, cost of food used cannot be derived simply by totaling issues for the month. However, the cost of food used can be derived by subtracting the ending inventory from the cost of food available.

Calculating cost of food used thus requires a physical count of the food products in the storeroom because there are no records of ending inventory under a periodic inventory system. Assume that after counting and pricing the products at cost, the inventory in the storeroom on June 30 is estimated to be $4,000.

Suppose that during the month of June, employee meals (provided at cost) totaled $180, distributed according to the following pattern:

Rooms Department Employees	$ 50
Food Department Employees	100
Beverage Department Employees	30
Total Employee Meals	$180

The cost of sales (also called cost of food sold) for June is computed as follows:

	Beginning Food Inventory	$ 3,800
Plus:	Food Purchases	12,200
Result:	Cost of Food Available for Sale	$16,000
Minus:	Ending Food Inventory	4,000
Result:	Cost of Food Used	$12,000
Minus:	Employee Meals (at cost)	180
Result:	Cost of Food Sold	$11,820

The procedure used to record the ending inventory under a periodic inventory system is more involved than the corresponding task under a perpetual inventory system. Coverage of this method is not within the scope of this text. However, *Understanding Hospitality Accounting II* presents an in-depth discussion of this specific topic.

Direct Purchases under a Periodic Inventory System. Under a periodic inventory system, all purchases are charged to the *Purchases* account regardless of whether they are direct purchases or storeroom purchases. Refer to Exhibit 6.1 for a summary of this bookkeeping treatment.

Inventories in Service Areas

The net income shown on the financial statements depends on the accuracy of the ending inventory dollar amount. In the hospitality industry, many items are requisitioned from the storeroom and stored temporarily in the bar or the kitchen in order to provide quality and prompt customer service.

Measuring inventory of bar stock is required in order for records to reflect accurate amounts of items not consumed and sold. Full and open bottles of liquor, wine and beer in kegs, and other beverage inventories on hand must be physically counted since these items are usually of material value.

Measuring inventory of food items in the kitchen area is performed by larger hotels at the end of each month, a required procedure due to its materiality to the financial statements. Small restaurant operations may not perform such procedures for various reasons; for instance, if the effort expended is likely to exceed the intended benefits (cost-benefit rule), or if the results are not expected to have any material effect on the net income.

Operating Expenses

Operating expenses include all expenses incurred by a business which are necessary in its day-to-day activities. Since payroll represents a significant expense, a business usually shows it first under Operating Expenses on its statement of income. Payroll is followed by payroll-related items such as payroll taxes and employee fringe benefits. Employee fringe benefits include the cost of employees' meals. Any payments from employees for these meals are used to *reduce* this expense account.

Larger hospitality firms also produce income or expense statements for the various departments which constitute its operations. In these cases, separate expense accounts are set up on a departmental basis. As already noted, the cost of employee meals may be divided into separate expense accounts and distributed among various departments. As another example, payroll may require the following departmental accounts:

- Payroll Expense—Rooms
- Payroll Expense—Restaurant
- Payroll Expense—Lounge
- Payroll Expense—Telephone
- Payroll Expense—Administrative and General
- Payroll Expense—Property Operation and Maintenance

According to the concept of *responsibility accounting*, only those expenses directly associated with a specific department are charged to that department. Departmental accounts will be discussed in greater detail in *Understanding Hospitality Accounting II* when the concept of responsibility accounting is presented in more detail.

The following list gives examples of operating expense accounts used in the hospitality industry:

Payroll	Kitchen Fuel
Payroll Taxes	Utilities
Employee Benefits	Repairs and Maintenance
Employee Meals	Rent
China, Glassware, and Silverware	Property Taxes
Supplies	Property Insurance
Advertising	Interest
Telephone	Depreciation

Depreciation

When a fixed asset is purchased, its cost is recorded in a specific property and equipment asset account. The periodic allocation of the cost of a fixed asset over its estimated useful life is recorded as Depreciation Expense or simply Depreciation.

In the hospitality industry, the depreciation expense associated with fixed assets is not charged to any specific department. Instead, Depreciation appears separately on the hotel's statement of income as a fixed charge.

For instance, the cost of a hotel building would be allocated (depreciated) over its estimated useful life and recorded in the expense account Depreciation. Rather than being charged to the rooms department, this expense would be presented on the hotel's statement of income as a fixed charge.

The depreciation of most fixed assets—specifically, buildings, furniture, and equipment—requires two accounts:

1. Depreciation (An expense account)

2. Accumulated Depreciation (A contra-asset account)

The expense account *Depreciation* records the allocation of the cost of an asset only for the current business year; at the end of the year, it is set to zero to start a new record. The account *Accumulated Depreciation* is a perpetual record which keeps a total of the depreciation charges until the asset has been disposed. The effect of Accumulated Depreciation is to reduce the basis of another asset; that is, its balance is deducted from another account in the financial statements. Such accounts are called contra-asset accounts.

For example, suppose that a vehicle is purchased for $12,000 at the beginning of the accounting year, and is estimated to have a useful life of three years. Because of this estimation, periodic allocation to Depreciation should be set at $4,000 per year until the $12,000 cost has been recorded in the Accumulated Depreciation account.

Normally depreciation entries are made monthly. To simplify the discussion, only the annual amounts are shown for each of the three years. The following example summarizes the transactions involved from date of purchase through annual computation of depreciation. In addition, the proper presentation of the asset *Vehicle* on the balance sheet is also illustrated.

AT PURCHASE:
    Vehicle (asset account) $12,000
        Cash paid out $12,000

———————

AT END OF FIRST YEAR:
    Depreciation (expense account) $ 4,000
        Accumulated Depreciation $ 4,000

At this time, the Accumulated Depreciation account for the vehicle would have a balance of $4,000 since this is its first year of useful life. The vehicle would be presented on the balance sheet as follows:

Vehicle (at cost) $12,000
Less Accumulated Depreciation   4,000
Book Value $ 8,000

———————

AT END OF SECOND YEAR:
    Depreciation (expense account)   4,000
        Accumulated Depreciation   4,000

Notice the effect of the straight-line depreciation method. Each full year's depreciation calculation is identical. At this time, the Accumulated Depreciation account for the vehicle would have a balance of $8,000 (this year's $4,000 entry plus last year's balance of $4,000). The vehicle would be presented on the balance sheet as follows:

Vehicle (at cost) $12,000
Less Accumulated Depreciation   8,000
Book Value $ 4,000

———————

AT END OF THIRD YEAR:
    Depreciation (expense account)   4,000
        Accumulated Depreciation   4,000

The Accumulated Depreciation account for the vehicle would now have a balance of $12,000 (this year's $4,000 entry plus last year's balance of $8,000). The vehicle would be presented on the balance sheet as follows:

Vehicle (at cost) $12,000
Less Accumulated Depreciation   12,000
Book Value $ 0

Each successive year would not require any further calculations because the asset has been fully depreciated. Until the vehicle is disposed, it would continue to be shown as it appears on the balance

Exhibit 6.6 Income Statement Accounts

REVENUE ACCOUNTS

Room Sales   Telephone Sales
Food Sales   Gift Shop Sales
Beverage Sales

_____

EXPENSE ACCOUNTS

Cost of Sales (if a perpetual   Purchases (if a periodic
inventory system is used):   inventory system is used):
    Cost of Food Sales   Food Purchases
    Cost of Beverage Sales   Beverage Purchases
    Cost of Gift Shop Sales   Gift Shop Purchases

Cost of Telephone Calls

Operating Expenses: Fixed Charges:
    Payroll   Rent
    Payroll Taxes   Property Taxes
    Employee Benefits   Property Insurance
    Employee Meals   Interest
    China, Glassware, Silverware   Depreciation
    Supplies   Amortization
    Advertising
    Telephone   Income Taxes
    Kitchen Fuel
    Utilities
    Repairs and Maintenance

sheet at the end of the third year. Upon disposal, the vehicle's asset account and its related accumulated depreciation would be set to zero.

A fixed asset such as a building, furniture, or equipment requires depreciation procedures to allocate the asset's cost over its useful life. By contrast, depreciation procedures are not used for the noncurrent asset

Land since land does not wear out in the normal course of business. Another exception to typical depreciation procedures is the treatment of china, glassware, silverware, uniforms, and linen. One or more accounts may be set up to handle these items. In depreciating these assets, the depreciable amount is computed and used to:

- directly reduce the associated asset account, and
- increase the associated expense account.

Income Taxes Expense

The expense for income taxes is reserved in a category by itself. It represents all taxes which are imposed on business income. Separate accounts may be established for federal, state, and municipal income taxes as necessary.

State and municipal income taxes are deductible for federal income tax purposes. However, federal income taxes are not deductible as a business expense for federal income tax purposes.

Of course, income taxes expense is not relevant to proprietorships and partnerships. For these forms of business organization, any income or loss of the business is reported on the personal income tax return(s) of the owner(s).

Throughout this chapter, the composition of the statement of income has been reduced to its most basic elements. This process fosters an understanding of the specific accounts and categories which make up this financial statement. Exhibit 6.6 is a list of the basic income statement accounts which should be closely examined before we address debits and credits in Chapter 8.

The primary objective up to this point has been to build the foundation necessary to understand the increase/decrease effect of business transactions on various accounts, which is the subject of the next chapter. Upcoming chapters will enable the reader to gain competence in the application of debits and credits and the use of accounting records.

Discussion Questions

1. How is the revenue classification defined?

2. How is the expense classification defined?

3. At what point is a sale recorded?

4. How does the Sales account differ from the Cost of Sales account?

5. What are the major differences between the perpetual and periodic inventory systems?

6. What are advantages and disadvantages of the two inventory systems discussed in this chapter?

7. How do accounting treatments of storeroom purchases and direct purchases differ under the two types of inventory systems?

8. What is the difference between the expense account Depreciation and the contra-asset account Accumulated Depreciation?

Problems

Problem 6.1
Calculate the cost of food sales under a periodic inventory system for the period ended October 31 given the following information:

Inventory on October 31 is $7,000.
Sales for the period were $200,000.
Purchases for the period were $69,000.
Inventory on September 30 was $8,000.
Free employee meals for the period were as follows:

Rooms Department	$500
Food Department	900
Administrative and General Department	375

Problem 6.2
Calculate the cost of food sales under a perpetual inventory system for the month ended March 31 given the following information:

Inventory on March 31 was $2,900.
Storeroom purchases for the month were $36,000.
Storeroom issues for the month were $36,500.
Direct purchases for the month were $626.
Free employee meals for the month were $225.

Problem 6.3
A building is purchased on January 1 for $240,000. The cost of this asset is to be allocated on the basis of $8,000 per year. What is its book value at the end of the first year?

Problem 6.4
Equipment is purchased on June 1 for $7,500 and its cost is to be allocated at $625 per month.

a.   What would be its book value on June 30?

b.   What would be its book value on July 31?

Problem 6.5
A vehicle is purchased for $10,200 and is estimated to have a useful life of three years. At the end of three years, its estimated book value is zero. What should be the annual charge to depreciation expense?

Problem 6.6
A hospitality company uses the perpetual inventory system. Its food inventory was $2,700 on August 1 and $3,000 on August 31. Total deliveries to the storeroom in August were $15,000. What were the food issues from the storeroom in August?

Problems *(continued)*

Problem 6.7
A hospitality business uses the perpetual inventory system. For October, storeroom issues (food used) totaled $25,875 and the cost of sales equaled $25,615. What was the amount for free employee meals for October?

Problem 6.8
A hospitality business uses the periodic inventory system. On November 1, the food inventory was $2,000. During November, food purchases totaled $9,000 and free employee meals were $200. The cost of food sales for the month equaled $4,000. What is the ending inventory on November 30?

7
Effects of Business Transactions

All business transactions must be recorded in the accounting records. Competence in carrying out this task requires an ability to analyze the effects of these transactions on the bookkeeping accounts.

Previous chapters have concentrated on the individual accounts composing the five major account classifications. The importance of this subject cannot be overestimated; indeed, a thorough comprehension of accounts and their corresponding classifications is required to understand this and upcoming chapters.

In order to understand the concept of debits and credits presented in the next chapter, it is first necessary to grasp the underlying logic which guides their application. Chapter 7 provides this necessary logic at its most fundamental level by demonstrating how business transactions affect bookkeeping accounts. In the process, this chapter provides answers to such questions as:

1. How are transactions categorized according to method of payment and involvement of outside parties?

2. What specific accounts are affected by a business transaction?

3. Why are bookkeeping accounts increased or decreased as a result of a business transaction?

4. What is the difference between a transaction which creates an asset and one which creates an expense in the current accounting period?

5. Why do procedures used in accounting for supplies differentiate between supplies used and supplies on hand?

This chapter presents an in-depth analysis of business transactions based on three preliminary steps: (a) identifying the accounts involved, (b) associating the accounts with their classifications, and (c) determining the increase/decrease effect on the accounts.

Special attention is focused on accounting for supplies. The discus-

Exhibit 7.1   Cash, Payables, and Receivables Transactions

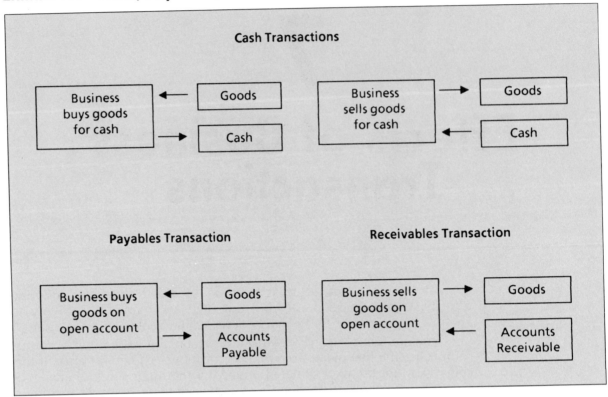

sion compares two different methods of accounting for these items: the expense method and the asset method.

Business Transactions

As previously defined, a business transaction is an exchange of property, goods, or services for cash or a promise to pay. A business may purchase goods, property, or services by the payment of cash (referred to as a *cash transaction*) or by the use of credit or borrowings (referred to as a *payables transaction*). A business may also sell goods, property, or services to another in return for cash (another type of cash transaction) or promise of payment (referred to as a *receivables transaction*). Exhibit 7.1 illustrates these activities in buying and selling goods.

Transactions involving outside parties are termed *external transactions*. Examples of external transactions with suppliers include purchases of services, property, equipment, inventory, and office supplies. Examples of external transactions with guests include room rentals and sales of food and beverage items. External transactions may also involve the sale or purchase of property and equipment between the hospitality company and outside parties.

External transactions are not the only transactions that must be recorded in the accounting records. Other business activities that require recording in the accounting records involve activities within the business, sometimes called *internal transactions*. Examples of internal transactions include issues of inventory from the storeroom and allocation of asset costs through depreciation.

Not all internal and external activities are recorded in the accounting records. One example is when a business issues a purchase order for goods or services. Until a business activity creates a change in a company's assets, liabilities, or equity, an event is not recorded in the accounting records.

Transactions are the raw material of the accounting process. Business papers and other documents provide proof that a transaction has taken place. As examples, cash register tapes serve as the basis for recording daily sales; when an invoice is paid, the check and the invoice become the basis for an entry in the accounting records. Business documents, especially those originating outside the business, are objective evidence of completed transactions. This is in accord with the *objectivity principle*, which states that all business transactions must be supported by objective evidence proving that the transactions did in fact occur.

Typical Transactions of a Business

Assets have been defined as items owned by a business which have commercial or exchange value. Initially, a business acquires assets through investments by the owner(s). Owner's investments may include property and equipment, but frequently involve only cash.

However, the mere holding of cash does not generate operating profits in the hospitality business; its main function is to serve as a medium of exchange. Later, the business can acquire property and equipment using cash and/or borrowings (liabilities) to generate profits from its operations.

In order to produce revenue (sales), a hospitality operation must purchase productive assets. These noncash assets are used to provide goods and services to guests in exchange for cash, or receivables which will later be converted to cash. From this cycle, the business pays its expenses. Any remaining cash may be distributed to owners in the form of dividends or used to pay off borrowings, finance future expansion, and replace inefficient assets.

Recording Business Transactions

According to *double-entry accounting*, each transaction affects a minimum of two bookkeeping accounts. A transaction is initially recorded on an accounting document called a journal. The journal entries are ultimately recorded in the bookkeeping accounts by a process called posting. These documents and procedures are discussed in Chapters 9 and 10.

A bookkeeping account is a form in which information is accumulated and summarized. A separate form is maintained for each bookkeeping account in the company's chart of accounts; for instance, Cash, Inventory, and Accounts Receivable are typically found in the chart of accounts for a hospitality operation. Each account is summarized and the resulting monetary amount is called the *account balance*.

Exhibit 7.2 "Bin" Concept of an Account

Account Title: Cash	
Increase	$1,000
Increase	2,000
Decrease	500
Increase	700
Decrease	1,000
Account Balance	$2,200

Collectively, these bookkeeping accounts are referred to as the *general ledger*. In a manual system, the general ledger is composed of a separate page for each account. In modern computer systems, the ledger accounts may be stored on magnetic tapes or disks, and can be viewed by means of an output device such as a printer or a video display terminal.

The design of an account has a technical format, which will be presented in Chapter 9. For purposes of the present discussion, an account may be imagined as a bin or container in which financial data are stored. Such financial data result from the effects of various business transactions. Exhibit 7.2 illustrates the "bin" concept of a bookkeeping account by showing several transaction entries and the resulting balance.

Analyzing Business Transactions

Before any transaction can be recorded in the accounting records, it must be properly analyzed by considering three basic questions:

1. Which accounts are affected by a transaction?
2. How are each of the affected accounts classified?
3. Does the transaction increase or decrease the account balance?

By addressing each of these considerations, it is possible to analyze the effects of a given transaction on the accounting records. Indeed, this critical thought process is required before a transaction can be properly recorded.

Which accounts are affected by a transaction? According to double-entry accounting, a minimum of two bookkeeping accounts are used to record any transaction. Accounts used to record transactions may include Cash, Accounts Receivable, Accounts Payable, or any other bookkeeping account found in the general ledger.

How are each of the affected accounts classified? After determining the bookkeeping accounts affected by a given transaction, it is necessary to classify each of the affected accounts. The five major account classifications are:

- Asset
- Liability
- Equity
- Revenue
- Expense

Several contra accounts have been previously discussed. For purposes of analyzing the increase/decrease effect, they are not treated any differently than the other accounts. Contra accounts will be discussed in more detail in Chapter 8.

Does the transaction increase or decrease the account balance? The increase/decrease effect is determined in the same manner for all classifications of accounts, including contra accounts. Furthermore, determining whether the effect of a business transaction is an increase or decrease does not require a knowledge of debits or credits.

The following guidelines offer a means of determining the increase/decrease effect:

1. If a transaction creates an asset, liability, equity, revenue, or expense, the effect is an *increase*.

2. If a transaction increments an account balance, the effect is an *increase*.

3. If a transaction reduces an account balance, the effect is a *decrease*.

Four Examples in Expanded Form

To further your understanding of this vital concept, four examples are presented in expanded form. These examples demonstrate the thought process involved in analyzing transactions.

Example A At a particular hospitality operation, cash food sales for the day are $500.

Which accounts are affected by the transaction? The two bookkeeping accounts involved are *Cash* and *Food Sales*. The restaurant has received cash from its guests in exchange for food goods and services.

How are each of the affected accounts classified? The account Cash is classified as an *asset* account. The account Food Sales is classified as a *revenue* account.

Does the transaction increase or decrease the account balance? The receipt of cash always *increases* the balance in the Cash account. The occurrence of new sales always *increases* the total sales of the business.

Example B B. Mercedes, the owner of a proprietorship, invests personal cash of $12,000 to start a new coffee shop.

Which accounts are affected by the transaction? The two bookkeeping accounts involved are *Cash* and *Capital, B. Mercedes*. The business has received cash from an equity transaction with the owner.

How are each of the affected accounts classified? The account Cash is classified as an *asset* account. Capital, B. Mercedes, is classified as an *equity* account.

Does the transaction increase or decrease the account balance? The receipt of cash *increases* the balance in the Cash account. An equity investment by the owner always *increases* the owner's claim on the assets of the business.

Example C

A restaurant purchases advertising on open account.

Which accounts are affected by the transaction? The two bookkeeping accounts involved are *Advertising Expense* and *Accounts Payable*. The restaurant has incurred an expense and has implied a promise to pay.

How are each of the affected accounts classified? The account Advertising Expense is classified as an *expense* account. Accounts Payable is classified as a *liability* account.

Does the transaction increase or decrease the account balance? Incurring a new advertising expense *increases* the balance in the Advertising Expense account. Any new purchases on open account always *increase* the balance in Accounts Payable.

Example D

The restaurant in Example C pays the open account.

Which accounts are affected by the business transaction? The two bookkeeping accounts involved are *Accounts Payable* and *Cash*. The restaurant is using cash to settle its open account balance with the vendor.

How are the affected accounts classified? Accounts Payable is classified as a *liability* account. Cash is classified as an *asset* account.

Does the transaction increase or decrease the account balance? The use of cash always *decreases* the cash account balance. Settlement of an open account always *decreases* Accounts Payable.

The preceding examples have provided the fundamental approach to analyzing the 18 transactions which appear in the next section. In analyzing a given transaction, keep in mind that it may fit any one of three alternatives:

- all accounts may be increased, or
- all accounts may be decreased, or
- there may be a combination of increases and decreases.

Analysis of 18 Common Transactions

The analysis involved in determining the increase/decrease effect of transactions on bookkeeping accounts may be best understood by studying a series of examples. These transactions cover a multitude of

Exhibit 7.3 Chart of Accounts for the Analysis of 18 Common Transactions

ASSET ACCOUNTS

Cash
Marketable Securities
Accounts Receivable
Food Inventory
Beverage Inventory
Prepaid Rent
Prepaid Insurance
Supplies Inventory
Land
Building
Furniture and Equipment

LIABILITY ACCOUNTS

Accounts Payable
Sales Tax Payable
Income Taxes Payable
Notes Payable
Mortgage Payable

EQUITY ACCOUNTS

Accounts used for a proprietorship:
    Capital, (owner's name)
    Withdrawals, (owner's name)

Accounts used for a corporation:
    Common Stock Issued
    Additional Paid-In Capital
    Retained Earnings

REVENUE ACCOUNTS

Room Sales
Food Sales
Beverage Sales

EXPENSE ACCOUNTS

If a perpetual inventory system is used:
    Cost of Food Sales
    Cost of Beverage Sales

If periodic inventory system is used:
    Food Purchases
    Beverage Purchases

Salaries and Wages
Payroll Taxes
Employee Benefits
Food Department--Employee Meals
Rooms Department--Employee Meals
Supplies
Advertising
Telephone
Utilities
Repairs and Maintenance
Rent
Property Insurance
Interest
Depreciation
Income Taxes

situations common to most hospitality businesses. Unless otherwise stated, these examples are unrelated and do not involve the same company.

Read each transaction carefully and determine whether it should be recorded. For those transactions which require recording, perform the following analysis:

- Identify the accounts affected by the transaction.

- List the classifications associated with the affected accounts.

- Indicate the increase/decrease effect on these accounts.

Compare your results with the solution which follows the initial description of the transaction. To assist you in selecting the proper account titles, Exhibit 7.3 lists the bookkeeping accounts available in analyzing these 18 transactions.

Example #1. A motel writes a check to pay its current monthly rent.

Account	Classification	Effect
Cash	Asset	*Decrease*
Rent Expense	Expense	*Increase*

Reason: An expense (Rent) has been incurred, which requires the use of cash. This reduces the balance in the Cash account. The account Rent Expense is incremented (increased) for the period.

Example #2. A lodging operation writes a check on April 15, paying its rent for May.

Account	Classification	Effect
Cash	Asset	*Decrease*
Prepaid Rent	Asset	*Increase*

Reason: When rent is paid in advance of the current accounting period, it cannot be charged to Rent Expense. Rather, the prepayment of rent creates an asset (an item which benefits more than one accounting period). This increments the asset account called Prepaid Rent. As in the previous example, the Cash balance is reduced.

Example #3. A lodging business writes a check on August 1, paying its rent for August.

Account	Classification	Effect
Cash	Asset	*Decrease*
Rent Expense	Expense	*Increase*

Reason: While this may appear to be paying the rent in advance, this is not actually the case. Since August is the current accounting period, payment of the August rent on August 1 is an expense incurred *within that period*.

Example #4. A customer pays cash to the restaurant for a meal.

Account	Classification	Effect
Cash	Asset	*Increase*
Food Sales	Revenue	*Increase*

Reason: The restaurant's account Food Sales is incremented by the sale of a meal. The Cash account of the business is incremented due to the receipt of cash. (For our purposes, cash could also include payment by bankcard, travelers check, or personal check.)

Example #5. A customer rents a guestroom and pays by charging the bill to an open account previously arranged with the lodging operation.

Account	Classification	Effect
Accounts Receivable	Asset	*Increase*
Room Sales	Revenue	*Increase*

Reason: This transaction is similar to the preceding example except that the purchase has been charged to an open account rather than paid by cash. In this case, the lodging operation has received a promise of payment at some future date, which increments Accounts Receivable by the amount charged. The account Room Sales is incremented by the rental of a room.

Example #6. A lodging operation receives a check from a customer who had charged goods and services to an open account.

Account	Classification	Effect
Cash	Asset	*Increase*
Accounts Receivable	Asset	*Decrease*

Reason: The receipt of the customer's check increases the Cash account. The lodging operation is receiving payment for a transaction which originally increased a sales account and increased an Accounts Receivable account. The customer's payment reduces this Accounts Receivable account.

Example #7. A hotel buys food provisions for its storeroom and pays cash on delivery. The perpetual inventory system is used.

Account	Classification	Effect
Cash	Asset	*Decrease*
Food Inventory	Asset	*Increase*

Reason: When the perpetual inventory system is employed, the account called Food Inventory is used to record purchases of food provisions. Food Inventory is incremented by this purchase. Since the hotel has paid cash, the balance in the Cash account is reduced.

Example #8. A hotel buys food provisions for its storeroom and uses an open account previously arranged with the supplier. The perpetual inventory system is used.

Account	Classification	Effect
Food Inventory	Asset	*Increase*
Accounts Payable	Liability	*Increase*

Reason: This transaction is similar to the preceding business transaction except that the purchase has been charged to an open account rather than paid by cash. In this case, the hotel has made a promise to pay at some future date; this has increased its liabilities. Purchases on open account are recorded as Accounts Payable.

If the purchase had involved signing a formal promissory note, then the Notes Payable account would have been affected.

Example #9. The hotel remits a check to the supplier in payment of inventory purchases that had been made on open account.

Account	Classification	Effect
Cash	Asset	*Decrease*
Accounts Payable	Liability	*Decrease*

Reason: When the purchases were initially made (see Example #8), Accounts Payable was increased to reflect the increase in the hotel's liabilities. The remittance of a check has now reduced this liability. The Cash account is decreased by this business transaction.

Example #10. A hotel buys food provisions for its storeroom and pays cash on delivery. The periodic inventory system is used.

Account	Classification	Effect
Cash	Asset	*Decrease*
Food Purchases	Expense	*Increase*

Reason: When the periodic inventory system is employed, the account called Food Purchases is used to record purchases of food inventory items. In this transaction, the Food Purchases account is incremented by the purchase of additional food provisions. Since the hotel has paid cash, the balance of the Cash account is reduced.

Example #11. A hotel buys food provisions for its storeroom and uses an open account previously arranged with the purveyor (supplier). The periodic inventory system is used.

Account	Classification	Effect
Food Purchases	Expense	*Increase*
Accounts Payable	Liability	*Increase*

Reason: This transaction is similar to the preceding business transaction except that the purchase has been charged to an open account rather than paid by cash. In this case, the hotel has made a promise to pay at some future date; this promise has increased its liabilities. Purchases on open account are recorded as Accounts Payable.

If the purchase had involved signing a formal promissory note, then the Notes Payable account would have been affected.

Example #12. Ken Thomas is starting a new business, a proprietorship called Ken's Restaurant Supply Company. In a single transaction, Ken invests personal cash, land, and a building into the business.

Account	Classification	Effect
Cash	Asset	*Increase*
Land	Asset	*Increase*
Building	Asset	*Increase*
Capital, Ken Thomas	Equity	*Increase*

Reason: The assets of the business have been increased by the owner's investment of cash, land, and a building. The Capital account of Ken Thomas is incremented since he has increased his ownership interest in the business. An alternate view is that Ken Thomas has increased his claim to the assets of the business by investing personal assets.

Example #13. Mae Brentwood is starting a new hospitality establishment called Brentwood, Inc. She invests $50,000 into the business for 4,000 shares of $1 par common stock.

Account	Classification	Effect
Cash	Asset	*Increase*
Common Stock Issued	Equity	*Increase*
Additional Paid-In Capital	Equity	*Increase*

Reason: Brentwood, Inc., has received cash, thus incrementing its Cash account. The corporation has also increased its issued and outstanding common stock. Since the corporation has received $50,000 for stock issued at a total par value of $4,000, the stock has been issued at a premium of $46,000. Therefore, the account Additional Paid-In Capital is incremented.

Example #14. Deb Stephens is starting a new lodging operation called Dotco, Inc. She invests $50,000 into the business for 4,000 shares of no-par common stock.

Account	Classification	Effect
Cash	Asset	*Increase*
Common Stock Issued	Equity	*Increase*

Reason: The corporation has received cash and increased its issued and outstanding common stock. There is no premium to record because the corporation issued no-par stock without any "stated" value.

Example #15. Ann Barry is starting a new restaurant called Dorco, Inc. She invests $50,000 into the business for 4,000 shares of no-par common stock which has a stated value of $8 per share.

Account	Classification	Effect
Cash	Asset	*Increase*
Common Stock Issued	Equity	*Increase*
Additional Paid-In Capital	Equity	*Increase*

Reason: The corporation has received cash and increased its issued and outstanding common stock. While the stock issued had no par value, the stock did have a stated value. Since the corporation has received $50,000 for stock issued at a total stated value of $32,000, the stock has been issued at a premium of $18,000. Therefore, the account Additional Paid-In Capital is incremented.

Example #16. A restaurant uses a perpetual inventory system. Issues from the storeroom total $15,000 for the month. This amount represents food used by the kitchen in generating sales and preparing employee meals.

Account	Classification	Effect
Cost of Food Sales	Expense	*Increase*
Food Inventory	Asset	*Decrease*

Reason: Under a perpetual inventory system, the inventory records reflect the cost of food issued from the storeroom. Issues are treated as a reduction to the Food Inventory account and an increase to the expense account called Cost of Food Sales. In the next example, this account is adjusted for the cost of free employee meals.

Example #17. Of the $15,000 total for food issued to the kitchen, $300 was used for free employee meals ($200 to Rooms Department Employees and $100 to Food Department Employees).

Account	Classification	Effect
Rooms Department— Employee Meals Expense	Expense	*Increase*
Food Department— Employee Meals Expense	Expense	*Increase*
Cost of Food Sales	Expense	*Decrease*

Reason: The Cost of Food Sales account should reflect only the cost of food used in the selling process. Therefore, an adjustment must be made for free employee meals, whose total reduces the Cost of Food Sales account. The costs of free employee meals increase departmental expense accounts.

Example #18. A restaurant uses a periodic inventory system. Issues from its storeroom total $15,000 for the month. This amount represents food used by the kitchen in generating sales and preparing employee meals.

Effect

No bookkeeping entries are made for issues under a periodic inventory system.

Reason: Under a periodic inventory system, inventory purchases are recorded as Purchases. Issues from the storeroom are not recorded as they are under a perpetual inventory system.

At the end of each accounting period, the inventory is physically counted and priced at cost, or it is estimated using a procedure such as the gross profit method. After ending inventory has been determined, the following procedure can be used (on either the financial statements or supporting schedules) to compute the cost of food sold:

	Beginning Food Inventory
Plus:	Food Purchases
Result:	Cost of Food Available for Sale
Minus:	Ending Food Inventory
Result:	Cost of Food Used
Minus:	Employee Meals, at cost
Result:	Cost of Food Sold

This section has considered which accounts are affected by a specific transaction, how the affected accounts are classified, and whether each account is increased or decreased due to the transaction. These considerations constitute the underlying logic required to understand debits and credits when they are presented in the next chapter.

Before addressing debits and credits, however, it is necessary to complete the presentation of preliminary topics by discussing two accounting methods used for supplies.

Accounting for Supplies

Supplies include items purchased for maintenance, office, restaurant, and other uses. Purchased supplies may be intended for either storeroom or direct use. Storeroom purchases are delivered directly to the storeroom for future use; direct purchases bypass the storeroom and are delivered directly to the user department. Direct purchases usually involve small expenditures, while storeroom purchases generally involve material amounts.

There are two major methods of accounting for the purchase of supplies: the *expense method* and the *asset method*. Procedures for these two accounting methods may be summarized as follows:

- Expense method—Record all purchases (both storeroom and direct) as Supplies Expense and make an adjusting entry at the end of the accounting period to reflect supplies on hand.

- Asset method—Record storeroom purchases as Supplies Inventory and make an adjusting entry at the end of the accounting period to reflect supplies used. Generally, any direct purchases are recorded in the Supplies Expense account.

Both methods produce similar results at the end of the month. Each reflects the expense portion (supplies used) and the asset portion (supplies on hand).

Unless otherwise indicated, the asset method is used throughout the remainder of this text.

Discussion Questions

1. How is double-entry accounting defined?

2. What is the difference between a receivables transaction and a payables transaction?

3. What is the difference between an internal transaction and an external transaction? Give examples of each.

4. What three steps are involved in analyzing the effects of business transactions?

5. How is the increase/decrease effect defined?

6. How are "supplies used" differentiated from "supplies on hand"?

7. What are the alternative methods of accounting for supplies?

Problems

Problem 7.1
Assume that a hospitality operation uses a perpetual inventory system. Name the accounts affected by the following transactions and specify whether the effect is an increase or a decrease.

a. Liquor sales for the day total $525, $400 of which was paid in cash with the balance charged to customers' open accounts.

b. A storeroom purchase of liquor totaling $725 is charged by the operation to an open account.

c. A direct purchase of liquor totaling $67 is made. Check number 978 is issued upon purchase.

d. Issues from the liquor storeroom for the month total $1,525.

Problem 7.2
Assume the hospitality operation instead uses a periodic inventory system. Name the accounts affected by the following transactions and specify whether the effect is an increase or a decrease.

a. Liquor sales for the day total $525, $400 of which was paid in cash with the balance charged to customers' open accounts.

b. A storeroom purchase of liquor totaling $725 is charged by the operation to an open account.

c. A direct purchase of liquor totaling $67 is made. Check number 978 is issued upon purchase.

Problem 7.3
A hospitality operation makes two separate purchases: one for storeroom supplies and another for supplies intended for direct use. Its accounting policy for supplies is to record storeroom purchases to an asset account and direct purchases to an expense account. Name the accounts affected by the following transactions and specify whether the effect is an increase or a decrease.

a. A $400 purchase of storeroom supplies made on open account.

b. A $25 purchase of supplies for direct use, which is paid in cash.

Problem 7.4
Name the accounts which would be affected by the following types of transactions and specify whether the affected accounts are increased or decreased.

a. Room sales for the day were as follows:

Cash	$500	Travelers Checks	$120
MasterCard	$400	American Express	$978
VISA	$325	Open Account	$110

Problems *(continued)*

b. The general ledger account called Office Supplies Inventory has a balance of $900. A physical count shows that inventory on hand totals $560.

Problem 7.5
Classify the following accounts as Asset (A), Liability (L), Equity (EQ), Revenue (R), or Expense (EX).

a. Accrued Payroll

b. Payroll

c. Prepaid Rent

d. Rent

e. Cash

f. Accounts Payable

g. Supplies Inventory

h. Supplies

i. Food Sales

j. Food Inventory

k. Retained Earnings

l. Building

m. Common Stock Issued

n. Owner's Capital

o. Owner's Withdrawals

p. Payroll Taxes

q. Accounts Receivable

r. Additional Paid-In Capital

8
Debits and Credits

The proper application of debits and credits is vital to the accuracy of accounting records. As tools of accounting, however, debits and credits are often misunderstood and incorrectly applied by beginning students. A careless approach to debits and credits would create numerous problems for accountants and auditors checking the validity of accounting procedures.

This chapter helps to eliminate any lingering misconceptions about debits and credits, sets forth the basic rules which guide their proper application, and provides answers to such questions as:

1. How are debits and credits applied in recording business transactions?

2. What is the significance of a normal account balance in checking the accuracy of recording and posting procedures?

3. How does the equality of debits and credits relate to the accounting equation?

4. What are the mathematical and descriptive forms of the accounting proof regarding the equality of debits and credits?

5. What are the limitations of the accounting proof for debits and credits?

6. What special treatment do contra accounts require regarding the application of debits and credits?

This chapter explains the meaning of debits and credits, describes their use and application, and derives the rules for their selection in the recording process. Contra accounts are introduced later in a separate discussion.

The discussion of debits and credits is based on three considerations: account classifications, the increase/decrease effect, and a simple *rule of increase*. This rule of increase relates the increase effect of business transactions with specific account classifications as a method of properly applying debits and credits.

The significance of a *normal account balance* is described and correlated to the rule of increase. Normal account balance refers to the type of balance (debit or credit) expected of a particular account based on its classification. This provides an alternative method for determining the application of debits and credits, as well as a means of investigating posting accuracy.

The examples introduced in Chapter 7 are repeated to demonstrate the application of debits and credits in the journalizing step. Additional examples illustrate accounting for supplies, treatment of expired assets, handling of sales tax, and declaration and payment of dividends.

An Introduction to Debits and Credits

The words "debit" and "credit" are used by the accounting profession to indicate whether an amount is to be recorded on the left side or the right side. To debit an account means to record an amount on the left side of an account; to credit an account means to record an amount on the right side of an account. Debit and credit may be abbreviated as "dr" and "cr," respectively.

To illustrate debits and credits, the two-column account format will be used. All account formats are designed so that debits are posted to the left side and credits to the right side. The two-column format is also referred to as a "T-account" because it looks like the letter "T."

Name of Account	
Debit	Credit

The difference between the total debits and the total credits of an account is called the account balance; an account may have either a debit balance or a credit balance. If the sum of debits exceeds the sum of credits, the result is a debit balance; conversely, if the sum of credits exceeds the sum of debits, the result is a credit balance.

Based on the classification of an account, a particular type of balance (debit or credit) is expected. The normal balance of accounts is discussed in a later section.

The Use of Debits and Credits

Misconceptions are prevalent regarding the use of debits and credits. One such misconception is that debits are used for addition while credits are reserved for subtraction. This notion is absolutely false! The meaning of debits and credits is *not* based on whether a plus or minus function is to be performed.

The terms debits and credits are sometimes misused in reference to positive vs. negative values. Such misconceptions must be dispelled if one is to become competent in the application of debits and credits.

Debits and credits are an accounting technique used to record business transactions. The selection of a debit or a credit is based on: (a) whether the bookkeeping accounts affected by a business transaction are increased or decreased, and (b) the classification of each affected account.

Applying Debits and Credits

Chapter 7 discussed at length the determination of the increase/ decrease effect on accounts. It explained that the increase effect applies if a transaction creates an asset, liability, equity, revenue, or expense; or increments an account balance. The decrease effect only applies if a transaction reduces an account balance.

Once the increase/decrease effect has been determined, the application of a debit or credit becomes a simple matter of correlating the effect with the account classification, and applying a few basic rules. An account may belong to one of the following "regular" classifications:

- Asset
- Liability
- Equity
- Revenue
- Expense

(The special treatment of contra accounts will be the focus of discussion later in this chapter.)

The use of a debit increases certain classifications of accounts, but decreases other classifications. Likewise, the use of a credit increases certain classifications of accounts, but decreases other classifications. *Yes!* Both debits and credits perform in the same manner.

The action of a debit or credit depends on the classification of the affected account. The proper use of debits and credits is guided by a few basic rules which are easy to learn and apply.

Debit and Credit Rules

Rules governing the proper use of debits and credits may be derived from one simple rule of increase:

Only use a debit to increase an asset or expense account.

For example, each time the account Cash (an asset account) is to be increased, use a *debit*. Likewise, whenever an expense is incurred (such as Rent Expense or Advertising Expense), use a *debit*.

This is the only rule you need to memorize: only use a debit to increase an asset or expense account. Equipped with this simple rule, one can apply debits and credits using logic rather than relying on memorization.

One fundamental trait of debits and credits should be kept in mind. For any particular account classification, a debit has the opposite effect of a credit. Those account classifications increased by use of a credit are decreased by use of a debit. Conversely, those account classifications increased by use of a debit are decreased by use of a credit.

What *decreases* an asset or expense account? Since a debit increases an asset or expense account, then it follows that a *credit* decreases an asset or expense account.

The basic rules governing the application of debits and credits may now be expanded and enumerated as follows:

1. Use a debit to increase an asset or expense account.

2. Use a credit to decrease an asset or expense account.

What increases a liability, equity, or revenue account? Since a debit is used to increase only asset and expense accounts, then it follows that a credit increases a liability, equity, or revenue account.

What decreases a liability, equity, or revenue account? Since a credit is used to increase a liability, equity, or revenue account, then it follows that a debit decreases a liability, equity, or revenue account.

The basic rules governing the application of debits and credits may be further expanded as follows:

1. Use a debit to increase an asset or expense account.

2. Use a credit to decrease an asset or expense account.

3. Use a credit to increase a liability, equity, or revenue account.

4. Use a debit to decrease a liability, equity, or revenue account.

The following list summarizes the basic rules relating the increase/decrease effect to debits and credits:

Account Classification	Rule of Increase	Rule of Decrease
Asset	*Debit*	Credit
Liability	Credit	*Debit*
Equity	Credit	*Debit*
Revenue	Credit	*Debit*
Expense	*Debit*	Credit

This list reaffirms two facts pointed out at the beginning of this section:

● Debits are used to increase only asset and expense accounts.

● For any given account classification, debits and credits have opposite effects.

By understanding these two statements, the proper application of debits and credits can be arrived at through logical analysis.

Exhibit 8.1 shows the relationship of debits and credits to the long form of the accounting equation. Note that revenue and expense appear in a separate line below equity; at the end of the accounting period, revenue and expense account balances are set to zero by transferring the resulting net income or loss to an equity account.

Normal Account Balances
 The difference between total credits and total debits of an account is called the balance. As previously explained, an account may have a debit balance or a credit balance.

The normal account balance refers to the type of balance (debit or credit) expected of an account *based on the account's classification.*

The normal balance of an account corresponds to the rule of increase associated with the account's classification. Since a debit is used to

Exhibit 8.1 Relationship of Debits/Credits to Accounting Equation

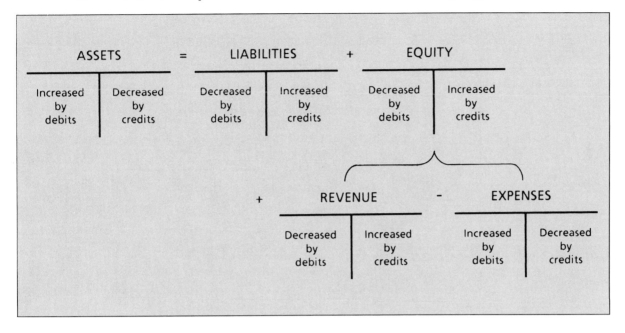

increase accounts within the asset classification, each asset account is expected to have a debit balance.

For example, the asset account Cash is increased by use of a debit entry. Therefore, the normal balance for the Cash account is expected to be a debit balance because this account is increased by the use of a debit. The normal account balance is illustrated in the following T-account for Cash:

Cash

Receipts	9,800	Payments	7,600
Balance	2,200		
(debit)		(credit)	

The normal balance of accounts follows the rule of increase associated with each account classification:

Account Classification	Normal Balance	Rule of Increase
Asset	*Debit*	*Debit*
Liability	Credit	Credit
Equity	Credit	Credit
Revenue	Credit	Credit
Expense	*Debit*	*Debit*

Some may prefer to memorize the normal balances of the accounts and use this knowledge to determine when to use a debit or credit. Others may prefer to use the logic behind the rule of increase. Both methods produce identical results; select the method with which you are

Exhibit 8.2 Summary of Normal Balances by Classification

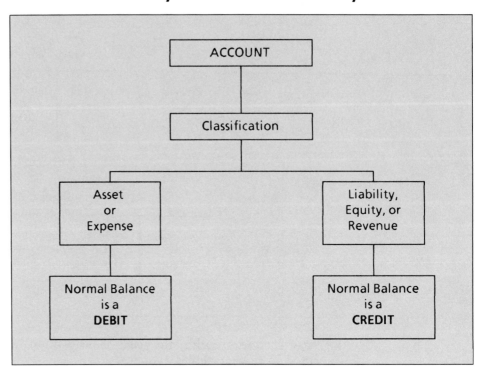

most comfortable. Exhibit 8.2 summarizes the normal balances for the five major account classifications.

An important application of the normal account balance is in the area of investigating posting accuracy. A normal balance is expected of any given account based on its classification. If an account does not show a normal balance, the usual cause is a posting error or omission; however, this situation may also result from an unusual business transaction. For example, if the Cash account results in a credit balance and all postings are valid and complete, then the checking account has been overdrawn.

The Debit and Credit Proof

As just noted, the normal balances of accounts provide accountants with a means to investigate posting accuracy. Debits and credits are also useful when an accountant must test the mathematical accuracy of the bookkeeper's journal entries and postings to the general ledger. Mathematical accuracy is assumed if the following condition exists:

$$DEBIT\$ = CREDIT\$$$

The dollar signs in this mathematical proof are used to illustrate an important point: it is not the *number* of debit and credit entries which is equal but the *dollar amounts* of these entries.

Double-entry accounting is based on the principle that every business transaction affects two or more accounts. Double-entry accounting also has another principle, which is based on the recording process:

every time a business transaction is recorded, the sum of the debit amounts must equal the sum of the credit amounts.

For instance, when a hospitality operation records a food sale, the sum of debit entries equals the sum of credit entries:

Cash	$42.40 (debit)
Food Sales	$40.00 (credit)
Sales Tax Payable	$ 2.40 (credit)

The equality of debits and credits is necessary to support the validity of the accounting equation:

$$\text{Assets} = \text{Liabilities} + \text{Equity}$$

When the totals of debit amounts and credit amounts are equal, the books are said to be *in balance*. This is a fundamental requirement in accounting procedures. When the totals of debit amounts and credit amounts are not equal, the books are said to be *out of balance*.

Books may be out of balance for any number of reasons. One or more amounts may have been journalized or posted in error, or part of a journal entry may not have been recorded. Chapter 11 discusses procedures used to determine the reason for an inequality of debit and credit totals.

Limitations of the Debit and Credit Proof

The proof that the debit totals are equal to the credit totals is only a mathematical proof, and, therefore, has several limitations. For instance, this proof does not verify that all transactions which should have been posted were in fact posted, nor does it verify that the correct accounts were used in the journalizing process or the posting process.

Checking whether business transactions were recorded to the correct accounts is a time-consuming process. At the end of the month, the accountant must prepare many reconciling and supporting schedules, especially for the balance sheet accounts. The bank reconciliation is one of these supporting schedules that forms part of an accountant's working papers.

An auditor or accountant may also analyze various accounts by tracing the entries in these accounts to the original source documents. This may be accomplished by conducting a detailed analysis, selecting entries on a test basis, or researching only those amounts considered material.

For instance, the expense accounts for repairs and maintenance are frequently analyzed. These accounts must at times be checked to determine whether items that should have been capitalized (charged to an asset account) were expensed in error.

An auditor or accountant uses independent documents (such as vendors' statements, bank statements, brokers' statements, invoices, loan amortization schedules, and contracts) to verify the validity of business transactions or account balances. This procedure is in compliance with the principle of objectivity, which states that all business transactions must be supported by objective evidence that the transactions did in fact occur.

Exhibit 8.3 Two-Column Journal

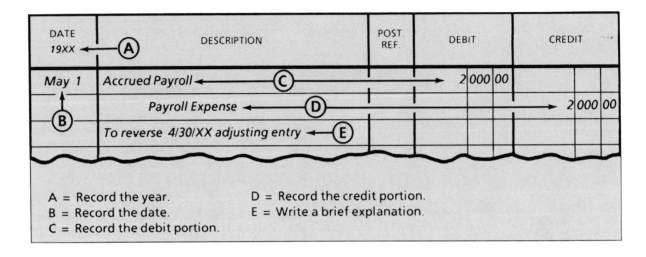

DATE 19XX	DESCRIPTION	POST. REF.	DEBIT	CREDIT
May 1	Accrued Payroll		2 000 00	
	Payroll Expense			2 000 00
	To reverse 4/30/XX adjusting entry			

A = Record the year.
B = Record the date.
C = Record the debit portion.

D = Record the credit portion.
E = Write a brief explanation.

Recording Business Transactions Using Debits and Credits

The business transactions presented in this chapter will be recorded on a two-column document called a journal or general journal. Later we will find that special journals are more convenient to use. For now, the two-column journal (Exhibit 8.3) provides a good format for learning the correct application of debits and credits.

Directions for Using a Two-Column Journal

Several steps are required to record business transactions in a two-column journal. These steps are outlined as follows:

A. Record the year in the space provided for the date heading (required only once per page).

B. Record the date of the business transaction. For subsequent entries on the same page, the month may be omitted if it is the same as the month for the previous transaction.

C. Write the debit portion of the journal entry first.

1. The exact account title is written at the start of the left margin.

2. The debit amount is written in the debit column.

D. Write the credit portion of the journal entry next.

1. The exact account title is indented to the right.

2. The credit amount is written in the credit column.

E. Write a brief explanation describing the event, reason, or purpose of the journal entry. The explanation may be started next to the left margin (as shown in Exhibit 8.3) or indented to the right.

F. It is customary to skip a line after each journal entry.

G. The posting reference column is left blank until the journal is posted to the accounts in the general ledger. The posting reference column is sometimes indicated as "PR" or "folio." The posting reference column will be discussed in Chapter 10.

Journal Entries for 18 Common Business Transactions

The 18 common business transactions introduced in Chapter 7 demonstrated how the increase/decrease effect is determined. The same examples are repeated here to illustrate the next step in the accounting process: recording (journalizing) the results of business transactions.

Rather than complicate the learning of debits and credits with format considerations, the following journal entries give an example number rather than the actual date. The entries also exclude any explanations describing the event, reason, or purpose of the journal entry. The posting reference column will not be used at this time as the present discussion is limited to journalizing.

This section should be approached in the same manner as the examples given in Chapter 7. For each transaction, review the initial presentation of facts and predict how the results of the transaction would be entered in journal form. Compare your prediction with the journal entry supplied, and refer to the analysis section as necessary.

When a transaction is journalized, the debit entries are written before the credit entries. The credit entries are indented as illustrated in each of the following transactions. However, in analyzing a transaction, it is not always preferable to analyze debits before credits. A general recommendation is to analyze and solve a transaction for those results which are immediately obvious.

Generally, the increase/decrease effect to the Cash account is the most obvious result in any transaction. Therefore, many accounting educators advocate the following guidelines when cash is present in a transaction:

1. Analyze the effect to the Cash account *first*.

2. Use logic to solve for the remaining account(s).

Example #1. A motel writes a check to pay its current monthly rent.

General Journal										
Date	Description	PR	Debit			Credit				
1.	Rent Expense		1	500	00					
	Cash						1	500	00	

Account	Classification	Effect	Debit/Credit
Cash	Asset	*Decrease*	Credit
Rent Expense	Expense	*Increase*	Debit

Example #2. A lodging operation writes a check on April 15, paying its rent for May.

				1	500	00				
2.	Prepaid Rent			1	500	00				
	Cash						1	500	00	

Account	Classification	Effect	Debit/Credit
Cash	Asset	*Decrease*	Credit
Prepaid Rent	Asset	*Increase*	Debit

Comment: When rent is paid in advance of the current accounting period, it cannot be charged to expense. The prepayment of rent creates an asset, an item that will benefit a future period.

Example #3. A lodging business writes a check on August 1, paying its rent for August.

3.	Rent Expense			1	500	00				
	Cash						1	500	00	

Account	Classification	Effect	Debit/Credit
Cash	Asset	*Decrease*	Credit
Rent Expense	Expense	*Increase*	Debit

Comment: August is the current accounting period; thus, payment of the August rent is an expense in the period.

Example #4. A customer pays cash to the restaurant for a meal.

4.	Cash			90	00				
	Food Sales						90	00	

Account	Classification	Effect	Debit/Credit
Cash	Asset	*Increase*	Debit
Food Sales	Revenue	*Increase*	Credit

Example #5. A customer rents a guestroom and pays by charging the bill to an open account previously arranged with the lodging operation.

5.	Accounts Receivable			75	00				
	Room Sales						75	00	

Account	Classification	Effect	Debit/Credit
Accounts Receivable	Asset	*Increase*	Debit
Room Sales	Revenue	*Increase*	Credit

Example #6. A lodging operation receives a check from a customer who had charged goods and services to an open account.

6.	Cash			75 00			
	Accounts Receivable					75 00	

Account	Classification	Effect	Debit/Credit
Cash	Asset	*Increase*	Debit
Accounts Receivable	Asset	*Decrease*	Credit

Example #7. A hotel buys food provisions for its storeroom and pays cash on delivery. The perpetual inventory system is used.

7.	Food Inventory			65 00			
	Cash					65 00	

Account	Classification	Effect	Debit/Credit
Cash	Asset	*Decrease*	Credit
Food Inventory	Asset	*Increase*	Debit

Comment: When the perpetual inventory system is employed, the account called Food Inventory is used to record purchases of inventory items.

Example #8. A hotel buys food provisions for its storeroom and uses an open account previously arranged with the supplier. The perpetual inventory system is used.

8.	Food Inventory		1 200 00				
	Accounts Payable				1 200 00		

Account	Classification	Effect	Debit/Credit
Food Inventory	Asset	*Increase*	Debit
Accounts Payable	Liability	*Increase*	Credit

Example #9. The hotel remits a check to the supplier in payment of inventory purchases that had been made on open account.

	9.	Accounts Payable			1	200	00				
		Cash							1	200	00

Account	Classification	Effect	Debit/Credit
Cash	Asset	*Decrease*	Credit
Accounts Payable	Liability	*Decrease*	Debit

Example #10. A hotel buys food provisions for its storeroom and pays cash on delivery. The periodic inventory system is used.

	10.	Food Purchases				55	00				
		Cash								55	00

Account	Classification	Effect	Debit/Credit
Cash	Asset	*Decrease*	Credit
Food Purchases	Expense	*Increase*	Debit

Comment: When the periodic system is employed, the account called Purchases is used to record purchases of inventory items.

Example #11. A hotel buys food provisions for its storeroom and uses an open account previously arranged with the purveyor (supplier). The periodic inventory system is used.

	11.	Food Purchases			900	00			
		Accounts Payable						900	00

Account	Classification	Effect	Debit/Credit
Food Purchases	Expense	*Increase*	Debit
Accounts Payable	Liability	*Increase*	Credit

Example #12. Ken Thomas is starting a new business, a proprietorship called Ken's Restaurant Supply Company. In a single transaction, Ken invests personal cash, land, and a building into the business.

	12.	Cash		55	000	00			
		Land		40	000	00			
		Building		175	000	00			
		Capital, Ken Thomas					270	000	00

Account	Classification	Effect	Debit/Credit
Cash	Asset	*Increase*	Debit
Land	Asset	*Increase*	Debit
Building	Asset	*Increase*	Debit
Capital, Ken Thomas	Equity	*Increase*	Credit

Example #13. Mae Brentwood is starting a new hospitality establishment called Brentwood, Inc. She invests $50,000 into the business for 4,000 shares of $1 par common stock.

13.	Cash		50 000 00	
	Common Stock Issued			4 000 00
	Additional Paid-In Capital			46 000 00

Account	Classification	Effect	Debit/Credit
Cash	Asset	*Increase*	Debit
Common Stock Issued	Equity	*Increase*	Credit
Additional Paid-In Capital	Equity	*Increase*	Credit

Comment: The total par value of the stock issued is $4,000. The excess paid represents the premium.

Example #14. Deb Stephens is starting a new lodging operation called Dotco, Inc. She invests $50,000 into the business for 4,000 shares of no-par common stock.

14.	Cash		50 000 00	
	Common Stock Issued			50 000 00

Account	Classification	Effect	Debit/Credit
Cash	Asset	*Increase*	Debit
Common Stock Issued	Equity	*Increase*	Credit

Comment: If no-par stock does not have a "stated" value, the stock issued account reflects the amount paid by the stockholders.

Example #15. Ann Barry is starting a new restaurant called Dorco, Inc. She invests $50,000 into the business for 4,000 shares of no-par common stock which has a stated value of $8 per share.

15.	Cash		50 000 00	
	Common Stock Issued			32 000 00
	Additional Paid-In Capital			18 000 00

Account	Classification	Effect	Debit/Credit
Cash	Asset	*Increase*	Debit
Common Stock Issued	Equity	*Increase*	Credit
Additional Paid-In Capital	Equity	*Increase*	Credit

Comment: This no-par stock was given a "stated" value. At stated value, the total stock issued was $32,000. The excess paid represents the premium.

Example #16. A restaurant uses a perpetual inventory system. Issues from the storeroom total $15,000 for the month. This amount represents food used by the kitchen in generating sales and preparing employee meals.

16.	*Cost of Food Sales*		15 000 00		
	Food Inventory			15 000 00	

Account	Classification	Effect	Debit/Credit
Cost of Food Sales	Expense	*Increase*	Debit
Food Inventory	Asset	*Decrease*	Credit

Example #17. Of the $15,000 total for food issued to the kitchen, $300 was used for free employee meals ($200 to rooms department employees and $100 to food department employees).

17.	*Rooms Dept. - Employee Meals*		200 00		
	Food Dept. - Employee Meals		100 00		
	Cost of Food Sales			300 00	

Account	Classification	Effect	Debit/Credit
Rooms Department— Employee Meals Expense	Expense	*Increase*	Debit
Food Department— Employee Meals Expense	Expense	*Increase*	Debit
Cost of Food Sales	Expense	*Decrease*	Credit

Example #18. A restaurant uses a periodic inventory system. Issues from its storeroom total $15,000 for the month. This amount represents food used by the kitchen in generating sales and preparing employee meals.

Effect

No bookkeeping entries are made for issues under a periodic inventory system.

Results of Business Transactions: Additional Examples

To foster a better understanding of the increase/decrease effect, the following section introduces new examples covering a wide range of topics, which include accounting for supplies, treatment of expired assets, handling of sales tax, and declaration and payment of dividends.

These examples also demonstrate the application of debits and credits using a two-column journal. Unless specifically stated, these examples are unrelated and involve different operations.

Example #19. A hospitality operation purchases office supplies totaling $875 from a vendor and charges the purchase to an open account. The purchase is intended for the storeroom.

19.	Office Supplies Inventory			875	00			
	Accounts Payable						875	00

Account	Classification	Effect	Debit/Credit
Office Supplies Inventory	Asset	*Increase*	Debit
Accounts Payable	Liability	*Increase*	Credit

Reason: Using the asset method, storeroom purchases of office supplies are recorded in a specific supplies inventory account, which is incremented by the purchase amount. Since the purchase is charged to an open account, Accounts Payable is also incremented.

Example #20. A hospitality operation is preparing its financial statements for the month of May. At the end of this accounting period, a physical count of the office supplies storeroom shows that $500 of office supplies are on hand. The Office Supplies Inventory account in the general ledger reflects a balance of $800.

20.	Office Supplies Expense			300	00			
	Office Supplies Inventory						300	00

Account	Classification	Effect	Debit/Credit
Office Supplies Expense	Expense	*Increase*	Debit
Office Supplies Inventory	Asset	*Decrease*	Credit

Reason: The bookkeeping account Office Supplies Inventory reflects a balance of $800 and office supplies totaling $500 are on hand in the storeroom. Therefore, $300 of supplies have been consumed during the accounting period.

The consumption of an asset reflects an expense. In such cases, the asset account is reduced by the amount used; the consumption is charged to the expense account.

Example #21. A restaurant is preparing its financial statements for the month of August. At the end of this accounting period, the Office Supplies Inventory account in the general ledger reflects a balance of $900. The account reflects last month's balance on hand plus any purchases during the current month. Issues for the current month, which have not yet been recorded, total $480.

21.	Office Supplies Expense			480	00			
	Office Supplies Inventory						480	00

Account	Classification	Effect	Debit/Credit
Office Supplies Expense	Expense	*Increase*	Debit
Office Supplies Inventory	Asset	*Decrease*	Credit

Reason: This type of transaction is typical of a company that maintains a perpetual inventory system for office supplies. A perpetual inventory system simplifies the determination of supplies issued and consumed. Again, the asset account is reduced by the amount used; the consumption is charged to the expense account.

Example #22. A check is issued for $1,200 on 3/1/X1 in payment of a property insurance policy with a term of 3/1/X1 to 3/1/X2.

22.	Prepaid Insurance		1	200	00			
	Cash					1	200	00

Account	Classification	Effect	Debit/Credit
Cash	Asset	*Decrease*	Credit
Prepaid Insurance	Asset	*Increase*	Debit

Reason: The effect of this business transaction is to increase the account Prepaid Insurance. The Cash account is reduced by the outlay of cash.

When an insurance policy is paid in advance, it cannot be charged to expense. Prepayment of insurance creates an *asset*, an item that will benefit a future accounting period. As time passes, part of the prepaid value will also expire; an adjusting entry will be recorded at the end of the accounting period to reflect the passage of time and resulting charge to expense.

Example #23. On 3/31/X1, the Prepaid Insurance account has a debit balance of $1,200, which reflects a property insurance policy with a term of 3/1/X1 to 3/1/X2.

23.	Insurance Expense			100	00			
	Prepaid Insurance						100	00

Account	Classification	Effect	Debit/Credit
Insurance Expense	Expense	*Increase*	Debit
Prepaid Insurance	Asset	*Decrease*	Credit

Reason: One month has expired on the prepaid insurance. The prepaid insurance represented 12 months of coverage at $1,200, or $100 per month. The book value of the asset has decreased by $100; this represents the expired portion of the asset "written off" to expense.

Example #24. A customer buys a meal from a restaurant and pays cash. The amount of the sale is $50 with an additional 6% sales tax totaling $3.

24.	Cash		53 00	
	Food Sales			50 00
	Sales Tax Payable			3 00

Account	Classification	Effect	Debit/Credit
Cash	Asset	*Increase*	Debit
Food Sales	Revenue	*Increase*	Credit
Sales Tax Payable	Liability	*Increase*	Credit

Reason: In this transaction, the restaurant has received cash, which increments its Cash account. The revenue account Food Sales is increased by the amount of the sale ($50).

Sales taxes are excluded from revenue since they represent a liability to the seller, who acts as a collection agent. The collection of sales taxes increments the liability account Sales Tax Payable.

Example #25. The sales taxes collected for the month are remitted to the taxing authority. A check is issued for $3,400.

25.	Sales Tax Payable		3 400 00	
	Cash			3 400 00

Account	Classification	Effect	Debit/Credit
Cash	Asset	*Decrease*	Credit
Sales Tax Payable	Liability	*Decrease*	Debit

Reason: At the end of every month, the restaurant files the appropriate sales tax return and remits tax collections to the taxing authority. In this transaction, two accounts are reduced—Cash and Sales Tax Payable. The restaurant has decreased its liabilities by the use of cash assets.

Example #26. Kenco, Inc., has 25,000 shares of common stock issued and outstanding. On May 15, 19XX, the Board of Directors issues a dividend notice (Exhibit 8.4) which declares a dividend of 10¢ per share on common stock held by stockholders as of May 31, 19XX.

Exhibit 8.4   Dividend Notice

KENCO, INC.

The Board of Directors has today declared a dividend of ten cents (10¢) per share on the common stock of this company, payable 6/15/XX, to stockholders of record at the close of business 5/31/XX.

W.A. Kens
Secretary
May 15, 19XX

This dividend notice tells us three important dates:

1. **DECLARATION DATE** is 5/15 -- the date that the company has created a liability.

2. **DATE OF RECORD** is 5/31 -- the company will pay the dividend to all stockholders on its records as of 5/31.

3. **PAYMENT DATE** is 6/15 -- the date that the company will send dividend checks to the stockholders (of 5/31).

	General Journal				
Date	Description	PR	Debit		Credit
May 15	Retained Earnings		2 500 00		
	Dividends Payable				2 500 00

Account	Classification	Effect	Debit/Credit
Retained Earnings	Equity	*Decrease*	Debit
Dividends Payable	Liability	*Increase*	Credit

Reason: The dividend notice gives a *declaration date* of May 15, 19XX. This is the date when the Board of Directors declares a dividend. At this point, a legal liability is created which increments the Dividends Payable account; the declaration of dividends reduces the equity account Retained Earnings. Notice that the date in the journal entry corresponds to the declaration date.

Date of record is a cut-off date to determine which stockholders will be entitled to receive the dividends declared. The dividend notice gives the date of record as May 31, 19XX. All shareholders owning stock as of that date will be entitled to the dividend. An accounting entry is not required for the date of record.

Example #27. The Board of Directors for Kenco, Inc., pays the cash dividend described in the previous example on June 15, 19XX—the payment date stated in the dividend notice.

June 15	Dividends Payable			2	500	00			
	Cash						2	500	00

Account	Classification	Effect	Debit/Credit
Cash	Asset	*Decrease*	Credit
Dividends Payable	Liability	*Decrease*	Debit

Reason: Cash dividends are paid on the stated *payment date* of June 15, 19XX, to those holding stock as of the date of record. The payment of dividends to stockholders reduces the asset account Cash, while reducing the liability account Dividends Payable.

Debit and Credit Rules for Contra Accounts

The major account classifications have been addressed throughout the course of this text. These "regular" classifications are as follows:

- Asset
- Liability
- Equity
- Revenue
- Expense

Contra accounts are "contrary" to the regular classifications of accounts. A contra account is opposite in function to the regular classification with which it is associated. Contra accounts require special attention because of their unique treatment with respect to the application of debits and credits.

Only a few contra accounts are required in hospitality accounting. Some of the more common contra accounts are as follows:

Contra Account	Classification
Allowance for Doubtful Accounts	Contra-*asset*
Accumulated Depreciation	Contra-*asset*
Withdrawals	Contra-*equity*
Treasury Stock	Contra-*equity*
Allowances	Contra-*revenue*

Because contra accounts function in an opposite manner to the regular accounts, the use of reverse logic is helpful in understanding the application of debit and credit rules for contra accounts. Earlier in this chapter, we presented the simple rule of increase for regular accounts as follows: only use a debit to increase an asset or expense account.

Using reverse logic, the following rule can be derived for contra accounts:

Use a credit to increase a contra-asset or contra-expense account.

The following list summarizes the debit and credit rules for contra accounts. Since there are only a few contra accounts, items are listed by contra account, rather than account classification.

Contra Account	Classification	To Increase
Allowance for Doubtful Accounts	Contra-*asset*	Credit
Accumulated Depreciation	Contra-*asset*	Credit
Withdrawals	Contra-*equity*	Debit
Treasury Stock	Contra-*equity*	Debit
Allowances	Contra-*revenue*	Debit

In every case, the rule of increase for the contra account is opposite to the rule of increase for the regular account classification.

In the following examples, business transactions involving contra accounts are analyzed in terms of the increase/decrease effect.

Withdrawals

Ken Thomas owns a proprietorship called Ken's Restaurant Supply Company. Because a proprietorship cannot pay salaries or wages to its owner, Ken Thomas must draw funds from the business as necessary. A business check is issued for $1,000, payable to Ken Thomas.

Account	Classification	Effect	Debit/Credit
Cash	Asset	*Decrease*	Credit
Withdrawals, Ken Thomas	Equity (Contra)	*Increase*	Debit

The journal entry used to record the $1,000 withdrawal of funds would appear as follows:

Withdrawals, Ken Thomas		1 000 00		
Cash			1 000 00	

Keep in mind that the Withdrawals account is closed at the end of the business year, its balance set to zero and transferred as a reduction to the Capital account.

Accumulated Depreciation

When a long-lived asset (for instance, a building) is purchased, the purchase cost is allocated over the asset's estimated useful life by a process known as depreciation. In the case of a building, the cost is initially recorded in an asset account called Buildings. Two accounts are set up to handle the depreciation process: Depreciation Expense and Accumulated Depreciation.

Depreciation Expense appears on the income statement. This account contains depreciation expense *for the current year only*.

Accumulated Depreciation is a contra-asset account that contains the depreciation amounts for the current period and prior years. Accumulated Depreciation appears on the balance sheet.

Each time depreciation is recorded, both Depreciation Expense and Accumulated Depreciation are increased. Since Accumulated Depreciation is a contra-asset account, a credit is used to record the increase.

Assume that a building was purchased for $100,000. Suppose that the balance in the Accumulated Depreciation account from prior entries is $6,000, and depreciation for the current period is calculated as $2,000. This $2,000 depreciation write-off would create the following events:

Account	Classification	Effect	Debit/Credit
Depreciation Expense	Expense	*Increase*	Debit
Accumulated Depreciation	Asset (Contra)	*Increase*	Credit

The entry used to record the $2,000 depreciation for the current period would appear as follows:

Depreciation Expense		2 000 00		
Accumulated Depreciation			2 000 00	

After posting the above journal entry, the Accumulated Depreciation account would have an $8,000 balance, represented as follows:

Accumulated Depreciation

6,000 (Prior Balance)
2,000 (Current Posting)
8,000 (New Balance)

The presentation of the building on the balance sheet would be as follows:

Building (cost)	$100,000
Less Accumulated Depreciation	8,000
Net Book Value	$ 92,000

It is important to remember that the cost of a fixed asset is *not* directly reduced by any depreciation calculations. The exception to this rule is depreciation of china, glassware, silver, uniforms, and linen, as previously discussed in Chapter 6.

Allowance for Doubtful Accounts

The contra-asset account called Allowance for Doubtful Accounts represents the portion of receivables estimated to be uncollectible. The account called Uncollectible Accounts Expense appears on the income statement and represents bad debts expense. Extensive coverage of this topic is provided in *Understanding Hospitality Accounting II*.

Assume that the estimate of Allowance for Doubtful Accounts is $1,000 for the period, with no prior balance in this account. Analysis of the increase/decrease effect would produce the following results:

Account	Classification	Effect	Debit/Credit
Uncollectible Accounts Expense	Expense	*Increase*	Debit
Allowance for Doubtful Accounts	Asset (Contra)	*Increase*	Credit

The journal entry used to record this estimate would appear as follows:

	Uncollectible Accounts Expense		1	000	00		
	Allowance for Doubtful Accounts					1 000 00

Assume that Accounts Receivable shows a $30,000 balance and no actual bad debts occurred during the period. The balance sheet would present Accounts Receivable as follows:

Accounts Receivable	$30,000
Less Allowance for Doubtful Accounts	1,000
Net Realizable Value	$29,000

Guest Discounts and Allowances

A contra-revenue account called Allowances is used to record guest discounts, rebates, and refunds. This account is subtracted from gross sales to arrive at net revenue (net sales).

Maintaining good customer relations is vital to any business. A hospitality business, by its nature, implies excellence of service and product. After presentation of the guest check, a guest may express a complaint regarding unsatisfactory service or a disputed charge. Under such circumstances, the hospitality operation may make a price adjustment or refund. Allowances would appear on the income statement as follows:

REVENUE	
Sales	$375,000
Allowances	1,000
Net Revenue	$374,000

Discussion Questions

1. What do the words "debit" and "credit" indicate?

2. What account classifications (other than contra accounts) are increased by a debit?

3. What account classifications (other than contra accounts) are increased by a credit?

4. How is the rule of increase related to the normal balance of an account?

5. How is the normal balance of an account used to prove posting accuracy?

6. How is equality of debits and credits used as a proof procedure in accounting? What are the limitations of this proof?

7. What is the definition of the term "contra account"?

8. What are the five common contra accounts mentioned in this chapter? Classify and state whether a debit or credit is used to increase the account.

9. How are the following dividend terms defined?

   a. Declaration Date

   b. Date of Record

   c. Payment Date

Problems

Problem 8.1
Assume that a hospitality operation uses a perpetual inventory system. Journalize the following transactions on a two-column journal.

a. Liquor sales for the day total $525, $400 of which was paid in cash with the balance charged to customers' open accounts.

b. A storeroom purchase of liquor totaling $725 is charged by the operation to an open account.

c. A direct purchase of liquor totaling $67 is made. Check number 978 is issued upon purchase.

d. Issues from the liquor storeroom for the month total $1,525.

Problem 8.2
Assume the hospitality operation instead uses a periodic inventory system. Journalize the following transactions on a two-column journal.

a. Liquor sales for the day total $525, $400 of which was paid in cash with the balance charged to customers' open accounts.

b. A storeroom purchase of liquor totaling $725 is charged by the operation to an open account.

c. A direct purchase of liquor totaling $67 is made. Check number 978 is issued upon purchase.

Problem 8.3
A hospitality operation makes two separate purchases: one for storeroom supplies and another for supplies intended for direct use. Its accounting policy for supplies is to record storeroom purchases to an asset account and direct purchases to an expense account. Journalize the following transactions on a two-column journal.

a. A $400 purchase of storeroom supplies made on open account.

b. A $25 purchase of supplies for direct use, which is paid in cash.

Problem 8.4
Assume that a hospitality operation uses a perpetual inventory system. Journalize the following transactions on a two-column journal.

a. Room sales for the day were as follows:

Cash	$500	Travelers Checks	$120
MasterCard	$400	American Express	$978
VISA	$325	Open Account	$110

b. The general ledger account called Office Supplies Inventory has a balance of $900. A physical count shows that inventory on hand totals $560.

Problems *(continued)*

Problem 8.5
The Blue Ribbon Steakhouse uses a perpetual inventory system for food and beverages. Supplies inventory and expense accounts are separately maintained for the following types of supplies: Guest, Cleaning, Office, and Kitchen. Purchases of supplies are charged to either an inventory (asset) account or an expense account based on the destination of the supplies (storeroom or direct use).

Journalize the following transactions on a two-column journal for the Blue Ribbon Steakhouse.

<u>19X1</u>

March 1: The sales report for the day presented the following information:

Food	$1,985.75
Beverage	425.00
Sales Tax	144.65
Cash received and bank credit cards	1,550.65
Non-bank credit cards	1,003.68
Cash shortage	1.07

(Cash shortages or overages are recorded to one account called Cash Short or Over.)

March 1: Issued check number 645 for $1,600 to Baker Realty in payment of the March rent.

March 1: Purchased $900 of food provisions for the storeroom on open account from Daxell Supply.

March 1: Purchased $250 of liquor on open account for the storeroom from Tri-State Distributors.

March 1: Paid for newspaper advertising to run on March 15. Issued check number 646 for $350 to *City News.*

March 2: The sales report for the day presented the following information:

Food	$1,856.50
Beverage	395.00
Sales Tax	135.09
Cash received and bank credit cards	1,495.84
Non-bank credit cards	891.13
Cash overage	.38

March 2: Issued check number 647 for $1,500 to Capital Insurance for a one-year policy on contents of building. Term of the policy is March 8, 19X1, to March 8, 19X2.

March 2: Paid for newspaper advertising to run on April 8. Issued check number 648 for $850 to *City News.*

March 2: Issued check number 649 for $225 to Eastern Telephone for the period March 1 to March 31.

Problems *(continued)*

March 2: Purchased (on open account) the following items from Kimble Supply, intended for the storerooms:

Kitchen utensils, paper, twine, pots, and pans	$980.00
Pens, pencils, cash register rolls, staplers, and pads	200.00
Matchbooks provided free to guests	150.00
Cleaning solvents and polish	175.00

March 2: Recorded the following issues reports from the storerooms:

Issues from the storeroom to the kitchen	$1,225
Issues from the storeroom to the bar	200

March 2: The cost of free employee meals is recorded in a Food Department Employees Meals Expense account and a Beverage Department Employees Meals Expense account for management information purposes. Record the food manager's report of free meals provided to employees for March 1 and 2, which provided the following information:

Free meals to bar employees, at cost	$15
Free meals to food department employees, at cost	40

Problem 8.6

The Sunshine Motel uses a perpetual inventory system for food and beverages. Inventory and expense accounts are separately maintained for the following types of supplies: Rooms, Restaurant, and Administrative Supplies. Purchases of supplies are charged to either an inventory (asset) account or an expense account based on the destination of the supplies (storeroom or direct use).

Journalize the following transactions involving the Sunshine Motel on a two-column journal.

19X8

May 1: The sales report for the day presented the following information:

Room Sales	$5,210.00
Food	1,863.25
Beverage	375.00
Sales Tax	372.41
Cash received and bank credit cards	2,125.83
Non-bank credit cards	5,695.68
Cash overage	.85

May 2: Purchased $875 of food provisions for the storeroom on open account from Prince Supply.

May 2: Purchased $315 of liquor for the storeroom on open account from Hodges Distributors.

May 2: Paid for newspaper advertising to run on May 9. Issued check number 864 for $350 to *State Tribune*.

Problems *(continued)*

May 2: The sales report for the day presented the following information:

Room Sales	$4,968.50
Food	2,265.95
Beverage	575.00
Sales Tax	390.47
Cash received and bank credit cards	5,365.38
Non-bank credit cards	2,834.09
Cash shortage	.45

May 2: Issued check number 865 for $4,200 to Zenith Insurance for a one-year workers' compensation policy. Term of the policy is May 1, 19X8 to May 1, 19X9.

May 2: Issued check number 866 for $625 to Central Telephone for the period May 1 to May 31.

May 2: Purchased (on open account) the following items from Kimble Supply, intended for the storerooms:

Amenities for room guests	$750.00
Pens, pencils, and other office supplies	500.00
Kitchen utensils, paper, twine, pots, and pans	600.00

May 3: Recorded the following issues reports from the storerooms:

Issues from the storeroom to the kitchen	$1,500
Issues from the storeroom to the bar	300

May 3: The cost of free employee meals is recorded to separate departmental expense accounts. Recorded the food manager's report of free meals furnished to employees for May 1 and 2, which provided the following information:

Free meals to rooms department employees, at cost	$75
Free meals to food and bar department employees, at cost	50
Free meals to administrative and general department employees, at cost	25

Problem 8.7

Judy Barnes starts a new proprietorship called the Rialto Bistro on April 5, 19X5. The operation does not serve liquor; it uses a periodic inventory system for food items. Inventory and expense accounts are set up for Operating Supplies and Office Supplies (four separate accounts). Purchases of storeroom supplies are recorded to an inventory account; direct purchases are recorded to an expense account.

19X5

April 5: Judy invested $75,000 into the business. This amount was used to open a business checking account.

April 5: Purchased the following property:

Land	$ 45,000
Building	165,000
	$210,000

Problems *(continued)*

Issued check number 101 for $40,000 to State Bank, and financed the balance by a mortgage with State Bank.

April 5: Issued check number 102 for $5,000 to National Supply and executed a $35,000 promissory note payable to National Supply in order to purchase the following items:

Operating Supplies	$ 1,200
Office Supplies	800
Furniture	18,000
Equipment	14,000
China, Glassware, Silver	6,000

April 5: Issued check number 103 for $1,400 to Fidelity Insurance for a one-year fire insurance policy.

April 5: Issued check number 104 for $200 to City Utilities as a deposit for utility services.

April 5: Purchased $2,500 of food provisions on open account from Statewide Purveyors.

April 8: Issued check number 105 for $500 to Judy Barnes for personal use.

Problem 8.8

Joshua Kim starts a new corporation called Jokim, Inc., on May 12, 19X7. The operation uses a periodic inventory system for food items. The inventory and expense accounts set up for supplies are Operating Supplies and Office Supplies. Purchases of storeroom supplies are recorded to an inventory account, and direct purchases are recorded to a supplies expense account.

19X7

May 12: Jokim, Inc., issues 200,000 authorized shares of $1 par common stock. Of this total, 10,000 shares are issued to the owner, Joshua Kim, for $80,000. The owner issues a personal check payable to Jokim, Inc., which is used to open a company checking account.

May 12: Purchased the following property:

Land	$ 35,000
Building	155,000
	$190,000

Issued check number 101 for $50,000 to County Bank, and financed the balance by a mortgage with County Bank.

May 12: Issued check number 102 for $7,000 to Provident Supply, and executed a $40,000 promissory note with Provident Supply in order to purchase the following items:

Problems *(continued)*

Operating Supplies	$ 900
Office Supplies	600
Furniture	19,500
Equipment	18,000
China, Glassware, Silver	8,000

May 12: Issued check number 103 for $400 to City Utilities as a deposit for utility services.

May 15: Issued check number 104 for $2,100 to Fidelity Insurance for a one-year fire insurance policy.

May 16: Purchased $6,700 of food provisions on open account from Star Purveyors.

9
Accounting Records

An accounting system consists of forms and procedures used to process business transactions. The ultimate objective of an accounting system is to produce reliable financial statements which can then be used to analyze the results of operations.

An accounting system can be viewed as a cycle composed of daily, monthly, and end-of-year activities. As part of the daily cycle, business transactions are recorded in journals. As part of the monthly cycle, information from the journal entries is transferred from a journal to a bookkeeping account in the general ledger by a process called *posting*. As part of the end-of-year process, closing entries are prepared and posted so that the temporary accounts start the new accounting year with a zero balance.

This chapter focuses on the initial activities associated with recording business transactions, and provides answers to such questions as:

1. What are the purposes and characteristics of special journals?

2. What is the purpose of the daily cashiers report?

3. What are the uses of a guest ledger, a city ledger, and other subsidiary ledgers?

4. What is the purpose of a bookkeeping account and what are its various formats?

5. How do accounting systems treat employee tips entered on credit card drafts?

6. Why is internal control important in the design of accounting records?

This chapter introduces the various accounting records constituting a hospitality accounting system, and explains the use of the general journal, the sales & cash receipts journal, the cash payments journal, the accounts payable journal, and the payroll journal. Special emphasis is given to the daily cashiers report as a source document in preparing the sales & cash receipts journal.

A clear distinction is made between the practical uses of the two-column journal and special journals. Various account formats are illustrated and explained as to their construction and application. Subsidiary ledgers are introduced with special attention to ledgers unique to hotels, such as the guest ledger, the city ledger, the advance deposits ledger, and the banquet ledger.

Internal control and accounting systems are introduced at this time because of their relationship to accounting forms and records. An ongoing example involving the Tower Restaurant is also introduced, and will be referred to throughout the remainder of the text.

Purpose of Accounting Records

Accounting records are a chronological history of the business transactions for a company. These documents are used to record and classify business transactions. Financial statements are prepared from such records.

The accounting records used by a business to document the history of its business transactions are:

- Journals
- Bookkeeping accounts
- Subsidiary ledgers

Types of Journals

All business transactions are first recorded in a journal by a process called *journalizing*. The format and design of journals may vary in style and content from one business to another. However, they are all based on the same accounting concepts and serve an identical objective: to record business transactions.

Before a business transaction may be recorded, *evidential matter* must exist; this is in accordance with the objectivity principle, which requires that all business transactions be supported by documents proving that a transaction did in fact occur. Typical documents include invoices from suppliers, billings to customers, bank deposits, rental agreements, bills of sale, promissory notes, bank statements, employee time cards, and issued checks (supported by proper documentation).

The format of a journal may vary from a two-column journal (referred to as a general journal) to multi-column journals (referred to as special journals).

The General Journal

The general journal (Exhibit 9.1) is a two-column, general purpose journal. It is not practical for large volumes of repetitive transactions such as cash, sales, and other transactions that occur daily or on some other frequent basis.

A general journal requires extensive clerical effort. The account names must be written in full, and every entry should have a supporting explanation. *Each entry in a general journal requires individual posting to the accounts.*

When special journals are part of the accounting system, entries recorded in the general journal (two-column journal) are usually limited to the following types of entries:

Exhibit 9.1   General Journal

DATE	DESCRIPTION	POST. REF.	DEBIT		CREDIT	
Apr. 30	Payroll Expense		2 000 00			
	Accrued Payroll				2 000 00	
	To record 4 days unpaid wages as of 4/30/XX					

- Entries to record transactions which have not been provided for in the special journals.

- Correcting entries: These are any entries to correct previous entries which were erroneous.

- Adjusting entries: These end-of-month entries are necessary to comply with the matching principle (accrual basis of accounting). On this basis, expenses incurred during an accounting period (but not actually paid until the following period) are matched with the revenue generated during the same period.

- Reversing entries: These beginning-of-month entries may be required due to certain types of adjusting entries recorded in the previous month.

- Closing entries: These end-of-year entries set the revenue, expense, and temporary contra-equity accounts (such as Withdrawals) to zero. The purpose of closing entries is to clear these accounts for the next accounting period.

Special Journals

A special journal is a multi-column journal which may be custom-designed by an accountant according to the particular needs of a business. A separate special journal is designed for each major repetitive activity or event.

Special journals are designed with a number of basic characteristics. A separate column is established for each type of transaction likely to occur repeatedly during the month (for instance, cash in, cash out, accounts receivable debits, accounts receivable credits, and sales). In addition to these specific columns, a *sundry or miscellaneous area* is established to record those transactions that do not have specially-assigned columns, usually because they occur infrequently during the month (for example, payment on a mortgage).

In the daily journalizing process, only the totals of certain transactions are recorded in the columns of special journals. For example, the cash register tapes provide information about sales and cash received for the day. Only the totals are recorded in the journal. The cash register tapes are stored to serve as evidential matter in compliance with the objectivity principle.

At the end of the month, each column on the journal is totaled and a mathematical proof is performed by comparing the debit and credit totals; the total debits must equal the total credits.

With the exception of the sundry column, only the totals of the specially labeled columns are posted to the applicable accounts. The entries in the sundry column are individually posted, or the items are recapped in a summary form for posting purposes.

Each journal is assigned an exclusive symbol which may be a number and/or letter(s) representing the name of the journal. When a special journal is posted, its symbol will be entered in the posting reference column of the account; it provides a means of cross-referencing an amount posted in an account to its source document.

Special Journals and Internal Control. Special journals are an important part of an operation's system of *internal control*. Internal control relates to the policies, procedures, and equipment used in a business to safeguard its assets and promote operational efficiency.

The objectives of an internal control system are to:

- protect assets against waste, fraud, and inefficiency;

- maintain the accuracy and reliability of a company's financial information; and

- ensure compliance with company policies and procedures.

Special journals offer benefits to an internal control system by providing increased efficiency in a number of instances. For example, the use of special journals eliminates the repeated writing of account titles (Sales, Cash, Accounts Receivable, and others).

Special journals have the advantage of grouping similar transactions chronologically on one source document; for example, all sales are entered on the sales & cash receipts journal. Special journals may be delegated to different individuals to distribute journalizing time and effort.

Special journals also increase efficiency in the posting process. By posting column totals to the general ledger accounts rather than individual items, the volume of posting is greatly reduced. Sundry items will still require individual posting unless they are recapped in summary form.

Besides providing increased efficiency, special journals provide several safeguards which improve the internal control system:

- The division of duties prevents the possibility of one employee handling a particular transaction from beginning to end (for example, from the receipt of cash to the payment of cash).

- Since the general ledger accounts have fewer entries, the potential for error is reduced.

- The sales & cash receipts journal provides information that may be conveniently compared to bank deposit slips, providing control over cash transactions.

The design and number of special journals will depend on the specific needs of a particular business. In our ongoing example, Tower Restaurant's accountant has determined that the following special journals will meet the needs of the business:

Special Journal	Journal Reference Symbol
Sales & Cash Receipts Journal	S
Accounts Payable Journal	AP
Cash Payments Journal	CP
Payroll Journal	PR

Input to Special Journals. The objectivity principle requires that all journal entries be supported by objective evidence proving that the transactions did in fact occur. A check should never be issued unless it is supported by an invoice, contract, or other independent evidential matter. For example, all entries in the accounts payable journal must be supported by vendor invoices.

Entries in the cash payments journal and the payroll journal are supported by the issuance of checks. Checks written on the regular checking account are entered in the cash payments journal; checks written on the payroll checking account are entered in the payroll journal.

Entries to the sales & cash receipts journal can be quite involved depending on the operation. A hotel will have cash receipts and sales from the Rooms Department and other revenue centers, thus requiring special reports from each department. The special reports are summarized on a daily report, which is then journalized to the sales & cash receipts journal.

The concept of the daily report is best explained by using the daily cashiers report for a restaurant operation.

Daily Cashiers Report

The daily cashiers report is prepared from the cash register readings, cash count, bank deposit, and records of other transactions handled by the cashier. An operation with several stations and shifts may find it more convenient to utilize several daily cashiers reports, and summarize the data on a single daily report. Exhibit 9.2 presents a daily cashiers report for the Tower Restaurant.

All daily cashiers reports are designed with common characteristics. These reports generally contain a heading showing the date and day of the week, and may contain information about the weather, number of guests, or other data helpful in analyzing and managing the operation. They usually consist of separate sections for register readings, accounting of cash register funds and transactions, and supporting schedules.

For internal control reasons, register readings are taken by the supervisor or a designated individual other than the cashier. The differences less any "voids" (voided register entries approved by the supervisor) represent Food Sales and Sales Taxes Collected.

The accounting for the cash register funds and transactions is

Exhibit 9.2   Daily Cashiers Report

Daily Cashiers Report		Key A (Sales)			Key B (Sales Tax)		
Date: _12/8/X2_ Day: _Sat._ Weather: _Rainy + Cold_							
Previous shift's closing reading		62	113	14	9	002	03
This shift's closing reading		63	463	81	9	083	07
Difference		1	350	67		81	04
Voids				-0-			-0-
Net		1	350	67		81	04
TOTAL TO BE ACCOUNTED FOR:							
Food Sales		1	350	67			
Sales Tax			81	04			
Tips Charged			50	00			
Customer Collections			185	00			
Change Fund (Start)			500	00			
CONTROL TOTAL		2	166	71			
TOTAL ACCOUNTED FOR:							
Cash for Deposit		1	407	06			
Purchases Paid Out			8	75			
Tips Paid Out			50	00			
Customer Charges			200	00			
Change Fund (Return)			500	00			
Total Receipts and Paid Outs		2	165	81			
Cash Short (+)				90			
Cash Over (−)							
TOTAL ACCOUNTED FOR		2	166	71			
EXPLANATION OF CUSTOMER COLLECTIONS & CHARGES:							

CUSTOMER	TAB	COLLECTION		CHARGE	
DEBCO, Inc.	1812			200	00
J.R. Rickles		185	00		
TOTAL		185	00	200	00

EXPLANATION OF PURCHASES PAID OUT:

PAID TO	PURPOSE	AMOUNT	
Ted's Market	Food items for kitchen	8	75
Total		8	75

divided into two sections: the "To Be Accounted For" section and the "Accounted For" section.

The "To Be Accounted For" section represents net register readings, tips entered by guests on credit cards or charge accounts, collections from guests toward prior balances of open accounts, and the initial change fund in the register. It may include the following items:

- Food sales

- Sales tax

- Tips charged

- Customer collections

- Change fund (start)

The result of this section provides a *control total*. The total of cash drawer funds and amounts represented on supporting documents should reconcile with this control total, except for minor cash shortages or overages. Minor shortages or overages are generally due to errors in processing the numerous transactions which an operation handles daily. Obviously, any large variances should be investigated for irregularities.

The "Accounted For" section represents the cash drawer funds, and includes bankcard drafts (VISA and MasterCard), documents supporting items paid out of the cash drawer, and the return of the initial change fund. It may be composed of the following items:

- Cash

- Purchases paid out

- Tips paid out

- Customer charges

- Change fund (return)

- Cash shortages or overages

These total receipts and amounts paid out are reconciled with the control total, and any minor cash shortages or overages are computed. The final "Total Accounted For" must reconcile with the total of the items "To Be Accounted For" (control total).

Processing the "To Be Accounted For" Section. The "To Be Accounted For" section is processed as follows:

1. Amounts for *food sales* and *sales tax* are the result of totals of cash register readings, less any void rings.

2. *Tips charged* are tips that guests entered on credit card drafts or open account transactions. Such tips represent a liability of the restaurant to its employees.

3. *Customer collections* are payments received from guests to be applied toward their prior charges on open accounts. These collections are explained in a listing on a separate section of the report.

4. *Change fund (start)* represents the cashier's initial funds provided at the start of the day. This fund is a predetermined, fixed amount (also termed "imprest amount") established by policy.

5. The total of the "To Be Accounted For" section serves as the control total. This control total will later be compared to the cash count and register documents to determine any cash shortages or overages.

Processing the "Accounted For" Section. The "Accounted For" section is processed as follows:

1. The *change fund* is restored to its imprest amount. The balance of the cash, personal checks, travelers checks, and bank credit card drafts form the *cash* deposit. (For purposes of our example, assume that the Tower Restaurant accepts no other credit cards.)

2. *Purchases paid out* represent incidentals that were paid from the cash drawer during the shift. The cashier supports these amounts paid out by including documented vouchers in the cash drawer. These vouchers are explained in a listing on a separate section of the report.

    This is a convenient method of paying for small COD deliveries and incidental needs. It saves the writing of checks for small items and eliminates the need for a separate cash fund.

3. *Tips paid out* represent payments to employees for the tips that were entered on credit card drafts or open accounts.

    Tower Restaurant's tip policy is to pay the server immediately upon receipt of the credit card draft or open account charge. In doing so, the restaurant has settled its liability, which was originally recorded in the previous section as tips charged.

    Because of Tower Restaurant's tip policy, the net result of tips charged and tips paid out will be zero. The Tower Restaurant enters the tip activity to maintain internal control of cash.

4. *Customer charges* represent charges made by guests on their house accounts, and include the total of the guest checks. These charges are explained in a listing on a separate section of the report.

5. The total of the above items, referred to as "Total Receipts and Paid Outs," is compared with the control total (the total of the "To Be Accounted For" section). Any difference between these two totals is due to a *cash shortage or overage*. A cash shortage has the same effect as an expense, and a cash overage creates an effect similar to revenue. Both are recorded in a single account called Cash Short or Over.

6. The resulting "Accounted For" total must agree with the "To Be Accounted For" total (control total).

Sales & Cash Receipts Journal

The purpose of the sales & cash receipts journal is to record all the sales and the cash receipts for the day. A large hospitality business may have several supplementary journals which are later summarized in one

Exhibit 9.3 Sales & Cash Receipts Journal

Date	Food Sales cr 401	Sales Tax Payable cr 211	Customer Collections cr 112	Cash to Bank dr 102	Customer Charges dr 112	Cash Short (Over) dr(cr)754	Sundry Items Account Title	Acct. No.	Amount dr
Dec. 8	1 350 67	81 04	185 00	1 407 06	200 00	90	Cost of Food Sales	501	8 75
15	1 268 52	76 11	---	1 286 93	48 65	(40)	Operating Supplies	727	9 45

(In actual practice, sales and cash receipts are entered daily; only two entries are used to simplify this illustration.)

sales & cash receipts journal (Exhibit 9.3) that will be used for posting purposes.

For a restaurant operation, the input information for this journal is taken from the daily cashiers report (Exhibit 9.2). The columns of the sales & cash receipts journal are arranged to correlate with the information on the daily cashiers report. Exhibit 9.3 shows the account number and indicates debit (dr) or credit (cr) at the top of each column. Showing the account number and indicating debit or credit is not required in day-to-day use of the sales & cash receipts journal. This information has been included in Exhibit 9.3 to facilitate the discussion of the special journals.

The accounting logic employed in the design of this journal and the assignment of debits and credits is as follows:

- The revenue account Food Sales is increased by a credit.

- The liability account Sales Tax Payable is increased by a credit.

- The customer collections column represents payments made by customers toward their open account balances which were previously recorded as Accounts Receivable. Customer payments reduce the asset account called Accounts Receivable; a credit decreases this asset account.

- The asset account Cash is increased by a debit.

- The customer charges column lists transactions charged by guests to their open accounts, representing Accounts Receivable. A debit increases this asset account.

- Only one column is provided to record a cash shortage or overage because the net result is posted to one account called Cash Short or Over. A cash shortage represents an expense; therefore, it is recorded with a debit entry. A cash overage is similar to revenue, and is recorded with a credit. Parentheses are used to indicate a cash overage.

- The sundry items area is a debit column used to record those items for which no special column is provided. Unusual items requiring a credit entry in this column may be indicated by the use of parentheses.

Exhibit 9.4 Accounts Payable Journal

Date	Vendor	Accounts Payable cr 201	Food Inventory dr 121	Supplies Inventory dr 131	Utilities dr 712	Sundry Items		
						Account Title	Acct.No	Amount dr
Dec.7	Star Purveyors	300 00	300 00					
14	Pompano Purveyors	500 00	500 00					

- It is not necessary to record the change fund unless its imprest amount is modified.

In our ongoing example involving the Tower Restaurant, the operation's tip policy and internal control procedures make it unnecessary to journalize the tips charged and tips paid out. Some companies may prefer to record these activities; the Tower Restaurant has determined that it is not necessary due to its limited volume of tips charged and paid out.

Accounts Payable Journal

The use of the accounts payable journal may vary from one company to another. Some companies have an accounting policy requiring that all invoices, upon receipt, be recorded in the accounts payable journal (Exhibit 9.4), regardless of whether they are paid immediately or at some later date. This procedure is similar to a *voucher register system*.

In our example, the Tower Restaurant uses another approach to the journal—an approach which is common for small operations. Upon receipt of an invoice, a determination is made whether to pay immediately or at some later date. Those invoices that will not be paid immediately are entered on the accounts payable journal. Invoices that are paid immediately upon receipt bypass the accounts payable journal and go directly to the cash payments journal.

The voucher register system provides better internal control on unpaid invoices; however, it increases clerical costs. Larger companies usually prefer a voucher register system, since greater volumes of invoices require an improved system of internal control.

The columns in the accounts payable journal are as follows:

- The accounts payable column is a credit entry because only unpaid invoices are entered on this journal. An unpaid invoice is a liability, increased by a credit to the Accounts Payable account.

- All other columns (food inventory, supplies inventory, utilities, and sundry items) are debit entries because they represent increases to asset or expense accounts.

Cash Payments Journal

The cash payments journal (Exhibit 9.5) is used to record checks issued from the regular checking account. The name of this journal may be misleading since it contains the word "cash" but is only concerned with the issuance of checks. The cash payments journal is sometimes called the disbursements journal.

Exhibit 9.5 Cash Payments Journal

Date	Paid To:	Check Number	Cash-- Checking cr 102	Food Inventory dr 121	Accounts Payable dr 201	Sundry Items Account Title	Acct. No.	Amount dr
Dec.2	DSK Realty	348	800 00			Rent Expense	801	800 00
2	Associated Insurance Co.	349	2 400 00			Prepaid Insurance	132	2 400 00
6	Star Purveyors	350	2 150 00		2 150 00			
6	VOID	351	---					
7	Tom's Seafood	352	75 00	75 00				
7	State Dept. of Taxation	353	1 216 75			Sales Tax Payable	211	1 216 75
9	Pompano Purveyors	354	2 450 00		2 450 00			
14	Tom's Seafood	355	125 00	125 00				
16	Tower Payroll Account	356	730 35			Cash--Payroll Checking	103	730 35
31	City Utilities	357	250 66			Utilities	712	250 66
31	Regional Telephone	358	65 16			Telephone	751	65 16

The cash payments journal serves as a check register showing all issued and voided checks. Additional columns may be set up to maintain a running bank balance to monitor the availability of cash for operating use.

The cash column is a credit to the regular checking account because the issuance of a check decreases the asset account Cash. The remaining columns are all debit entries which are explained as follows:

- Payments made immediately upon delivery of storeroom provisions increase Food Inventory (an asset account).

- Payments of prior purchases on open account decrease Accounts Payable (a liability account).

- The sundry items area is for debit entries that increase asset or expense accounts, or debit entries that decrease liability accounts for which no special column has been provided.

Payments of certain invoices require only an entry in the accounts payable debit column because they were previously entered in the accounts payable journal. Invoices that are entered in the accounts payable journal represent those which will not be paid immediately. When the entry was originally made in the accounts payable journal, the invoice amount was entered as a credit to Accounts Payable.

The following examples will trace the events involving the accounts payable and cash payments journals. The entries are shown in general journal format for illustration.

Example #1. Upon receipt of an invoice for food provisions (to be paid at a later date), a restaurant using a perpetual inventory system records the transaction as follows:

Entry in Accounts Payable Journal

dr	Food Inventory	$780	
	cr	Accounts Payable	$780

When the invoice is paid, the transaction is recorded as follows:

Entry in Cash Payments Journal

dr	Accounts Payable	$780	
	cr	Cash	$780

Example #2. An invoice accompanying a delivery of food provisions is paid immediately upon receipt. No entry was previously made in the accounts payable journal. The transaction is recorded as follows:

Entry in Cash Payments Journal

dr	Food Inventory	$75	
	cr	Cash	$75

Payroll Journal

The payroll journal (Exhibit 9.6) is a check register used to record all payroll checks issued.

The Tower Restaurant maintains a separate checking account for its payroll payments. Some small operations may prefer to pay their employees directly from regular checking accounts. The use of a separate account improves internal control and simplifies reconciliation of the regular and payroll checking accounts.

The payroll account is maintained on an imprest system. A predetermined amount is deposited to open the account. This amount is nominal; it may be $100 or any amount depending on the bank's requirements or the company's decision. It is seldom significant or sufficient to cover the wages for any payroll period.

When the payroll liability is calculated, a transfer is made from the regular account to the payroll account to cover the total amount of the current payroll checks. This transfer is made by issuing a check from the regular account and depositing it in the payroll account.

If a company uses a $100 imprest amount, the reconciled payroll checking account balance should always have a balance of $100.

There are many formats for a payroll journal; however, they share common characteristics. The first two columns are used to indicate the recipient of the check and the check number. A payroll journal typically includes columns for gross wages, FICA taxes, federal income tax withheld, and net pay.

Gross Wages. The total of the gross wages column represents the payroll expense of the hotel to its employees. As an expense, it is increased by a debit entry.

FICA Taxes. Under the Federal Insurance Contributions Act (FICA), an

Exhibit 9.6 Payroll Journal

Paid To:	Check No.	Gross Wages dr 601		FICA cr 215		FIT cr 215		Net Pay cr 103	
		1		**2**		**3**		**4** / **5**	
Christine Robert	621	32	16	7	85	2	00	22	31
Elizabeth David	622	30	15	7	36	6	00	16	79
Ann Tasha	623	42	00	9	94	10	00	22	06
Mary Alcrep	624	24	40	2	41	---		21	99
Tom Paul	625	140	00	9	80	6	00	124	20
Steve Towe	626	600	00	42	00	35	00	523	00

Table title:
> Tower Restaurant
> PAYROLL REGISTER (PR)
> December 16, 19X2

employer withholds certain amounts commonly known as social security deductions from each employee's gross wages. The FICA column is a credit entry because the employer owes this amount to the Internal Revenue Service, creating a liability which is increased by use of a credit. By withholding these deductions, the employer is acting as a collection agent for the IRS.

Federal Income Taxes (FIT). The FIT column is for federal income taxes withheld from the employee's gross wages. The withholding of these taxes creates a liability for the employer, similar to that created under FICA.

Some companies may establish separate accounts for the FICA and FIT taxes withheld. The Tower Restaurant records both of these liabilities in the same account: Employee Withheld Taxes.

Net Pay. The net pay column lists each employee's payroll check, and the column total represents the amount to be paid out of the payroll checking account. It is a credit column because its effect is to decrease the payroll checking account's cash balance.

Bookkeeping Accounts

Accounts are separate bookkeeping records kept for each individual item in the asset, liability, equity, revenue, and expense classifications. Sometimes, these accounts are called ledger accounts. The entire group of accounts is called the general ledger.

A ledger account is a means of accumulating information in a single place. This information relates to increases and decreases to an account, and its resulting balance. For example, by maintaining a Cash account, a

Exhibit 9.7 Two-Column Account

ACCOUNT ACCOUNTS RECEIVABLE							ACCOUNT NO. 122	
Date 19XX	ITEM	PR	DEBIT	DATE	ITEM	PR	CREDIT	
Jan. 1	Bal Fwd	✓	8 000 00	Jan.31		S	5 600 00	
31		S	3 700 00					
	6,100		11,700					

record is provided showing total cash receipts, total cash payments, and the cash balance for an accounting period.

Daily business transactions are initially recorded in journals. Information is later transferred from these journals to the general ledger accounts by the process of posting, which is generally performed at the end of each month.

There are several account formats, namely:

● Two-column format

● Three-column format

● Four-column format

The following sections discuss these three formats in more detail and explain their uses.

Two-Column Account

The two-column format is shown in Exhibit 9.7. It is often referred to as a T-account because its shape is similar to the letter "T."

Debits are posted on the left side and credits are entered on the right side. An account balance is computed by subtracting the totals of the debit and credit amounts. If total debits exceeds total credits, the difference is a debit balance. Conversely, if total credits exceeds total debits, the difference is a credit balance. Exhibit 9.7 provides an example of an account with a debit balance.

The two-column format (T-account) is not popular today because of the use of computers in business applications. However, it is still an important tool in solving accounting problems. Accountants use a modified format of the T-account to serve as a working tool, as shown in the following example:

Utilities

6/10 Heat	500	6/15 Water Rebate 50
6/12 Electric	900	
6/30 Water	100	
Total Debits	1500	
Balance	1450	

Exhibit 9.8 Three-Column Account

DATE 19XX	ITEM	POST. REF.	DEBIT	CREDIT	BALANCE
NAME ACCOUNTS RECEIVABLE					Account No. 122
Jan. 1	Bal Fwd	✓			8 000 00
31		S	3 700 00	5 600 00	6 100 00

Exhibit 9.9 Four-Column Account

DATE 19XX	ITEM	POST. REF.	DEBIT	CREDIT	BALANCE DEBIT	BALANCE CREDIT
NAME ACCOUNTS RECEIVABLE						Account No. 122
Jan. 1	Bal Fwd	✓			8 000 00	
31		S	3 700 00	5 600 00	6 100 00	

Three-Column Account

The three-column account (Exhibit 9.8) is popular in both computer and manual systems. The debits and credits still maintain their left and right relationship. A column is separately assigned to enter the balance of the account. Because of this special balance column, any credit balance must be "signed" by the use of either parentheses (typical in manual systems) or a negative sign (typical in computer systems).

For example, a $100.00 credit balance might be shown as (100.00), 100.00−, or 100.00 cr.

Four-Column Account

The four-column account (Exhibit 9.9) is similar to the three-column format except that there are two columns for the balance. One column is used for recording a debit balance, and another is used for recording a credit balance.

Using two columns for the account balance eliminates the necessity of signing the balance as debit or credit. However, if the four-column format is used, caution must be exercised to avoid entering the balance in the wrong column.

The General Ledger

General ledger is a term that represents all of the accounts used in the accounting system. It is sometimes referred to as the "book of accounts."

Exhibit 9.10 Accounts Receivable Subsidiary Ledger

NAME ___DEBCO, Inc.___

ADDRESS_____

DATE 19X2	ITEM	POST. REF.	DEBIT	CREDIT	BALANCE
Dec. 8	Tab 1812	S	200 00		200 00

NAME ___J.R. Rickles___

ADDRESS_____

DATE 19X2	ITEM	POST. REF.	DEBIT	CREDIT	BALANCE
Nov. 18	Tab 1511	S	185 00		185 00
Dec. 8	Payment	S		185 00	-0-
15	Tab 1849	S	48 65		48 65

The general ledger may be a binder housing all accounts, or, in the case of a computerized general ledger, it may be all accounts printed on a continuous form.

The accounts in the general ledger are arranged according to their sequence in the chart of accounts.

Subsidiary Ledgers

A subsidiary ledger is a separate ledger that provides the supporting detail of an account in the general ledger. For example, the Accounts Receivable account in the general ledger does not tell us *which* customers owe amounts to the business; it merely tells us the total amount owed to the business by all customers. The accounts receivable subsidiary ledger provides the information arranged by customer and by invoice.

The two most common types of subsidiary ledgers are as follows:

- Accounts receivable subsidiary ledger
- Accounts payable subsidiary ledger

Accounts Receivable Subsidiary Ledger

The accounts receivable subsidiary ledger (Exhibit 9.10) provides detailed information on amounts due the business from its customers. This information is usually arranged alphabetically by customer and chronologically by invoice within each customer category. The total of all the customers' balances must agree with the balance of the Accounts

Receivable account in the general ledger. For this reason, the Accounts Receivable account in the general ledger is called a *control account*.

In the hotel industry, there may be several different types of accounts receivable subsidiary ledgers. Some common types are:

- Guest ledger
- City ledger
- Advance deposits ledger
- Banquet ledger

Guest Ledger. A guest ledger is a type of ledger used for registered guests staying at the hotel. This ledger provides up-to-the-minute status on guest charges and payments made by guests. The guest ledger may also be referred to as a front office ledger, transient ledger, or room ledger.

The guest ledger is usually maintained by room number because that arrangement is more convenient for processing guest transactions.

City Ledger. A city ledger is a type of ledger used for all customers other than those classified as registered guests staying at the hotel.

For example, it would contain accounts receivable transactions for rental of conference rooms. Transfers are also made to this ledger from the guest ledger for registered guests who have checked out of the hotel and charged their bills using open account privileges or nonbank credit cards.

In a manual system, the city ledger is usually maintained in alphabetical sequence by customer name.

Advance Deposits Ledger. Some hotels maintain a separate advance deposits ledger to record reservation deposits. When the guest arrives, the deposit is transferred from the advance deposits ledger to the guest ledger. An alternative method used by some hotels is to record advance deposits in the city ledger and, when guests arrive, transfer the deposits from the city ledger to the guest ledger.

Hotels doing a large banquet business might have a separate *banquet ledger* to record banquet deposits. The advance deposits ledger and advance payments recorded in a banquet ledger represent credit balances, because the hotel has received funds for services not yet rendered. It does not have legal claim to these funds until service is completed or contract terms have expired.

Accounts receivable represent money due the hotel for services rendered. Therefore, the advance deposits ledger and advance payments in the banquet ledger are not accounts receivable for purposes of financial statement reporting.

Additionally, any credit balances in the guest ledger or city ledger are not considered accounts receivable because such balances usually arise from overpayments or advance payments.

For financial statement reporting purposes, the advance deposits ledger, advance payments in the banquet ledger, and credit balances in the city and guest ledgers are combined into one amount. This amount would appear in the Current Liabilities section of the balance sheet as a

Exhibit 9.11 Accounts Payable Subsidiary Ledger

NAME	Star Purveyors							Terms: n/10 EOM		
ADDRESS										

DATE 19X2	ITEM	POST. REF.	DEBIT		CREDIT		BALANCE	
Nov. 4	INV 4865	AP			500	00	(500	00)
11	INV 4934	AP			700	00	(1 200	00)
20	INV 5519	AP			950	00	(2 150	00)
Dec. 6	CK 350	CP	2 150	00			-0-	
7	INV 6245	AP			300	00	(300	00)

NAME	Pompano Purveyors							Terms: n/10 EOM		
ADDRESS										

DATE 19X2	ITEM	POST. REF.	DEBIT		CREDIT		BALANCE	
Nov. 30		✓					(2 450	00)
Dec. 6	CK 356	CP	2 450	00			-0-	
14	INV 1642	AP			500	00	(500	00)

line item which may be called Unearned Revenue or Deposits and Credit Balances.

The accounts receivable subsidiary ledger may be in the form of posting machine ledger cards, manual ledger cards, or computerized listings. A smaller restaurant may simply use the unpaid guest checks as its subsidiary ledger.

Accounts Payable Subsidiary Ledger

The accounts payable subsidiary ledger (Exhibit 9.11) provides detailed information about amounts owed by the business to its suppliers. This information is arranged alphabetically by vendor and chronologically by invoice within each vendor account. The accounts payable subsidiary ledger is also referred to as the *creditors ledger*.

The total of all the vendors' balances must agree with the balance of the Accounts Payable account in the general ledger. For this reason, the Accounts Payable account in the general ledger is also called a control account.

The accounts payable subsidiary ledger may be in the form of posting machine ledger cards, manual ledger cards, or computerized listings. A smaller hotel may simply use the unpaid vendor invoices as its subsidiary ledger.

It is not necessary to sign the balance in the accounts payable subsidiary ledger because it is implied that the balance is a credit balance. Should a debit balance result due to overpayment or some other reason, the balance is then signed with a minus (−) sign, or the amount is enclosed in parentheses to indicate that it is not a normal credit balance.

While it is not necessary to sign credit balances in the accounts payable subsidiary ledger, we will sign credit balances in this text because it simplifies the computation of account balances for individuals learning basic accounting practices.

Input to Subsidiary Ledgers

Postings are made to the subsidiary ledgers as the transactions occur to provide instantaneous information on the receivables and payables of the business. As previously noted, two subsidiary ledgers are used to record this information:

1. An accounts receivable subsidiary ledger to record all guest open account charges and guest payments thereon.

2. An accounts payable subsidiary ledger to record unpaid invoices and subsequent payment of these invoices.

The special journals that provide input to the subsidiary ledgers are the accounts payable journal, the cash payments journal, and the sales & cash receipts journal. In determining whether posting to the subsidiary ledgers is required, the following guidelines will be helpful:

*   Always post a corresponding entry to the accounts payable subsidiary ledger whenever an entry is made on any journal that affects the Accounts Payable account (a control account) in the general ledger.

*   Always post a corresponding entry to the accounts receivable subsidiary ledger whenever an entry is made on any journal that affects the Accounts Receivable account (a control account) in the general ledger.

Accounts Payable Journal. Entries in the accounts payable column of this journal must always be posted immediately to the proper record in the accounts payable subsidiary ledger. Since the column on the journal is a credit entry, a corresponding credit entry is posted to the subsidiary account.

Cash Payments Journal. Entries in the accounts payable column of this journal must always be posted immediately to the proper record in the accounts payable subsidiary ledger. Since the column on the journal is a debit entry, a corresponding debit entry is posted to the subsidiary account.

Sales & Cash Receipts Journal. This journal contains two columns affecting Accounts Receivable; one is a credit column and the other is a debit column. An entry in either of these columns requires an immediate corresponding entry in the guest's account in the accounts receivable subsidiary ledger.

Exhibit 9.12   The Accounting System

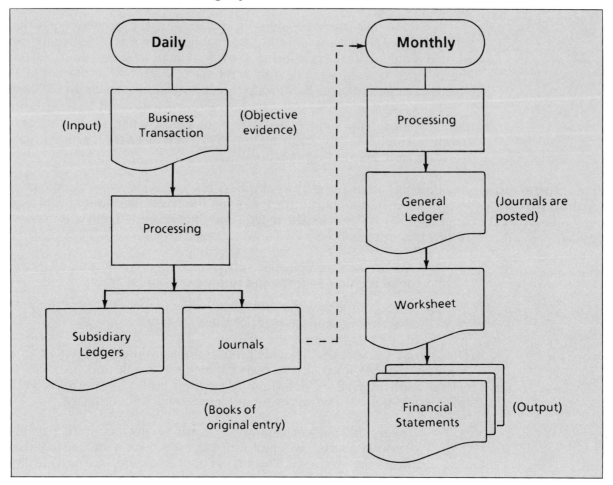

The Accounting System

Accounting systems are transaction-oriented. They are designed to record and classify the volume of business transactions that occur daily and summarize the results to produce financial information.

The procedures and forms used in an accounting system depend upon the size, nature of operations, and complexity of a business. While the use of computers may require modification of certain forms and procedures, the basic concepts and objectives of an accounting system remain unchanged.

The accounting cycle under a computerized system is identical to that under a manual system. An analysis of a portion of the accounting cycle is presented in Exhibit 9.12. This analysis is based on inputs, processing, and outputs.

An accounting cycle is repetitive throughout the accounting year. On a daily basis, business transactions are journalized and the subsidiary ledgers for receivables and payables are updated. These processes are explained in Chapter 10.

Most transactions are recorded in special journals. The following list associates typical transactions with the special journals used to record them:

Type of Transaction	Special Journal
Sales and cash receipts	S
Purchases on open account	AP
Checks issued on regular account	CP
Checks issued on payroll account	PR

In addition to these special journals, a general journal is used for recording transactions which do not fit in any special journal.

At the end of each month, the journals are posted to the general ledger accounts. After all journals have been posted, a balance is computed for each general ledger account. The posting process is discussed in Chapter 10.

The month-end activities include the preparation of a comprehensive working document called a *worksheet*, which is explained in Chapter 11. This worksheet is used by the accountant to prove the equality of debits and credits in the general ledger accounts and to determine adjusting entries. It also serves as a basis in preparing the financial statements.

This cycle is repeated for each month of the accounting year. At the end of the year, closing entries are recorded in the general ledger to set the temporary accounts to zero and record the profit (or loss) for the year to an equity account. Subsequently, a new general ledger must be set up for the new accounting year. These procedures are explained in Chapter 12.

Discussion Questions

1. What are the advantages of using special journals?
2. What is the purpose of each of the following special journals?

    a. Sales & cash receipts journal
    b. Cash payments journal
    c. Accounts payable journal
    d. Payroll journal

3. What purpose do accounting records serve?
4. What is the usefulness of the accounts receivable subsidiary ledger? How is it related to the control account for accounts receivable?
5. What are the guest ledger and the city ledger?
6. What are the daily and monthly functions in an accounting system?
7. How are the following accounting documents defined?

    a. Journal
    b. Account
    c. General ledger
    d. Subsidiary ledger

8. How are the following types of journal entries used?

    a. Adjusting entries
    b. Reversing entries
    c. Closing entries

9. What are the objectives of an internal control system?

Problems

Problem 9.1

As the food and beverage supervisor, your responsibility is to reconcile the transactions for the day with the cash register readings. Following are the results of your check-out procedures for the bar.

Register Readings:

	Sales	Sales Tax
This shift's close	126,875.95	6,343.90
Prior shift's close	126,195.45	6,309.77

There are no voids to consider for this shift. The change fund is on a $200 imprest system. Following are the contents of the cash drawer:

Return of change fund	$200.00
Cash for deposit	620.00
Bank credit cards	29.36
Travelers checks	50.00

In addition to register funds, there is a paid-out voucher of $12.76 for supplies.

What is the cash shortage or overage for this shift?

Problem 9.2

Indicate the journal in which the following transactions will be recorded by making a checkmark under the appropriate heading.

	Sales	Accounts Payable	Payroll	Cash Payments
a. Payroll checks	___	___	___	___
b. Checks to suppliers	___	___	___	___
c. Sales for the day	___	___	___	___
d. Invoice to be paid next week	___	___	___	___
e. Issued check for rent payment	___	___	___	___
f. The voucher system is used. An invoice is received and will be immediately paid.	___	___	___	___

Problems *(continued)*

Problem 9.3
Determine the balance of the following accounts:

ACCOUNT A

Date	PR	Amount	Date	PR	Amount
Apr 1	Bal	120.00	Apr 30	J3	375.00
Apr 30	J1	260.00	Apr 30	J3	216.00
Apr 30	J2	75.00	Apr 30	J4	162.75

ACCOUNT B

Date	PR			Balance
May 1	Bal			515.36
May 31	J6	968.52		
May 31	J8		1,125.69	
May 31	J9	12.67		

ACCOUNT C

Date	PR			Balance
Apr 1	Bal			968.47
Apr 30	J1	485.33		
Apr 30	J2		785.25	
Apr 30	J3	1,101.11		

Problem 9.4
A payroll journal shows the following information:

Gross Wages Due	$10,500.80
FICA Withheld	750.81
Federal Income Tax Withheld	860.00
Group Insurance Withheld	560.20

The payroll checking account is on an imprest system. What check amount must be written from the regular checking account and deposited into the payroll checking account?

Problems *(continued)*

Problem 9.5
Specify whether the columns on the following special journals are a debit or a credit. Wherever a column is not applicable to a particular journal, an "x" has been inserted.

Journal Column	Sales & Cash Receipts	Accounts Payable	Cash Payments
Cash	___	x	___
Sales Tax Payable	___	x	___
Customer Collections	___	x	x
Customer Charges	___	x	x
Accounts Payable	x		
Food Sales	___	x	x
Food Inventory	x		
Allowances	___	x	x
Cash Shortage	___	x	x
Sundry Items	___	___	___

Problem 9.6
A hotel uses three accounts receivable subsidiary ledgers as follows:

	Guest Ledger	City Ledger	Banquet Ledger
Total accounts with debit balances	$105,895.25	$164,566.28	$ 0
Total accounts with credit balances	1,286.33	196.88	5,200.00
Total Accounts Receivable	$104,608.92	$164,369.40	$5,200.00 cr

What amount will appear as Accounts Receivable on the balance sheet?

10
Journalizing and Posting

Transactions begin the accounting process; each day, a business generates sales, receives cash, issues checks, and makes purchases on open account. An accounting system must include the necessary forms and procedures to accumulate data for this large volume of business activity in order to produce reliable financial information.

Years ago, most accounting systems were manual, requiring tedious handwriting and time-consuming computations. Today, even small businesses can afford to use computerized applications to perform many of the functions required in an accounting system.

Nevertheless, a mastery of accounting principles is best accomplished by studying a manual system. The advantage of this approach is that the learner can personally experience the many different accounting procedures and appreciate the necessity of accurately processing financial data.

With these benefits comes another plus: there is little need to re-learn accounting under automated procedures because computer systems emulate manual systems. In analyzing the accounting process in greater detail, this chapter will address such questions as:

1. How are business transactions recorded in special journals?

2. How is the daily cashiers report used as input to the sales & cash receipts journal?

3. How is posting to the subsidiary ledgers performed?

4. How is posting to the general ledger accounts performed?

5. How are footing and crossfooting performed?

This chapter presents the processes of journalizing business transactions on the special journals, posting to the subsidiary ledgers, and posting the special journals to the general ledger. The discussion of special journals (sales & cash receipts, cash payments, accounts payable, and payroll journals) is expanded to show how journalizing and posting are accomplished.

The Tower Restaurant is further discussed in terms of a case study developed in this chapter and continued in subsequent chapters through the end of the accounting cycle. The accounting policies and chart of accounts of the restaurant are furnished prior to illustrating how the business transactions are processed.

In this chapter, the business transactions of the Tower Restaurant are journalized in special journals and posted to the subsidiary and general ledgers. The resulting general ledger will form the basis of the ongoing case study which demonstrates the month-end and year-end accounting processes.

The Journalizing Process

All business transactions are first recorded on an accounting document called a journal. These journals may be referred to as the *book of original entry*. Journalizing is the process of writing (recording) a business transaction in a journal; each recorded transaction is called a journal entry.

Every entry must have objective evidence—a document such as an invoice or contract—to support the validity of the entry. These documents are inputs to the accounting system because they introduce data into the system. The journalizing procedure is referred to as processing.

The process of journalizing is performed on special journals or a two-column journal. The following journals are used as the books of original entry in Tower Restaurant's accounting system:

Journal	Journal Reference Symbol
Sales & Cash Receipts Journal	S
Accounts Payable Journal	AP
Cash Payments Journal	CP
Payroll Journal	PR
General Journal	J

A sequential page number may follow the journal reference symbol to facilitate cross-referencing to a journal.

Because special journals are part of Tower Restaurant's accounting system, entries recorded in the general journal (two-column journal) are limited to the following types of entries:

- Entries for transactions not provided for in the special journals

- Correcting entries (any entries used to correct previous entries which were erroneous)

- Adjusting entries (end-of-month entries required to comply with the accrual basis of accounting)

- Reversing entries (beginning-of-month entries which may be required due to certain types of adjusting entries recorded in the previous month)

- Closing entries (end-of-year entries to set the revenue, expense, and temporary contra-equity accounts to zero)

The purpose of closing entries is to clear certain accounts for the next accounting period. The account called *Income Summary* is used in the closing process, as more fully explained in Chapter 12.

Policies for the Tower Restaurant

The Tower Restaurant is a proprietorship owned by Ann Dancer. The business rents its land and building. Since December is the off-season, the restaurant operated only December 8 and 15. At the end of business on December 15, 19X2, it closed for the remainder of the year, to later re-open on January 1, 19X3. Its fiscal year is from January 1 to December 31. The previous accountant had completed the accounting records as of November 30, 19X2.

Assume that you have been engaged to perform the December 19X2 accounting duties for the restaurant. First, you must learn Tower Restaurant's accounting policies with respect to credit cards, payroll, inventory, accounts payable, and other relevant topics.

Bank Credit Cards. Only MasterCard and VISA credit cards are accepted; they are treated as cash and deposited into the regular checking account.

Payroll. A separate checking account is maintained for payroll. The payroll checking account is on a $200 imprest system. When the payroll checks are written, the payroll checking account is reimbursed for the total net payroll. This is accomplished by issuing a check from the regular checking account and depositing it in the payroll checking account.

Payrolls are paid twice a month (semimonthly). The restaurant pays minimum wage less the allowable maximum tip credit to all tipped employees.

Accounts Payable. The accounts payable journal is used to record only those invoices which are not paid immediately upon receipt. Any invoices that are immediately paid upon receipt are recorded in the cash payments journal, bypassing the accounts payable journal.

Guest Charge Privileges. Open account arrangements are restricted to selected guests by prior management approval. The restaurant has never experienced any bad debts; therefore, it does not provide for any estimate of uncollectible accounts.

Tips Policy. The policy for tips entered on credit cards or guest charges is as follows:

- The server submits the credit card or guest charge to the cashier and the tip is immediately paid out of the cash drawer.

- The server initials the tip entry on the credit card or charge document to indicate receipt of the tip from the cashier.

Inventory System. The food inventory is maintained on a perpetual system. Storeroom purchases are recorded as Food Inventory; direct purchases are recorded as Cost of Food Sales.

Amounts Paid Out. Minor COD deliveries are paid out of the cash drawer. The invoice is placed in the cash drawer as evidential matter. Any large COD deliveries are paid by check.

Cash Register Funds. The Cash on Hand account represents cash for the register drawer and a spare change fund. These funds are on an imprest system, replenished from the daily cash receipts as necessary.

Accounting for Supplies. Storeroom purchases of cleaning supplies, paper supplies, and guest supplies are recorded in a Supplies Inventory account. Direct purchases of these items are recorded in an expense account called Operating Supplies Expense.

At the end of the month, an inventory is taken, the consumed supplies are charged to Restaurant Supplies Expense, and the Supplies Inventory account is adjusted to properly reflect the inventory of supplies on hand.

Menus and replacement of small kitchen utensils are charged directly to the Operating Supplies expense account upon purchase.

Insurance. Workers' compensation insurance is charged to the Employee Benefits account. Property insurance and liability insurance are charged to the Insurance account.

Kitchen Fuel. Kitchen fuel is not separately identified from the utility costs because all utilities are on one meter, and management has determined that separate information on kitchen fuel consumption is not needed.

Tower Restaurant's Accounting System

Exhibit 10.1 shows Tower Restaurant's chart of accounts. Before beginning to process the restaurant's business transactions, you should be familiar with the chart of accounts and accounting policies of the business.

The business transactions are recorded daily in the proper journals in accordance with accounting policy. When making a journal entry that affects a control account in the general ledger (either Accounts Payable or Accounts Receivable), a corresponding entry is always posted to the proper subsidiary ledger.

Read each transaction and trace the processing to the respective journal and subsidiary ledger. The exhibits which illustrate the journalizing process are as follows:

Special Journal	Exhibit
Sales & Cash Receipts Journal	10.2
Accounts Payable Journal	10.3
Cash Payments Journal	10.4
Payroll Journal	10.5

Posting to subsidiary ledgers is performed immediately whenever a business transaction affects Accounts Receivable or Accounts Payable. This process is illustrated in the following exhibits:

Subsidiary Ledger	Exhibit
Accounts Receivable	10.6
Accounts Payable	10.7

Exhibit 10.1 Chart of Accounts for the Tower Restaurant

ASSET ACCOUNTS

Cash on Hand	101
Cash--Regular Checking	102
Cash--Payroll Checking	103
Accounts Receivable	112
Food Inventory	121
Supplies Inventory	131
Prepaid Insurance	132
Furniture & Equipment	147
China, Glassware & Silver	149
Accumulated Depreciation--F & E	157

LIABILITY ACCOUNTS

Accounts Payable	201
Sales Tax Payable	211
Employee Taxes Withheld	215
Accrued Payroll	231
Accrued Payroll Taxes	232

EQUITY ACCOUNTS

Capital, Ann Dancer	301
Withdrawals, Ann Dancer	302
Income Summary	399

REVENUE ACCOUNTS

Food Sales	401

EXPENSE ACCOUNTS

Cost of Food Sales	501
Payroll	601
Payroll Taxes	602
Employee Benefits	605
Employee Meals	607
Utilities	712
China, Glassware & Silver	721
Operating Supplies	727
Telephone	751
Office Supplies	752
Credit Card Fees	753
Cash Short or Over	754
Repairs & Maintenance	764
Rent	801
Insurance	821
Depreciation	891

A Study Guide for the Tower Restaurant Case Study

Thus far, we have dealt with preliminary topics related to the Tower Restaurant case study, including its accounting policies, chart of accounts, special journals, and subsidiary ledgers. Our discussion has been leading toward the first step in this case study: processing the December business transactions for the Tower Restaurant.

Before proceeding directly with these activities, however, the following study guide is presented. It sets forth the recommended approach to analyzing this case study, which, in many respects, demands more than a casual reading. In fact, active participation and analysis are the best methods of understanding this extended example.

1. Read the business transaction and supporting comments.

2. Before looking at the exhibits, mentally select the proper special journal and determine how the business transaction should be recorded.

3. Check your results with those in the corresponding exhibit. If your conclusions do not agree, read the business transaction again and analyze the logic behind the resulting journal entry.

4. Ensure that debits equal credits for each journal entry before proceeding to the next business transaction.

5. If any transaction recorded in a special journal affects either Accounts Receivable or Accounts Payable, a posting is required to the subsidiary ledger. Trace these transactions to the subsidiary ledger.

    When a posting is traced to the subsidiary ledger, perform the computation of the new balance to become familiar with this procedure.

6. After completing steps 1 through 5, checkmarks should be made next to the journal entries and subsidiary ledger postings (Exhibits 10.2 to 10.7) affected by the December processing of business transactions. This will indicate that you have successfully traced the processing explained in the above steps.

7. After you have traced each business transaction, review your checkmarks in each journal and subsidiary ledger account. Any December entry that does not have a checkmark will indicate an area which requires further review as part of your learning process.

The Transaction Log for the Tower Restaurant

This section presents the business transactions (in chronological sequence) which are to be processed for December 19X2. These transactions are to be journalized in accordance with Tower Restaurant's accounting policies.

Some transactions provide comments to supplement the learning experience. Exhibits 10.2 through 10.7 illustrate how the transactions were processed. Trace the processing of each transaction as explained previously in the study guide section.

Exhibit 10.2 Sales & Cash Receipts Journal

								Sundry Items		
Date	Food Sales cr 401	Sales Tax Payable cr 211	Customer Collections cr 112	Cash to Bank dr 102	Customer Charges dr 112	Cash Short (Over) dr(cr)754		Account Title	Acct. No.	Amount dr
Dec.8	1 350 67	81 04	185 00	1 407 06	200 00	90		Cost of Food Sales	501	8 75
15	1 268 52	76 11	---	1 286 93	48 65	(40)		Operating Supplies	727	9 45

Tower Restaurant
SALES & CASH RECEIPTS JOURNAL (S)
December 19X2

Exhibit 10.3 Accounts Payable Journal

						Sundry Items		
Date	Vendor	Accounts Payable cr 201	Food Inventory dr 121	Supplies Inventory dr 131	Utilities dr 712	Account Title	Acct.No	Amount dr
Dec.7	Star Purveyors	300 00	300 00					
14	Pompano Purveyors	500 00	500 00					

Tower Restaurant
ACCOUNTS PAYABLE JOURNAL (AP)
December 19X2

December 2: Paid the rent for December. Issued check number 348 for $800 to DSK Realty.

December 2: Received invoice for property insurance policy; the policy covers the period of 12/1/X2 to 12/1/X3. Immediately issued check number 349 for $2,400 to Associated Insurance Company.

Comment: Invoices to be paid immediately are recorded in the cash payments journal (Exhibit 10.4). This transaction is for property insurance that will benefit this period and future accounting periods. It is recorded as Prepaid Insurance. At the end of the month, the premiums that have expired will be recorded as Insurance Expense, and the Prepaid Insurance account will be adjusted accordingly.

Observe the entry in the sundry area. While writing the account number is unnecessary, doing so at this time will improve efficiency and

Exhibit 10.4   Cash Payments Journal

<table>
<tr>
<td colspan="13" align="center">Tower Restaurant
CASH PAYMENTS JOURNAL (CP)
<u>December 19X2</u></td>
</tr>
<tr>
<td rowspan="2">Date</td>
<td rowspan="2">Paid To:</td>
<td rowspan="2">Check Number</td>
<td colspan="2" rowspan="2">Cash--
Checking
cr 102</td>
<td colspan="2" rowspan="2">Food
Inventory
dr 121</td>
<td colspan="2" rowspan="2">Accounts
Payable
dr 201</td>
<td colspan="4" align="center">Sundry Items</td>
</tr>
<tr>
<td>Account Title</td>
<td>Acct.
No.</td>
<td colspan="2">Amount
dr</td>
</tr>
<tr>
<td>Dec.2</td><td>DSK Realty</td><td>348</td><td>800</td><td>00</td><td></td><td></td><td></td><td></td><td>Rent Expense</td><td>801</td><td>800</td><td>00</td>
</tr>
<tr>
<td>2</td><td>Associated Insurance Co.</td><td>349</td><td>2 400</td><td>00</td><td></td><td></td><td></td><td></td><td>Prepaid Insurance</td><td>132</td><td>2 400</td><td>00</td>
</tr>
<tr>
<td>6</td><td>Star Purveyors</td><td>350</td><td>2 150</td><td>00</td><td></td><td></td><td>2 150</td><td>00</td><td></td><td></td><td></td><td></td>
</tr>
<tr>
<td>6</td><td>VOID</td><td>351</td><td>---</td><td></td><td></td><td></td><td></td><td></td><td></td><td></td><td></td><td></td>
</tr>
<tr>
<td>7</td><td>Tom's Seafood</td><td>352</td><td>75</td><td>00</td><td>75</td><td>00</td><td></td><td></td><td></td><td></td><td></td><td></td>
</tr>
<tr>
<td>7</td><td>State Dept. of Taxation</td><td>353</td><td>1 216</td><td>75</td><td></td><td></td><td></td><td></td><td>Sales Tax Payable</td><td>211</td><td>1 216</td><td>75</td>
</tr>
<tr>
<td>9</td><td>Pompano Purveyors</td><td>354</td><td>2 450</td><td>00</td><td></td><td></td><td>2 450</td><td>00</td><td></td><td></td><td></td><td></td>
</tr>
<tr>
<td>14</td><td>Tom's Seafood</td><td>355</td><td>125</td><td>00</td><td>125</td><td>00</td><td></td><td></td><td></td><td></td><td></td><td></td>
</tr>
<tr>
<td>16</td><td>Tower Payroll Account</td><td>356</td><td>730</td><td>35</td><td></td><td></td><td></td><td></td><td>Cash--Payroll Checking</td><td>103</td><td>730</td><td>35</td>
</tr>
<tr>
<td>31</td><td>City Utilities</td><td>357</td><td>250</td><td>66</td><td></td><td></td><td></td><td></td><td>Utilities</td><td>712</td><td>250</td><td>66</td>
</tr>
<tr>
<td>31</td><td>Regional Telephone</td><td>358</td><td>65</td><td>16</td><td></td><td></td><td></td><td></td><td>Telephone</td><td>751</td><td>65</td><td>16</td>
</tr>
</table>

Exhibit 10.5   Payroll Journal

<table>
<tr>
<td colspan="11" align="center">Tower Restaurant
PAYROLL REGISTER (PR)
<u>December 16, 19X2</u></td>
</tr>
<tr>
<td rowspan="2">Paid To:</td>
<td rowspan="2">1
Check No.</td>
<td colspan="2">2</td>
<td colspan="2">3</td>
<td colspan="2">4</td>
<td colspan="2">5</td>
</tr>
<tr>
<td colspan="2">Gross Wages
dr 601</td>
<td colspan="2">FICA
cr 215</td>
<td colspan="2">FIT
cr 215</td>
<td colspan="2">Net Pay
cr 103</td>
</tr>
<tr>
<td>Christine Robert</td><td>621</td><td>32</td><td>16</td><td>7</td><td>85</td><td>2</td><td>00</td><td>22</td><td>31</td>
</tr>
<tr>
<td>Elizabeth David</td><td>622</td><td>30</td><td>15</td><td>7</td><td>36</td><td>6</td><td>00</td><td>16</td><td>79</td>
</tr>
<tr>
<td>Ann Tasha</td><td>623</td><td>42</td><td>00</td><td>9</td><td>94</td><td>10</td><td>00</td><td>22</td><td>06</td>
</tr>
<tr>
<td>Mary Alcrep</td><td>624</td><td>24</td><td>40</td><td>2</td><td>41</td><td>---</td><td></td><td>21</td><td>99</td>
</tr>
<tr>
<td>Tom Paul</td><td>625</td><td>140</td><td>00</td><td>9</td><td>80</td><td>6</td><td>00</td><td>124</td><td>20</td>
</tr>
<tr>
<td>Steve Towe</td><td>626</td><td>600</td><td>00</td><td>42</td><td>00</td><td>35</td><td>00</td><td>523</td><td>00</td>
</tr>
<tr>
<td></td><td></td><td>868</td><td>71</td><td>79</td><td>36</td><td>59</td><td>00</td><td>730</td><td>35</td>
</tr>
</table>

accuracy in the posting process, which is performed at the end of the month.

December 6: Issued check number 350 for $2,150 to Star Purveyors in payment of the open account balance of November 30.

Exhibit 10.6   Accounts Receivable Subsidiary Ledger

NAME	DEBCO, Inc.					
ADDRESS						

DATE 19X2	ITEM	POST. REF.	DEBIT	CREDIT	BALANCE
Dec. 8	Tab 1812	S	200 00		200 00

NAME	J.R. Rickles					
ADDRESS						

DATE 19X2	ITEM	POST. REF.	DEBIT	CREDIT	BALANCE
Nov. 18	Tab 1511	S	185 00		185 00
Dec. 8	Payment	S		185 00	-0-
15	Tab 1849	S	48 65		48 65

Comment: This check is in payment of a prior liability (an accounts payable). Refer to the accounts payable subsidiary ledger (Exhibit 10.7) and verify that this balance does in fact exist as of November 30.

The balance due Star Purveyors represents invoices received in the prior month (November) which had been entered in the November accounts payable journal. The entries made in November debited Food Inventory and credited Accounts Payable. This check is in payment of the Accounts Payable balance.

After tracing this business transaction to the cash payments journal (Exhibit 10.4), refer again to the accounts payable subsidiary ledger for the posting of this payment. Observe that the payment is entered in the debit column; a debit decreases a liability account.

A balance is computed in the subsidiary ledger accounts each time a transaction occurs; this provides instantaneous reference capability.

December 6: Voided check number 351.

Comment: Internal control procedures require that all checks are accounted for by consecutive check number. All checks of the Tower Restaurant contain a preprinted check number. A voided check is entered on the cash payments journal (Exhibit 10.4) and noted as "void" to account for the check number. No amounts are entered since the check is not issued.

December 7: Issued check number 352 for $75.00 to Tom's Seafood for a storeroom purchase delivered today.

Exhibit 10.7 Accounts Payable Subsidiary Ledger

NAME _____ *Star Purveyors* _____ ADDRESS _____				Terms: _n/10 EOM_		
DATE 19X2	ITEM	POST. REF.	DEBIT	CREDIT	BALANCE
Nov. 4	INV 4865	AP		500 00	(500 00)
11	INV 4934	AP		700 00	(1 200 00)
20	INV 5519	AP		950 00	(2 150 00)
Dec. 6	CK 350	CP	2 150 00		-0-
7	INV 6245	AP		300 00	(300 00)

NAME _____ *Pompano Purveyors* _____ ADDRESS _____				Terms: _n/10 EOM_		
DATE 19X2	ITEM	POST. REF.	DEBIT	CREDIT	BALANCE
Nov. 30		✓			(2 450 00)
Dec. 9	CK 354	CP	2 450 00		-0-
14	INV 1642	AP		500 00	(500 00)

Comment: The invoice accompanied the food provisions and the terms are COD. The food items were not delivered directly to the kitchen for immediate use; they were placed in the storeroom.

December 7: Received $300 of food provisions from Star Purveyors; the invoice number is 6245, and terms of payment are "n/10 EOM" (no discount, payment due in full ten days after the end of the month). The food provisions were for the storeroom.

Comment: Refer to the accounts payable journal (Exhibit 10.3) and the accounts payable subsidiary ledger (Exhibit 10.7) for the effect of this transaction.

December 7: Issued check number 353 for $1,216.75 to the State Department of Taxation in payment of the November sales tax liability.

Comment: The November sales tax collections were credited to the Sales Tax Payable account when the November sales & cash receipts journal was posted.

December 8: The daily cashiers report for this day provides the following information:

Food Sales	$1,350.67
Sales Taxes	81.04
Tips Charged	50.00
Customer Collections (J.R. Rickles)	185.00
Change Fund (Start)	500.00
TOTAL TO BE ACCOUNTED FOR	$2,166.71
Cash Deposited in Bank	$1,407.06
Cash Paid Out (Direct Purchase: Food Provisions)	8.75
Tips Paid Out	50.00
Customer Charges (DEBCO, Inc., Tab No. 1812)	200.00
Change Fund (Return)	500.00
Cash Short	.90
TOTAL ACCOUNTED FOR	$2,166.71

Comment: The change fund information does not require any entry unless the imprest amount is modified. Tower Restaurant's tip policy, limited volume, and internal control procedures make it unnecessary to journalize tips charged and tips paid out. The $8.75 paid out of the cashier's drawer represents a COD purchase of incidental food items delivered directly to the kitchen (direct purchase) for immediate use. Direct purchases are recorded as Cost of Food Sales because the Tower Restaurant uses the perpetual inventory system.

Refer to the sales & cash receipts journal (Exhibit 10.2) for the recording of the daily cashiers report. Ensure that the total of the debits equals the total of the credits for the recorded journal entry.

Also refer to the accounts receivable subsidiary ledger (Exhibit 10.6) for the effect of the transactions regarding J.R. Rickles and DEBCO, Inc.

December 9: Issued check number 354 for $2,450 to Pompano Purveyors in payment of the open account balance of November 30.

Comment: Refer to the account in the accounts payable subsidiary ledger (Exhibit 10.7) for Pompano Purveyors and observe the balance as of November 30. In November, the ledger form was completely filled and the accountant had to start a new record. One method to bring a balance forward is to enter the date, checkmark the posting reference column, and enter the amount brought forward in the balance column.

December 14: Issued check number 355 for $125 to Tom's Seafood for a COD storeroom purchase of food provisions.

December 14: Received $500 of storeroom food provisions from Pompano Purveyors; the invoice number is 1642, and terms of payment are n/10 EOM.

December 15: The daily cashiers report for this day provides the following information:

Food Sales	$1,268.52
Sales Taxes	76.11
Tips Charged	7.50
Customer Collections	—
Change Fund (Start)	500.00
TOTAL TO BE ACCOUNTED FOR	$1,852.13
Cash Deposited in Bank	$1,286.93
Cash Paid Out (Kitchen Utensils)	9.45
Tips Paid Out	7.50
Customer Charges (J.R. Rickles, Tab No. 1849)	48.65
Change Fund (Return)	500.00
Cash Over	(.40)
TOTAL ACCOUNTED FOR	$1,852.13

Comment: A cash overage in the sales & cash receipts journal is indicated by the use of parentheses.

December 16: Issued payroll check numbers 621 to 626 in payment of salaries and wages for the period of December 1 to December 15.

Comment: Refer to the payroll journal shown in Exhibit 10.5. The basic entries are gross wages due the employees by the restaurant, withholding of payroll taxes, and net pay due the employees. (Gross wages less taxes withheld equals net pay.)

The payroll checking account will be decreased by $730.35 when the Net Pay column is posted to the Cash—Payroll Checking account at the end of the period. Check number 356 will be deposited in the payroll checking account to maintain the imprest amount.

December 16: Issued check number 356 for $730.35 to Tower Restaurant's Payroll account covering the payroll from December 1 to December 15. The check was deposited into the payroll checking account.

Comment: An entry is required only in the cash payments journal (Exhibit 10.4). This entry reduces the cash in the regular checking account and increases the cash in the payroll checking account.

December 31: Issued check number 357 for $250.66 to City Utilities for the December utilities invoice.

December 31: Issued check number 358 for $65.16 to Regional Telephone for the December telephone invoice.

The Posting Process

The process of transferring information from the journals to the general ledger accounts is called posting. In actual practice, posting from the special journals to the general ledger accounts is usually performed at the end of the month. General journals may be posted at any time, but the posting process is usually performed in a batch process at one time.

The posting process is performed only after the special journals are totaled and the equality of debits and credits is verified to ensure that the journals are "in balance." In accounting terminology, the process of totaling a column is called *footing* and the process of horizontally adding or subtracting numbers is called *crossfooting*.

Whether an operation uses a manual general ledger system or a computerized system, the posting policies are identical in concept. Computer systems are designed to either reject or signal journals that are "out of balance."

The equality of debits and credits is a fundamental mathematical proof that must occur at each step of the accounting cycle. When the journals are in balance, the posting process for special journals involves the following steps.

Step 1: Fill in the Date Column. The date column of the account to be posted is filled in; the date used is that of the source document. Since special journals contain the transactions for the month, the date entered is the end-of-the-month date.

Step 2: Fill in the Posting Reference Column. The posting reference column of the account is filled in to cross-reference the posting process to the source document (input)—in this case, a journal. The posting reference entered is the symbol of the journal.

The posting reference column in an account format may have a heading such as POST. REF., PR, or Folio.

Step 3: Post the Column Total. The total of a special journal column is posted to the proper account in the general ledger. An account balance is generally not computed at this time because it would not serve any useful purpose. Account balances are generally performed only after the posting of all journals is complete.

To illustrate the posting process, Exhibit 10.8 shows how a December 31 entry from the Cash column of the sales & cash receipts journal is posted to the Cash—Regular Checking account in the general ledger.

Step 4: Identify Columns as Posted. The processing is not completed until the amount in the journal (source document) is identified as having been posted to an account. One method of indicating that an amount has been posted is to enter the account number under the special column total of the special journal. This procedure also cross-references the

Exhibit 10.8 Posting to an Account

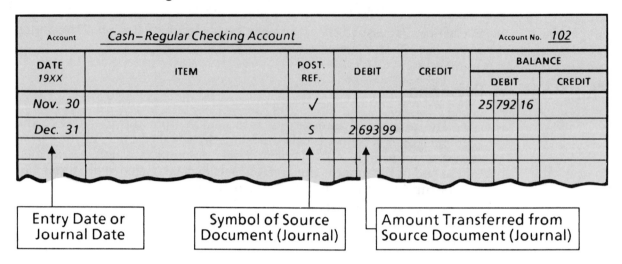

Account	*Cash–Regular Checking Account*				Account No. _102_	
DATE 19XX	ITEM	POST. REF.	DEBIT	CREDIT	BALANCE DEBIT	BALANCE CREDIT
Nov. 30		✓			25 792 16	
Dec. 31		S	2 693 99			

Entry Date or Journal Date

Symbol of Source Document (Journal)

Amount Transferred from Source Document (Journal)

Exhibit 10.9 Cross-Referencing on a Journal

Date	Food Sales	Sales Tax Payable	Customer Collections	Cash to Bank	Customer Charges	Cash Short (Over)	Sundry Items Account Title	Acct. No.	Amount dr
Dec.8	1 350 67	81 04	185 00	1 407 06	200 00	90	*Cost of Food Sales*	501	8 75
15	1 268 52	76 11	---	1 286 93	48 65	(40)	*Operating Supplies*	727	9 45
Total	2 619 19	157 15	185 00	2 693 99	248 65	50			18 20
	(401)	(211)	(112)	(102)	(112)	(754)			

amount on the special journal to the account to which it was posted in the general ledger.

Exhibit 10.9 presents how a special journal is cross-referenced after the amount has been posted (transferred) to an account in the general ledger.

Since the Tower Restaurant heads each column of its special journals with the account title and account number, it uses an alternative method to indicate that a journal amount has been posted. The method used by the Tower Restaurant is to enter a checkmark under the amount.

Step 5: Repeat the Process for Other Columns. Steps 1 through 4 are repeated for each special column on the journal.

Step 6: Post Entries from the Sundry Area. The column total of the sundry area is not posted because it is a summary amount of unrelated accounts. Each entry in the sundry area will require individual posting.

Since the Tower Restaurant indicates the account number next to the account title, a checkmark next to the amount serves the purpose of indicating that the entry has been posted to the general ledger.

Exhibit 10.10 Sales & Cash Receipts Journal with Footings

Date	Food Sales cr 401	Sales Tax Payable cr 211	Customer Collections cr 112	Cash to Bank dr 102	Customer Charges dr 112	Cash Short (Over) dr(cr)754	Sundry Items Account Title	Acct. No.	Amount dr
							Tower Restaurant SALES & CASH RECEIPTS JOURNAL (S) December 19X2		
Dec.8	1 350 67	81 04	185 00	1 407 06	200 00	90	Cost of Food Sales	501 √	8 75
15	1 268 52	76 11	---	1 286 93	48 65	(40)	Operating Supplies	727 √	9 45
Total	2 619 19	157 15	185 00	2 693 99	248 65	50			18 20
	√	√	√	√	√	√			

Step 7: Repeat the Process for Other Journals. The posting process is repeated for each journal (book of original entry). When all journals have been posted, account balances are computed.

The Posting Process for the Tower Restaurant

Earlier in this chapter, the business transactions involving the Tower Restaurant were journalized. In this section, Tower Restaurant's accounting cycle continues. The journalized transactions are used in the next step of the accounting cycle: the posting process. The December 19X2 special journals have been totaled in Exhibits 10.10 through 10.13.

Exhibit 10.14 shows the results of the completed posting process as reflected in the general ledger as of December 31, 19X2. Account balances are computed and entered only after all journals have been posted.

To facilitate understanding of posting procedures, the following suggestions are provided:

1. Foot each special journal shown in Exhibits 10.10 through 10.13 and compare your results with those shown.

2. Ensure that debits equal credits for each journal by crossfooting the debits and credits. A convenient method when using a calculator is to add the debit amounts and subtract the credit amounts; equality is verified when the result is zero.

3. Trace the posting process and observe the activity in each account, including the cross-referencing on the special journal after the account has been posted.

4. After all postings are performed, compute the balance of each account in the general ledger and compare your results with those shown in Exhibit 10.14.

Exhibit 10.11   Accounts Payable Journal with Footings

						Sundry Items		
Date	Vendor	Accounts Payable cr 201	Food Inventory dr 121	Supplies Inventory dr 131	Utilities dr 712	Account Title	Acct.No.	Amount dr
Dec.7	Star Purveyors	300 00	300 00					
14	Pompano Purveyors	500 00	500 00					
	TOTAL	800 00	800 00	---	---			---
		✓	✓					

Tower Restaurant — ACCOUNTS PAYABLE JOURNAL (AP) — *December 19X2*

Exhibit 10.12   Cash Payments Journal with Footings

Tower Restaurant — CASH PAYMENTS JOURNAL (CP) — *December 19X2*

Date	Paid To:	Check Number	Cash-- Checking cr 102	Food Inventory dr 121	Accounts Payable dr 201	Sundry Items		
						Account Title	Acct. No.	Amount dr
Dec.2	DSK Realty	348	800 00			Rent Expense	801 ✓	800 00
2	Associated Insurance Co.	349	2 400 00			Prepaid Insurance	132 ✓	2 400 00
6	Star Purveyors	350	2 150 00		2 150 00			
6	VOID	351	---					
7	Tom's Seafood	352	75 00	75 00				
7	State Dept. of Taxation	353	1 216 75			Sales Tax Payable	211 ✓	1 216 75
9	Pompano Purveyors	354	2 450 00		2 450 00			
14	Tom's Seafood	355	125 00	125 00				
16	Tower Payroll Account	356	730 35			Cash--Payroll Checking	103 ✓	730 35
31	City Utilities	357	250 66			Utilities	712 ✓	250 66
31	Regional Telephone	358	65 16			Telephone	751 ✓	65 16
	TOTAL		10 262 92	200 00	4 600 00			5 462 92
			✓	✓	✓			

Exhibit 10.13   Payroll Journal with Footings

Paid To:	Check No	Gross Wages dr 601	FICA cr 215	FIT cr 215	Net Pay cr 103
		1	2	3	4	5
Christine Robert	621	32 16	7 85	2 00	22 31
Elizabeth David	622	30 15	7 36	6 00	16 79
Ann Tasha	623	42 00	9 94	10 00	22 06
Mary Alcrep	624	24 40	2 41	---	21 99
Tom Paul	625	140 00	9 80	6 00	124 20
Steve Towe	626	600 00	42 00	35 00	523 00
TOTAL		868 71	79 36	59 00	730 35
		✓	✓	✓	✓

Tower Restaurant
PAYROLL REGISTER (PR)
December 16, 19X2

Exhibit 10.14 General Ledger for the Tower Restaurant

Title: Cash on Hand — Account No.: 101

Date	Explanation	Ref.	Dr	Cr	Balance
Nov 30		✓			1 000 00

Title: Cash--Regular Checking — Account No.: 102

Date	Explanation	Ref.	Dr	Cr	Balance
Nov 30		✓			25 792 16
Dec 31		S	2 693 99		
31		CP		10 262 92	18 223 23

Title: Cash--Payroll Checking — Account No.: 103

Date	Explanation	Ref.	Dr	Cr	Balance
Nov 30		✓			200 00
Dec 31		CP	730 35		
31		PR		730 35	200 00

Title: Accounts Receivable — Account No.: 112

Date	Explanation	Ref.	Dr	Cr	Balance
Nov 30		✓			185 00
Dec 31		S	248 65	185 00	248 65

Title: Food Inventory — Account No.: 121

Date	Explanation	Ref.	Dr	Cr	Balance
Nov 30		✓			4 875 00
Dec 31		CP	200 00		
31		AP	800 00		5 875 00

Title: Supplies Inventory — Account No.: 131

Date	Explanation	Ref.	Dr	Cr	Balance
Nov 30		✓			1 100 00

Title: Prepaid Insurance — Account No.: 132

Date	Explanation	Ref.	Dr	Cr	Balance
Dec 31		CP	2 400 00		2 400 00

Title: Furniture & Equipment — Account No.: 147

Date	Explanation	Ref.	Dr	Cr	Balance
Nov 30		✓			45 000 00

Title: China, Glassware & Silver — Account No.: 149

Date	Explanation	Ref.	Dr	Cr	Balance
Nov 30		✓			9 000 00

Exhibit 10.14 (continued)

Title: Accumulated Depreciation--F&E		Ref.	Dr	Cr	Account No.: 157 Balance
	Explanation	Ref.	Dr	Cr	Balance
Nov 30		✓			(27 000 00)

Title: Accounts Payable					Account No.: 201
	Explanation	Ref.	Dr	Cr	Balance
Nov 30		✓			(4 600 00)
Dec 31		CP	4 600 00		
31		AP		800 00	(800 00)

Title: Sales Tax Payable					Account No.: 211
	Explanation	Ref.	Dr	Cr	Balance
Nov 30		✓			(1 216 75)
Dec 31		S		157 15	
31		CP	1 216 75		(157 15)

Title: Employee Taxes Withheld					Account No.: 215
	Explanation	Ref.	Dr	Cr	Balance
Dec 31		PR		79 36	
31		PR		59 00	(138 36)

Title: Accrued Payroll					Account No.: 231
	Explanation	Ref.	Dr	Cr	Balance

Title: Accrued Payroll Taxes					Account No.: 232
	Explanation	Ref.	Dr	Cr	Balance

Title: Capital, Ann Dancer					Account No.: 301
	Explanation	Ref.	Dr	Cr	Balance
Nov 30		✓			(74 324 73)

Title: Withdrawals, Ann Dancer					Account No.: 302
	Explanation	Ref.	Dr	Cr	Balance
Nov 30		✓			38 000 00

Title: Income Summary					Account No.: 399
	Explanation	Ref.	Dr	Cr	Balance

Exhibit 10.14 (continued)

Title: Food Sales		Account No.: 401		
	Explanation	Ref.	Dr	Cr	Balance
Nov 30		✓			(162 590 75)
Dec 31		S		2 619 19	(165 209 94)

Title: Cost of Food Sales		Account No.: 501		
	Explanation	Ref.	Dr	Cr	Balance
Nov 30		✓			57 150 00
Dec 31		S	8 75		57 158 75

Title: Payroll		Account No.: 601		
	Explanation	Ref.	Dr	Cr	Balance
Nov 30		✓			48 906 16
Dec 31		PR	868 71		49 774 87

Title: Payroll Taxes		Account No.: 602		
	Explanation	Ref.	Dr	Cr	Balance
Nov 30		✓			4 788 75

Title: Employee Benefits		Account No.: 605		
	Explanation	Ref.	Dr	Cr	Balance
Nov 30		✓			2 164 18

Title: Employee Meals		Account No.: 607		
	Explanation	Ref.	Dr	Cr	Balance
Nov 30		✓			2 875 00

Title: Utilities		Account No.: 712		
	Explanation	Ref.	Dr	Cr	Balance
Nov 30		✓			3 094 65
Dec 31		CP	250 66		3 345 31

Title: China, Glassware & Silver		Account No.: 721		
	Explanation	Ref.	Dr	Cr	Balance
Nov 30		✓			1 650 00

Title: Operating Supplies		Account No.: 727		
	Explanation	Ref.	Dr	Cr	Balance
Nov 30		✓			2 898 66
Dec 31		S	9 45		2 908 11

Exhibit 10.14 (continued)

Title: Telephone   **Account No.:** 751

	Explanation	Ref.	Dr	Cr	Balance
Nov 30		✓			850 28
Dec 31		CP	65 16		915 44

Title: Office Supplies   **Account No.:** 752

	Explanation	Ref.	Dr	Cr	Balance
Nov 30		✓			923 14

Title: Credit Card Fees   **Account No.:** 753

	Explanation	Ref.	Dr	Cr	Balance
Nov 30		✓			1 868 75

Title: Cash Short or Over   **Account No.:** 754

	Explanation	Ref.	Dr	Cr	Balance
Nov 30		✓			137 16
Dec 31		S	50		137 66

Title: Repairs & Maintenance   **Account No.:** 761

	Explanation	Ref.	Dr	Cr	Balance
Nov 30		✓			2 489 34

Title: Rent   **Account No.:** 801

	Explanation	Ref.	Dr	Cr	Balance
Nov 30		✓			8 800 00
Dec 31		CP	800 00		9 600 00

Title: Insurance   **Account No.:** 821

	Explanation	Ref.	Dr	Cr	Balance
Nov 30		✓			1 859 00

Title: Depreciation   **Account No.:** 891

	Explanation	Ref.	Dr	Cr	Balance
Nov 30		✓			4 125 00

Discussion Questions

1. How are the following terms defined?

   a. Journalizing

   b. Journal entry

   c. Posting

   d. Footing

   e. Crossfooting

2. How are the following journal entries described?

   a. Correcting entries

   b. Adjusting entries

   c. Reversing entries

   d. Closing entries

3. Which of the following statements are true and which are false?

   a. Journal entries are prepared daily or as activity requires.

   b. Special journals are posted only at the end of the month.

   c. Each journal entry on a special journal is individually posted to the general ledger.

   d. A journal that is not in balance may be posted to the general ledger if a comment is made to that effect.

   e. Equality of the totals on a special journal may be verified by adding the debit amounts and subtracting the credit amounts; equality is proven if the result is zero.

   f. Any journal entry that affects the Accounts Receivable or Accounts Payable general ledger accounts also requires a posting to a subsidiary ledger.

   g. Adjusting, reversing, and closing entries are recorded in a special journal.

   h. If the perpetual inventory accounting system is used, food storeroom purchases are debited to Cost of Sales.

Problems

Problem 10.1
Complete the following daily cashiers report for December 15.

Food Sales	$2,542.62
Sales Taxes	127.13
Tips Charged	15.00
Customer Collections	102.00
Change Fund (Start)	800.00
TOTAL TO BE ACCOUNTED FOR	$_____
Cash Deposited in Bank	$2,675.09
Cash Paid Out	18.95
Tips Paid Out	15.00
Customer Charges	78.65
Change Fund (Return)	800.00
TOTAL ACCOUNTED FOR	$_____

Problem 10.2
Identify whether entries in the columns of the following special journals are debits or credits.

Cash Payments Journal

Sundry	Accounts Payable	Food Inventory	Beverage Inventory	Supplies Inventory	Cash
____	____	____	____	____	____

Accounts Payable Journal

Sundry	Advertising	Food Inventory	Beverage Inventory	Accounts Payable
____	____	____	____	____

Payroll Journal

Gross Wages	FICA Withheld	FIT Withheld	Group Life Withheld	Group Health Withheld	Cash
____	____	____	____	____	____

Sales & Cash Receipts Journal

Sundry	Cash	Cash Short	Cash Over	Customer Charges	Customer Collections
____	____	____	____	____	____

Food Sales	Beverage Sales	Sales Tax
____	____	____

Problems *(continued)*

Problem 10.3
Record the following daily cashiers report on the special journal provided below.

Food Sales	$1,500.95
Coffee, Tea, Milk Sales	160.00
Beer Sales	150.00
Wine Sales	200.00
Cocktails and Mixed Drink Sales	175.00
Sales Taxes	120.23
Tips Charged	25.00
Customer Collections	65.00
Change Fund (Start)	600.00
TOTAL TO BE ACCOUNTED FOR	$2,996.18
Cash Deposited in Bank	$2,240.31
Cash Paid Out (Office Supplies)	35.16
Tips Paid Out	25.00
Customer Charges	95.50
Change Fund (Return)	600.00
Cash Short	.21
TOTAL ACCOUNTED FOR	$2,996.18

Sales & Cash Receipts Journal

Sundry	Cash	Cash Short	Cash Over	Customer Charges	Customer Collections
___	___	___	___	___	___

Food Sales	Beverage Sales	Sales Tax
___	___	___

11

The Month-End Accounting Process

A major objective of accounting activities is to produce timely and reliable financial information to enable management to make day-to-day and long-term business decisions. This financial information may be informal reports (such as schedules and analyses) or more formal ones (such as financial statements).

In previous chapters, the main focus was on the recording process. In this chapter, the emphasis is on processing bookkeeping records to produce financial statements.

Most companies require monthly financial statements as part of their management information systems. Some very small operations either do not require or cannot afford monthly financial statements. The month-end procedures described in this chapter are performed only when financial statements are to be prepared. For smaller operations, these month-end procedures might be performed on a less frequent basis, such as quarterly or on demand.

In discussing the month-end accounting process, Chapter 11 will address such questions as:

1. What are the uses and limitations of a trial balance?

2. What are the components of an accountant's working papers?

3. What is the purpose of adjusting entries?

4. How is a worksheet completed?

5. How are financial statements prepared from the worksheet?

6. What are reversing entries?

This chapter continues through the accounting cycle. It discusses such tasks as determining adjustments, completing the worksheet, and preparing reliable financial statements.

The accounting system is presented using a modular approach, since this reflects the procedure employed in actual practice. For instance, the worksheet is explained and illustrated at each independent phase of its preparation.

Other parts of the accounting system discussed include the trial balance, reconciliations, and supporting schedules. The optional use of reversing entries as the first step of the next accounting period is also discussed.

The continued use of the Tower Restaurant as a case study reinforces the flow of procedural activities in an accounting system.

Month-End Procedures

During the month, business transactions are journalized. At the end of the accounting month, these journalized transactions are posted to the general ledger accounts. Companies requiring monthly financial statements will perform month-end procedures similar to those described in this section.

The general steps an accountant must perform at the end of each month are as follows:

1. Prepare a trial balance on a worksheet.

2. Prepare reconciliations and supporting schedules to verify the accuracy of the account balances shown in the trial balance.

3. Determine which accounts require adjustment. This process will be the basis for adjusting entries.

4. Enter the adjustments on the worksheet.

5. Complete the worksheet to aid in the preparation of the financial statements.

6. Prepare the financial statements for the period.

7. Forward the adjusting entries to the bookkeeper for posting to the current period's general ledger.

8. Determine and prepare any reversing entries that are to be posted in the next period because of certain types of adjusting entries journalized in the period just ended.

The Trial Balance

A trial balance is a listing of all of the accounts with their account balances in the order they appear in the general ledger. Its purpose is to verify the equality of debit and credit balances in the general ledger. The accountant copies each account name and balance from the general ledger to the trial balance.

The trial balance may be on a separate schedule or may be a component of a multi-column worksheet. This worksheet is part of the accountant's working papers used in the preparation of financial statements. The trial balance uses the first two columns of the worksheet, one column for debit balances and the other for credit balances.

Exhibit 11.1 presents a trial balance on a worksheet for Motel Consultants, a small hospitality consulting firm. Motel Consultants will be discussed in Chapter 12 when closing entries are explained.

Exhibit 11.1 Motel Consultants—Trial Balance on a Worksheet

		1 Trial Balance Dr	2 Trial Balance Cr	9 Balance Sheet Dr	10 Balance Sheet Cr
	Cash	2 700 00			
	Accounts Receivable	1 800 00			
	Supplies Inventory	300 00			
	Furniture & Equipment	2 000 00			
	Accum. Depreciation-- F&E		500 00		
	Capital, J. Daniels		2 282 51		
	Withdrawals, J. Daniels	8 000 00			
	Sales		15 000 00		
	Rent	2 000 00			
	Supplies	250 00			
	Telephone	160 21			
	Travel	497 30			
	Depreciation	75 00			
	Total	17 782 51	17 782 51		

Uses of the Trial Balance

The major purpose of the trial balance is to provide *proof* that the general ledger is mathematically in balance. "In balance" means that the debit dollars equals the credit dollars for all recorded transactions. If the debit and credit columns are not equal the cause may be due to one or more of the following errors:

- The debit column, the credit column, or both columns were incorrectly added.

- An account balance in the general ledger was incorrectly transferred to the trial balance.

- An account balance in the general ledger was incorrectly computed.

A trial balance does not prove that business transactions were posted to the correct bookkeeping accounts. For example, a purchase of food inventory for $1,000 may have been erroneously recorded as Supplies Inventory in the journalizing or posting process; a trial balance would not indicate this type of error. A trial balance would also fail to disclose a business transaction that had been completely omitted in the journalizing process.

Unequal Totals in the Trial Balance

A trial balance requires transferring numerous amounts from the general ledger to the worksheet, then totaling the debit and credit columns. A trial balance is "out-of-balance" when the total of the debits does not equal the total of the credits. This condition indicates an error in processing which must be located and corrected before any further activity may be performed.

Before checking each journal for proper debit and credit entries or recalculating the account balances in the general ledger, the following sequence of procedures may save time and effort in locating the reason for an inequality of the debit and credit totals.

1. Check the accuracy of the trial balance totals by adding the columns again.

2. If step 1 does not reveal the cause, determine the difference between the debit and credit totals. This difference may provide a clue to the reason for the error.

    a. If the difference is evenly divisible by 9, the error may be due to a transposition or slide in copying the amounts from the general ledger to the trial balance.

        A *transposition* means that two digits in a number have been mistakenly reversed. For example, an amount of $890.00 in the general ledger may have been transposed as $980.00 on the trial balance. The $90.00 difference between the two numbers is divisible by 9 with no remainder.

        A *slide* means that the decimal point in a number has been incorrectly moved to the left or right. For example, an amount of $890.00 in the general ledger may have been entered as $89.00 on the trial balance. The $801.00 difference between the two numbers is divisible by 9 with no remainder.

        From a practical standpoint, a difference divisible by 9 is more often due to a transposition than a slide.

    b. If the difference is not divisible by 9, the error may be due to entering a debit amount as a credit amount in the trial balance (or vice versa).

        To find errors of this type, simply divide the difference by 2 and scan the debit/credit columns in the trial balance for this amount. For example, if the account Prepaid Insurance had a debit balance of $240 in the general ledger but was entered as a $240 *credit* on the trial balance, this error would cause an out-of-balance difference of $480.

        Another way to find whether a debit or credit was incorrectly copied in the trial balance is to scan the accounts on the trial balance for their normal balances. However, an account may not have a normal balance due to an unusual business transaction or a recording error made by the bookkeeper.

3. If none of the above steps reveal the cause of the inequality, compare each amount in the general ledger to each amount in the trial balance to verify that they were correctly copied.

4. If the cause of the inequality still cannot be determined, recompute the balance of each account in the general ledger to verify its accuracy.

5. If an inequality still remains after performing these steps,

return to each journal and trace all entries to the general ledger to verify posting accuracy.

Reconciliations and Supporting Schedules

The accountant prepares reconciliations and supporting schedules of numerous accounts in the general ledger to verify that the balances are accurate, current, and in compliance with generally accepted accounting principles (especially the matching, realization, and objectivity principles).

These reconciliations and schedules are part of the accountant's working papers which support the information used in preparing the financial statements.

Generally, most or all of the balance sheet accounts are analyzed and documented in the working papers. Significant or troublesome expense accounts are also analyzed. For instance, Repairs and Maintenance is analyzed for any errors in recording as expenses those expenditures which should have been capitalized (recorded in an asset account).

Bank reconciliations, vendor statements, and other independent documents are fundamental parts of the working papers. Control accounts such as Accounts Receivable and Accounts Payable are reconciled to the subsidiary ledgers by the preparation of a schedule of accounts receivable and a schedule of accounts payable.

The subsidiary ledger schedules are prepared by listing the balance of each customer or vendor on a schedule, totaling the schedule, and comparing the total of the subsidiary ledger schedule with the balance in the control account.

In our example, Motel Consultants has accounts receivable, for which a supporting schedule is required. To prepare its schedule of accounts receivable, the accountant for Motel Consultants reviews the accounts receivable subsidiary ledger (Exhibit 11.2) and records the balances for each individual account. By totaling these balances, a schedule of accounts receivable (Exhibit 11.3) is produced. This total is confirmed with the control account in the general ledger, which was shown in the trial balance section of the worksheet (Exhibit 11.1).

Integrated Computer Applications

Integrated computerized accounting systems are capable of producing subsidiary schedules as a by-product of the information stored in the data base file. Today's technology has provided inexpensive microcomputers which are affordable to many small hospitality firms.

An integrated accounting system generally contains the following basic accounting applications:

- General ledger

- Accounts receivable

- Accounts payable

If a transaction is entered into one application, the other applications affected by it will be automatically updated. For example, a cash receipt from collection of an accounts receivable would automatically update the

Exhibit 11.2   Motel Consultants—Accounts Receivable Subsidiary Ledger

NAME ___COMPUTRON Inc.___

ADDRESS _____

DATE 19XX	ITEM	POST. REF.	DEBIT	CREDIT	BALANCE
Apr. 12	Tab 1470	S	1 250 00		1 250 00

NAME ___SUPERIOR OFFICE FORMS___

ADDRESS _____

DATE 19XX	ITEM	POST. REF.	DEBIT	CREDIT	BALANCE
Mar. 31	Tab 2115	S	390 00		390 00
Apr. 2	Payment	S		390 00	-0-
15	Tab 2345	S	550 00		550 00

Cash account in the general ledger, the accounts receivable control account in the general ledger, and the accounts receivable subsidiary file. The steps involved are similar to those performed in a manual system.

Specific applications of computers to the accounting function are discussed in much greater detail in *Managing Computers in the Hospitality Industry* by Michael L. Kasavana and John J. Cahill, published by the Educational Institute of the American Hotel & Motel Association.

Adjusting Entries

Accrual basis accounting is required to comply with the matching principle; revenue is recorded when earned (services performed) and expenses are recorded when incurred, regardless of whether cash was received or paid. The purpose of adjusting entries is to bring the revenue and expenses up-to-date on a matching basis. Adjusting entries may be necessary for recorded and unrecorded items.

Before preparing financial statements, adjustments are prepared because the statement of income must contain all revenue and expenses applicable to the period, and the balance sheet must contain all assets and liabilities as at the close of business on the last day of the period. Whenever an adjustment is determined, a revenue or expense account should be part of the adjusting entry.

Adjustments may be required for the following conditions:

Exhibit 11.3   Motel Consultants—Schedule of Accounts Receivable

Motel Consultants SCHEDULE OF ACCOUNTS RECEIVABLE *April 30, 19X2*	
Computron, Inc.	1,250.00
Superior Office Forms	550.00
Total	1,800.00

1. Expired assets (allocation of the cost of expired assets to expense)
2. Unrecorded expenses (expenses incurred but not yet recorded)
3. Unrecorded revenue (income earned but not yet recorded)
4. Unearned revenue (collections in advance)

Adjustments are generally required for the following areas:

Prepaid Insurance
Prepaid Rent
Other Prepaid Items
Accumulated Depreciation
China, Glassware & Silver
Supplies Inventory
Food Inventory

Beverage Inventory
Employee Meals
Potential Bad Debts
Unpaid Wages (at end of month)
Unrecorded Revenue and Expenses
Unearned Revenue

Expired Assets

An account may have a balance that is partly balance sheet amount and partly income statement amount. This type of account is sometimes called a *mixed account*. For example, the Supplies Inventory account (before adjustment) is made up of two elements: one element represents supplies inventory at the end of a period, which is an *unexpired cost* (asset); the other element represents supplies used for the period, which is an *expired cost* (expense).

Unexpired costs usually become expired costs through consumption or passage of time. The number of mixed accounts varies with the nature and size of an operation. The examples presented in this section cover the following areas: prepaid insurance; prepaid rent; accumulated depreciation; china, glassware, and silver; supplies inventory; and food inventory.

Prepaid Insurance

Assume that a lodging business paid $2,400 on June 1 for one year's insurance in advance. On June 1, Cash would have been credited for $2,400 and Prepaid Insurance debited for $2,400.

Prepaid Insurance

	Prepaid Insurance	
6/1	2,400	

On June 30, the passage of time causes part of the asset to expire; the expired portion of an asset's cost is recorded to expense. One-twelfth, or $200, has expired. The adjusting journal entry (AJE) is:

June 30	Insurance Expense			200	00			
	Prepaid Insurance						200	00

After posting, the Prepaid Insurance account properly reflects the 11 months ($2,200) of unexpired insurance premiums.

	Prepaid Insurance			
6/1	2,400	6/30 AJE	200
Balance	2,200		

Prepaid Rent   Assume that a lodging operation paid $2,700 on May 1 for three month's rent in advance. On May 1, Cash would have been credited for $2,700 and Prepaid Rent debited for $2,700.

	Prepaid Rent	
5/1	2,700	

On May 31, the passage of time causes part of the asset to expire; the expired portion of an asset's cost is recorded to expense. One-third, or $900, has expired. The adjusting journal entry is:

May 31	Rent Expense			900	00			
	Prepaid Rent						900	00

After posting, the Prepaid Rent account properly reflects two months ($1,800) of unexpired rent.

	Prepaid Rent			
5/1	2,700	5/31 AJE	900
Balance	1,800		

Accumulated Depreciation

With the exception of land, china, glassware, silver, linen, and uniforms owned by a hospitality business, property and equipment accounts have a contra-asset account called Accumulated Depreciation to record the allocation of the cost of a fixed asset over its estimated useful life.

In the hospitality industry, this allocation is generally based on the passage of time rather than units of production or hours of usage, which are methods used in other industries. The specific methods used to calculate depreciation expense are discussed in greater detail in *Understanding Hospitality Accounting II.*

Assume that the building depreciation calculation for the month of November is $1,000. The adjusting journal entry is:

Nov. 30	Depreciation Expense			1	000	00			
	Accum. Depreciation--Building						1	000	00

China, Glassware, and Silver

There is one major difference in allocating the cost of china, glassware, and silver compared to buildings or equipment: the allocation of these asset costs to expense does not involve an Accumulated Depreciation account. The amount transferred to expense is offset directly against the asset account.

Assuming that the cost to be allocated to expense for November is $180, the adjusting entry is:

Nov. 30	China, Glassware & Silver (Expense)			180	00			
	China, Glassware & Silver (Asset)					180	00

A similar procedure applies to uniforms and linen owned by the hospitality business. Methods used to allocate the cost of china, glassware, silver, and other items are discussed in greater detail in *Understanding Hospitality Accounting II.*

Supplies Inventory

Using the asset method of accounting for supplies, purchases are charged to the Supplies Inventory account. At the end of any period, a physical inventory of supplies is required unless a perpetual record-keeping system is maintained for them.

Assume that on July 31, the balance in the Supplies Inventory account is as follows:

Supplies Inventory

7/31 Bal	1,600	

On July 31, a physical count of the supplies on hand results in a value of $1,100 (at cost). Therefore, $500 of supplies inventory has been consumed; the consumption of an asset requires that it be transferred to expense.

The adjusting journal entry is:

July 31	Supplies Expense			500 00		
	Supplies Inventory				500 00	

After posting, the Supplies Inventory account properly reflects the $1,100 of supplies on hand per the physical inventory.

Supplies Inventory

7/31 Bal	1,600	7/31 AJE	500
Balance	1,100		

Food Inventory

The following discussion pertains to a hospitality business that uses the perpetual system of accounting for food inventory. When food provisions are purchased for the storeroom, the Food Inventory account is debited and either Cash or Accounts Payable is credited.

As food is issued from the storeroom, requisition forms are completed and forwarded to the accounting department. The day-to-day cost of food issued is tallied and may be recorded at various intervals during the month. Some companies may wait until the month-end procedure and record these issues with the adjusting entries. For purposes of discussion, a month-end recording procedure will be used.

When food is issued from the storeroom, an asset has been used; the consumption of an asset creates an expense. In this case, the asset called Food Inventory is used, creating an expense called Cost of Food Sales (Cost of Food Sold).

Assume that the total food issued from the storeroom is $6,000 for the month of November. The adjusting entry is:

Nov. 30	Cost of Food Sales			6 000 00		
	Food Inventory				6 000 00	

After this entry, the Cost of Food Sales account reflects the cost of food used for sales to customers and the cost of food provided to employees. Therefore, the Cost of Food Sales account is inflated by food that was not sold. A subsequent journal entry is required to transfer the cost of employee meals from Cost of Food Sales to an expense account called Employee Meals. This is presented as an example in the next section.

Unrecorded Expenses

Another type of adjustment is providing for any expenses that have been incurred during the month, but not yet recorded. These expenses are usually *not* associated with vendor invoices, since unpaid invoices for the period should be processed through the accounts payable journal.

Invoices not yet received should be estimated and recorded using an adjusting entry which debits the expense account and credits either an "accrued" liability account or the Accounts Payable account. The actual method used depends on the accounting system of the business.

The typical unrecorded expenses at the end of any period are usually related to the following areas: employee meals; uncollectible accounts; unpaid salaries and wages; and unrecorded interest expense.

Employee Meals

Some hospitality firms provide meals free of charge to employees on duty as a convenience for the employer. The actual cost of each meal is difficult to determine on a day-to-day basis for each employee. However, management should make an attempt to monitor this employee benefit because of its effect on food cost control and gross profit on food sales. A large operation may have significant employee meal costs; without proper accounting, the expense of employee meals would be intermingled with the expense called Cost of Food Sales.

Technically, accounting for employee meals is not an unrecorded expense but merely a transfer from one expense account (Cost of Food Sales) to another (Employee Benefits or Employee Meals).

Many restaurant operations develop a standard cost for employee meals. This standard meal cost represents an average estimated cost and is separately computed for breakfast, lunch, and dinner. These standard costs are modified whenever costs change significantly. Each day, employee meals are totaled by type of meal. At the end of the month, the total of each type of meal is multiplied by its standard cost to arrive at the monthly employee meals expense.

Assume that a restaurant uses the perpetual system for food inventories. The issues from the storeroom were charged to the Cost of Food Sales account which, at this point, contains the cost of employee meals. In November, employee meals at cost were $350; the adjusting entry is:

Nov. 30	Employee Meals			350	00			
	Cost of Food Sales						350	00

The journal entry for employee meals is different if the periodic system is used. In a periodic system, there is no account for cost of food sales. The periodic system is discussed in a separate chapter in *Understanding Hospitality Accounting II*.

Uncollectible Accounts

A company doing a large business providing open account privileges to its customers or issuing an in-house credit card may reasonably expect some losses due to bad debts. The business cannot predict which specific accounts will become uncollectible, but experience provides a ratio which may be used to calculate a reasonable estimate of the total of possible bad debts.

The actual loss on uncollectible accounts may not be realized for the present and possibly for many months, but an estimated loss attributable to the current month's sales must be recorded.

Potential losses due to bad debts may be estimated based on an analysis of sales or accounts receivable. Estimating procedures are discussed in *Understanding Hospitality Accounting II*.

Assume that a lodging operation estimates that its potential bad debts expense (uncollectible accounts) for the month of October is $375. The adjusting entry is:

Oct. 31	Uncollectible Accounts Expense			375	00			
	Allowance for Doubtful Accounts						375	00

Unpaid Salaries and Wages

At the end of an accounting month, it is typical that a portion of the wages earned by employees are not yet paid or entered in the accounting records. Even with today's computers, it is improbable that payroll checks will be issued on the last day of the workweek.

Two important terms to keep in mind are *workweek* and *payroll payment date*. For example, a company may have a workweek (payroll week) of Sunday to Saturday. The weekly payroll is paid on each Wednesday, which is then referred to as the payroll payment date.

Assume that the calendar for August is as follows:

S	M	T	W	T	F	S
	1	2	3	4	5	6
7	8	9	10	11	12	13
14	15	16	17	18	19	20
21	22	23	24	25	26	27
28	29	30	31			

↑
Payroll paid for workweek
of 8/21–8/27

On August 31, employees were paid for the workweek of August 21 to 27. The payroll days of August 28 to 31 will be included in the paycheck for the first Wednesday in September. Therefore, on August 31, there are four days of payroll expenses not recorded in the accounting month of August.

One estimating procedure is to multiply the average week's payroll by the fraction of days worked (in this case, 4/7). In practice, the accountant usually has access to the next week's payroll because the month-end process generally requires many days to complete.

Using the payroll information just presented, assume that the average payroll is $7,000 per week. The adjusting entry computed at 4/7 of $7,000 is:

Aug. 31	Payroll Expense			4	000	00			
	Accrued Payroll						4	000	00

Depending on the company's chart of accounts, the liability account credited may be called Accrued Payroll, Accrued Salaries and Wages, Payrolls Payable, or Salaries and Wages Payable. These terms are all interchangeable.

Unrecorded Interest Expense

As with payroll, interest expense on loans may not coincide with the accounting cutoff date. If the amounts are material, they should be provided for in the accounting records.

The most obvious example of unrecorded interest expense relates to notes payable for which the principal and interest are due only upon maturity (due date) of the note.

Assume that a $10,000 one-year note with 12% interest is executed on January 1. At maturity, the business will pay $10,000, plus interest of $1,200. To properly reflect expenses incurred in the period, it is necessary to record the accrued interest on a monthly basis by using an adjusting entry.

On January 31, 1/12 of the $1,200 interest is accrued; the adjusting entry is:

Jan. 31	Interest Expense			100	00			
	Accrued Interest Payable						100	00

Unrecorded Revenue

Unrecorded revenue generally relates to revenue generated from items other than typical sales transactions occurring on a daily basis. Investments in money market accounts or interest-bearing securities may result in unrecorded interest income; the date on which such investments pay interest seldom coincides with the accounting cutoff date. The accountant has to estimate the interest earned but not yet received.

Assume that on March 31, $300 in interest has been earned but not yet received. The adjusting entry is:

Mar. 31	Accrued Interest Receivable			300	00			
	Interest Income						300	00

Hotels may have contractual arrangements with concessionaires wherein the concessionaire pays a commission to the hotel. If commissions earned in the period have not yet been received, an adjusting entry is prepared.

Assume that on March 31, $500 in commissions has been earned but not yet received. The adjusting entry is:

Mar. 31	Accrued Commissions Receivable			500	00			
	Commissions Income						500	00

Unearned Revenue

Unearned revenue is a liability that is initially recorded when money is received for services not yet rendered. Some hotels lease space to office tenants or concessionaires and may receive rental payments several months in advance in accordance with lease terms. An advance rental payment from store or office tenants represents unearned revenue.

The receipt of cash does not represent revenue in accordance with the realization principle, which states that revenue resulting from business transactions should be recorded only after it is earned.

Assume that a hotel leases space with rental terms of three months rent due in advance on the first day of each quarter. On April 1, the hotel receives $3,600 from a concessionaire in payment of the rent for April, May, and June. On April 1, a journal entry shows $3,600 debited to cash and $3,600 credited to Unearned Rents. The Unearned Rents account is a current liability account because money has been received for services not yet rendered.

On April 30, the hotel has earned 1/3 of the advance rental payment in accordance with the realization principle. The adjusting entry is:

Apr. 30	Unearned Rents		1	200	00			
	Rental Income					1	200	00

Tower Restaurant's Month-End Procedures

The accounting records developed in the previous chapters will be used to perform the month-end procedures for the Tower Restaurant.

In Chapter 10, all business transactions were journalized and posted as of December 31, 19X2. The month-end procedures required are as follows:

1. Prepare a trial balance on a worksheet.
2. Prepare reconciliations and supporting schedules.
3. Determine the adjustments and adjusting entries.
4. Enter the adjustments on the worksheet.
5. Complete the worksheet.
6. Prepare the financial statements.
7. Post the adjusting entries.
8. Prepare any necessary reversing entries.

The Trial Balance for the Tower Restaurant

Tower Restaurant's trial balance has been prepared on a worksheet and is presented in Exhibit 11.4. It was prepared by copying each account

Exhibit 11.4 Tower Restaurant—Trial Balance on a Worksheet

Tower Restaurant
Worksheet
December 31, 19X2

		1 Trial Balance Dr	2 Trial Balance Cr	3 Adjustments Dr	4 Adjustments Cr	5 Adjusted Trial Balance Dr	6 Adjusted Trial Balance Cr	7 Income Statement Dr	8 Income Statement Cr	9 Balance Sheet Dr	10 Balance Sheet Cr
101	Cash on Hand	1 000 00									
102	Cash--Regular Checking	18 223 23									
103	Cash--Payroll Checking	200 00									
112	Accounts Receivable	248 65									
121	Food Inventory	5 875 00									
131	Supplies Inventory	1 100 00									
132	Prepaid Insurance	2 400 00									
147	Furniture & Equipment	45 000 00									
149	China, Glassware & Silver	9 000 00									
157	Acc. Depreciation--F&E		27 000 00								
201	Accounts Payable		800 00								
211	Sales Tax Payable		157 15								
215	Employee Taxes Withheld		138 36								
231	Accrued Payroll										
232	Accrued Payroll Taxes										
301	Capital, Ann Dancer		74 324 73								
302	Withdrawals, Ann Dancer	38 000 00									
401	Food Sales		165 209 94								
501	Cost of Food Sales	57 158 75									
601	Payroll	49 774 87									
602	Payroll Taxes	4 788 75									
605	Employee Benefits	2 164 18									
607	Employee Meals	2 875 00									
712	Utilities	3 345 31									
721	China, Glassware & Silver	1 650 00									
727	Operating Supplies	2 908 11									
751	Telephone	915 44									
752	Office Supplies	923 14									
753	Credit Card Fees	1 868 75									
754	Cash Short or Over	137 66									
761	Repairs & Maintenance	2 489 34									
801	Rent	9 600 00									
821	Insurance	1 859 00									
891	Depreciation	4 125 00									
	TOTAL	267 630 18	267 630 18								

Exhibit 11.5   Tower Restaurant—Schedule of Accounts Receivable

Tower Restaurant SCHEDULE OF ACCOUNTS RECEIVABLE December 31, 19X2	
DEBCO, Inc.	$200.00
J.R. Rickles	48.65
TOTAL	$248.65

Exhibit 11.6   Tower Restaurant—Schedule of Accounts Payable

Tower Restaurant SCHEDULE OF ACCOUNTS PAYABLE December 31, 19X2	
Pompano Purveyors	$500.00
Star Purveyors	300.00
TOTAL	$800.00

and its balance from the general ledger; the Income Summary account was not copied because it is a temporary year-end account used only during the closing entries process.

An adjustment may require a bookkeeping account not provided for in the company's chart of accounts. At this point, it is necessary to add the account to the chart of accounts. For purposes of completing the worksheet, any new accounts may be entered at the bottom of the worksheet.

Refer to the general ledger in Chapter 10 and trace the balances to the worksheet. Total the debit and credit columns of the trial balance to verify equality, then check your results with Exhibit 11.4.

Reconciliations and Schedules for the Tower Restaurant

With the exception of the subsidiary ledgers, all of the balance sheet accounts and selected income statement accounts have been reconciled and analyzed.

Refer to Exhibits 10.6 and 10.7 in Chapter 10 for the accounts receivable and accounts payable subsidiary ledgers for the Tower Restaurant. These ledgers are used to prepare the schedule of accounts receivable (Exhibit 11.5) and the schedule of accounts payable (Exhibit 11.6).

The next step is to verify the totals on these schedules with the general ledger control accounts. The trial balance in Exhibit 11.4 shows that Accounts Receivable has a balance of $248.65, and Accounts Payable has a balance of $800. Observe that the balances in the control accounts reconcile with the totals on the supporting schedules.

Adjustments for the Tower Restaurant

The adjustments to the accounts for the month of December will be determined for a number of situations presented in this section. As they are determined, they will be entered on the worksheet.

Some accountants journalize the adjustments as they are determined. Other accountants wait until financial statements are prepared. Tower Restaurant's adjustments will be journalized as they are determined during the preparation of the worksheet. This method fits conveniently into the flow of month-end procedures.

While Tower Restaurant's adjustments are *journalized* during worksheet preparation, they will not be *posted* to the general ledger until the financial statements are completed.

The Tower Restaurant does not require an adjusting entry to provide for potentially uncollectible accounts because its open account volume is minimal. It has never experienced any bad debts because of management's selectivity and control of open account privileges.

As each adjustment is prepared, trace it to the adjustments columns of the worksheet in Exhibit 11.7. Observe that each adjustment is cross-referenced on the worksheet by the use of a key letter to the left of each amount. This key letter serves to relate the debit and credit parts of each adjustment.

(a) Requisitions of food issued from the stockroom for the month total $718, at cost. The adjusting entry is:

Dec. 31	Cost of Food Sales			718 00			
	Food Inventory					718 00	

(b) The tally sheet for meals provided free of charge to employees shows a total of $35 at standard cost. The adjusting entry is:

Dec. 31	Employee Meals			35 00			
	Cost of Food Sales					35 00	

(c) A physical inventory of supplies at the close of business in December shows that supplies on hand total $1,000 (at cost). The general ledger account Supplies Inventory has a balance of $1,100 before adjustment. The adjusting entry is:

Exhibit 11.7 Tower Restaurant—Worksheet with Adjustments

Tower Restaurant
Worksheet
December 31, 19X2

	Account	Trial Balance Dr	Trial Balance Cr	Adjustments Dr	Adjustments Cr	Adjusted Trial Balance Dr	Adjusted Trial Balance Cr	Income Statement Dr	Income Statement Cr	Balance Sheet Dr	Balance Sheet Cr
101	Cash on Hand	1000 00									
102	Cash--Regular Checking	223 23									
103	Cash--Payroll Checking	200 00									
112	Accounts Receivable	248 65									
121	Food Inventory	5875 00			(a) 718 00						
131	Supplies Inventory	1100 00			(c) 100 00						
132	Prepaid Insurance	2400 00			(d) 200 00						
147	Furniture & Equipment	45000 00									
149	China, Glassware & Silver	9000 00			(f) 150 00						
157	Acc. Depreciation--F&E		27000 00		(e) 375 00						
201	Accounts Payable		800 00								
211	Sales Tax Payable		157 15								
215	Employee Taxes Withheld		138 36								
231	Accrued Payroll				(g) 385 00						
232	Accrued Payroll Taxes				(h) 366 00						
301	Capital, Ann Dancer		74324 73								
302	Withdrawals, Ann Dancer	38000 00									
401	Food Sales		165209 94								
501	Cost of Food Sales	57158 75		(a) 718 00	(b) 35 00						
601	Payroll	49774 87		(g) 385 00							
602	Payroll Taxes	4788 75		(h) 366 00							
605	Employee Benefits	2164 18									
607	Employee Meals	2875 00		(b) 35 00							
712	Utilities	3345 31									
721	China, Glassware & Silver	1650 00		(f) 150 00							
727	Operating Supplies	2908 11		(c) 100 00							
751	Telephone	915 44									
752	Office Supplies	923 14									
753	Credit Card Fees	1868 75									
754	Cash Short or Over	137 66									
761	Repairs & Maintenance	2489 34									
801	Rent	9600 00									
821	Insurance	1859 00		(d) 200 00							
891	Depreciation	4125 00		(e) 375 00							
	TOTAL	267630 18	267630 18	2329 00	2329 00						

Dec. 31	Operating Supplies			100	00		
	Supplies Inventory					100	00

(d) The Prepaid Insurance account balance of $2,400 reflects an insurance policy with a term of December 1, 19X2, to December 1, 19X3. One month's term, or 1/12 of the value, has expired. The adjusting entry for December is:

Dec. 31	Insurance			200	00		
	Prepaid Insurance					200	00

(e) Depreciation of furniture and equipment for the month of December is $375. The adjusting entry is:

Dec. 31	Depreciation			375	00		
	Accumulated Depreciation					375	00

(f) Depreciation of china, glassware, and silver for the month of December is $150. The adjusting entry is:

Dec. 31	China, Glassware & Silver (Expense)			150	00		
	China, Glassware & Silver (Assest)					150	00

(g) Since the Tower Restaurant was closed during the off-season, all operations personnel were paid to date.

However, one employee was assigned the duty of maintaining the physical plant and monitoring temperatures of food storage facilities prior to reopening. Wages pertaining to this December period will not be paid until the first week in January 19X3.

The unpaid gross wages as of December 31 are $385. The adjusting entry is:

Dec. 31	Payroll			385	00		
	Accrued Payroll					385	00

(h) The payroll taxes (FICA and FIT) imposed on employees have been journalized in the payroll journal. However, there are also various payroll taxes that are imposed on the *employer*. Hospitality companies are subject to federal and state payroll taxes based on the amount of salaries and wages paid to their employees.

The federal government requires the employer to pay a FICA tax and a federal unemployment tax. The state government also imposes an unemployment tax on the employer. Payroll taxes are thoroughly discussed in *Understanding Hospitality Accounting II*. Tower Restaurant's unpaid payroll taxes at the end of the period are $366, and the adjusting entry is:

Dec. 31	Payroll Taxes			366	00			
	Accrued Payroll Taxes						366	00

Proving Equality in the Adjustments Section

After all of the adjustments are entered on the worksheet, the next step is to total the debits and credits in the adjustments section. Proving the equality of debits and credits will disclose mathematical errors and prevent them from being continued through the remainder of the worksheet process.

Refer to Exhibit 11.7 and find the totals of the adjustments columns of the worksheet to verify the equality of debits and credits.

Completing the Worksheet for the Tower Restaurant

In review, worksheets contain the following sections:

- Trial balance

- Adjustments

- Adjusted trial balance

- Income statement

- Balance sheet

Thus far, the trial balance and adjustments sections of Tower Restaurant's worksheet have been completed. The sections of the worksheet remaining to be completed are the adjusted trial balance, income statement, and balance sheet sections.

Adjusted Trial Balance

The amounts in the trial balance section are combined with the amounts in the adjustment section and are entered in the adjusted trial balance section. (This crossfooting process is not used on the totals of these sections.)

For example, Cash on Hand is entered at its original amount of $1,000 since no adjustments affected this account. Food Inventory had an original balance of $5,875 (debit) and an adjustment of $718 (credit); therefore, Food Inventory is entered as $5,157 in the adjusted trial balance.

After all account balances have been crossfooted to the adjusted trial balance section, the debit and credit columns are then totaled. An equality of debits and credits will prove that no mathematical errors have been made in this section. Exhibit 11.8 presents the worksheet completed to the adjusted trial balance stage.

Income Statement and Balance Sheet Sections

From the adjusted trial balance columns, the amounts are transferred to either the income statement columns or the balance sheet columns according to the classification of each account. The transfer process is based on the following criteria:

- Asset, liability, and equity accounts—transfer to balance sheet columns

- Revenue and expense accounts—transfer to income statement columns

Exhibit 11.9 shows the result of transferring amounts to the income statement columns and balance sheet columns. After all amounts are entered, a total of the debits and credits is computed for each of these sections.

Note that the first pair of totals for the income statement columns and for the balance sheet columns are not in balance at this particular stage. Equality of debits and credits for either section at this time would indicate that the business had no profit and no loss, or exactly zero results (to the penny) from operations. This is an extremely improbable event.

Computing Net Income (Loss). The totals of the *income statement columns* are used to compute the income or loss for the year-to-date period. The difference between these totals represents income (loss) for the period. If the credit total exceeds the debit total, then the operating result is income. Conversely, if the total debits exceed the total credits in the income statement section, then the operating result is a loss.

The logic associated with this principle is as follows:

- Income statement accounts are composed of accounts in the revenue and expense classifications.

- Revenue accounts are increased by credits, and expense accounts are increased by debits.

- Income is the result of revenue (credits) exceeding expenses (debits).

Entering Net Income (Loss). Refer to the income statement section of Exhibit 11.9 and note that the total credits exceed the total debits, which indicates a net income for the period. Observe how the difference between the totals was entered on the worksheet. The caption Net Income is written in the left-most column of the worksheet; the net income amount is entered in the debit column of the income statement section and in the credit column of the balance sheet. The reason for crediting net income in the balance sheet column is that it increments owners' equity (a balance sheet classification), and increases in owners' equity are recorded by use of a credit.

The next step is to update the previous totals in the income statement and balance sheet columns for the net income entry. The

Exhibit 11.8 Tower Restaurant—Worksheet to the Adjusted Trial Balance Stage

Tower Restaurant
Worksheet
December 31, 19X2

	Account	1 Trial Balance Dr	2 Trial Balance Cr	3 Adjustments Dr	4 Adjustments Cr	5 Adjusted Trial Balance Dr	6 Adjusted Trial Balance Cr	7 Income Statement Dr	8 Income Statement Cr	9 Balance Sheet Dr	10 Balance Sheet Cr
101	Cash on Hand	1000 00				1000 00					
102	Cash--Regular Checking	18223 23				18223 23					
103	Cash--Payroll Checking	200 00				200 00					
112	Accounts Receivable	248 65				248 65					
121	Food Inventory	5875 00			(a) 718 00	5157 00					
131	Supplies Inventory	1100 00			(c) 100 00	1000 00					
132	Prepaid Insurance	2400 00			(d) 200 00	2200 00					
147	Furniture & Equipment	45000 00				45000 00					
149	China, Glassware & Silver	9000 00			(f) 150 00	8850 00					
157	Acc. Depreciation--F&E		27000 00		(e) 375 00		27375 00				
201	Accounts Payable		800 00				800 00				
211	Sales Tax Payable		157 15				157 15				
215	Employee Taxes Withheld		138 36				138 36				
231	Accrued Payroll				(g) 385 00		385 00				
232	Accrued Payroll Taxes				(h) 366 00		366 00				
301	Capital, Ann Dancer		74324 73				74324 73				
302	Withdrawals, Ann Dancer	38000 00				38000 00					
401	Food Sales		165209 94				165209 94				
501	Cost of Food Sales	57158 75		(a) 718 00	(b) 35 00	57841 75					
601	Payroll	49774 87		(g) 385 00		50159 87					
602	Payroll Taxes	4788 75		(h) 366 00		5154 75					
605	Employee Benefits	2164 18				2164 18					
607	Employee Meals	2875 00		(b) 35 00		2910 00					
712	Utilities	3345 31				3345 31					
721	China, Glassware & Silver	1650 00		(f) 150 00		1800 00					
727	Operating Supplies	2908 11		(c) 100 00		3008 11					
751	Telephone	915 44				915 44					
752	Office Supplies	923 14				923 14					
753	Credit Card Fees	1868 75				1868 75					
754	Cash Short or Over	137 66				137 66					
761	Repairs & Maintenance	2489 34				2489 34					
801	Rent	9600 00				9600 00					
821	Insurance	1859 00		(d) 200 00		2059 00					
891	Depreciation	4125 00		(e) 375 00		4500 00					
	TOTAL	267630 18	267630 18	2329 00	2329 00	268756 18	268756 18				

Exhibit 11.9 Tower Restaurant—Completed Worksheet

Tower Restaurant
Worksheet
December 31, 19X2

No.	Account	Trial Balance Dr	Trial Balance Cr	Adjustments Dr	Adjustments Cr	Adjusted Trial Balance Dr	Adjusted Trial Balance Cr	Income Statement Dr	Income Statement Cr	Balance Sheet Dr	Balance Sheet Cr
101	Cash on Hand	1000 00				1000 00				1000 00	
102	Cash--Regular Checking	18223 23				18223 23				18223 23	
103	Cash--Payroll Checking	200 00				200 00				200 00	
112	Accounts Receivable	248 65				248 65				248 65	
121	Food Inventory	5875 00			(a) 718 00	5157 00				5157 00	
131	Supplies Inventory	1100 00			(c) 100 00	1000 00				1000 00	
132	Prepaid Insurance	2400 00			(d) 200 00	2200 00				2200 00	
147	Furniture & Equipment	45000 00				45000 00				45000 00	
149	China, Glassware & Silver	9000 00			(f) 150 00	8850 00				8850 00	
157	Acc. Depreciation--F&E		27000 00		(e) 375 00		27375 00				27375 00
201	Accounts Payable		800 00				800 00				800 00
211	Sales Tax Payable		157 15				157 15				157 15
215	Employee Taxes Withheld		138 36				138 36				138 36
231	Accrued Payroll				(g) 385 00		385 00				385 00
232	Accrued Payroll Taxes				(h) 366 00		366 00				366 00
301	Capital, Ann Dancer		74324 73				74324 73				74324 73
302	Withdrawals, Ann Dancer	38000 00				38000 00				38000 00	
401	Food Sales		165209 94				165209 94		165209 94		
501	Cost of Food Sales	57158 75		(a) 718 00	(b) 35 00	57841 75		57841 75			
601	Payroll	49774 87		(g) 385 00		50159 87		50159 87			
602	Payroll Taxes	4788 75		(h) 366 00		5154 75		5154 75			
605	Employee Benefits	2164 18				2164 18		2164 18			
607	Employee Meals	2875 00		(b) 35 00		2910 00		2910 00			
712	Utilities	3345 31				3345 31		3345 31			
721	China, Glassware & Silver	1650 00		(f) 150 00		1800 00		1800 00			
727	Operating Supplies	2908 11		(c) 100 00		3008 11		3008 11			
751	Telephone	915 44				915 44		915 44			
752	Office Supplies	923 14				923 14		923 14			
753	Credit Card Fees	1868 75				1868 75		1868 75			
754	Cash Short or Over	137 66				137 66		137 66			
761	Repairs & Maintenance	2489 34				2489 34		2489 34			
801	Rent	9600 00				9600 00		9600 00			
821	Insurance	1859 00		(d) 200 00		2059 00		2059 00			
891	Depreciation	4125 00		(e) 375 00		4500 00		4500 00			
	TOTAL	267630 18	267630 18	2329 00	2329 00	268756 18	268756 18	148877 30	165209 94	119878 88	103546 24
	Net Income							16332 64			16332 64
	TOTAL							165209 94	165209 94	119878 88	119878 88

income statement and balance sheet sections should now show an equality of debits and credits; otherwise a mathematical error has been made on the worksheet. If an inequality occurs, first check the accuracy of the initial totals in the income statement section, because an error in totaling either debits or credits would affect the accuracy of the net income computation.

Refer to the worksheet in Exhibit 11.9 and observe that there is equality of debits and credits for the income statement and balance sheet sections of the worksheet.

Financial Statements for the Tower Restaurant

The income statement and balance sheet columns on the worksheet can now be used to prepare the following financial statements:

- Statement of Income

- Statement of Owner's Equity (for a proprietorship), *or* Statement of Retained Earnings (for a corporation)

- Balance Sheet

An experienced accountant is able to prepare the financial statements in almost any sequence. From a practical approach, it is easier to prepare the statements in the sequence just presented.

The statement of income is prepared first because the net income (loss) is required to prepare the statement of owner's equity (or the statement of retained earnings); the end result on the equity statement is then transferred to the balance sheet.

All of the amounts on the income statement columns and balance sheet columns must be used to prepare the financial statements. However, various accounts may be consolidated for presentation on the financial statements. For example, the Tower Restaurant has three different general ledger accounts for Cash. On the balance sheet, the amounts of these accounts may be combined and presented in a single caption called Cash.

A major reason for consolidating certain accounts is to improve the readability of the financial statements and eliminate unimportant details which only confuse the reader. The prepaid asset accounts in the general ledger may also be combined and presented under a single caption called Prepaid Items. Certain nominal operating expenses are sometimes combined and presented under a single caption called Other Operating Expenses on the statement of income.

Preparing the Statements

Refer to the worksheet (Exhibit 11.9) and trace how Tower Restaurant's financial statements were prepared in accordance with the following steps:

1. Take the amounts from the income statement columns and prepare the statement of income (Exhibit 11.10).

2. Prepare the statement of owner's equity (Exhibit 11.11):

Exhibit 11.10 Tower Restaurant—Income Statement

Tower Restaurant
INCOME STATEMENT
For the Year Ended December 31, 19X2

Food Sales	$165,209.94
Cost of Food Sales	57,841.75
Gross Profit	107,368.19
OPERATING EXPENSES:	
Payroll	50,159.87
Payroll Taxes	5,154.75
Employee Meals and Other Benefits	5,074.18
Utilities	3,345.31
China, Glassware & Silver	1,800.00
Operating Supplies	3,008.11
Telephone	915.44
Office Supplies	923.14
Credit Card Fees	1,868.75
Cash Short or Over	137.66
Repairs & Maintenance	2,489.34
Total Operating Expenses	74,876.55
INCOME BEFORE FIXED CHARGES	32,491.64
FIXED CHARGES:	
Rent	9,600.00
Insurance	2,059.00
Depreciation	4,500.00
Total Fixed Charges	16,159.00
NET INCOME	$16,332.64

Exhibit 11.11 Tower Restaurant—Statement of Owner's Equity

Tower Restaurant
STATEMENT OF OWNER'S EQUITY
For the Year Ended December 31, 19X2

Ann Dancer, Capital, January 1, 19X2	$74,324.73
Net income for the year	16,332.64
Total	$90,657.37
Less: Withdrawals during the year	38,000.00
Ann Dancer, Capital, December 31, 19X2	$52,657.37

a. The beginning capital amount comes from the Capital account balance in the trial balance section of the worksheet.

Exhibit 11.12 Tower Restaurant—Balance Sheet

Tower Restaurant
BALANCE SHEET
December 31, 19X2

CURRENT ASSETS

Cash	$19,423.23	
Accounts Receivable	248.65	
Food Inventory	5,157.00	
Supplies Inventory	1,000.00	
Prepaid Insurance	2,200.00	
Total Current Assets		$28,028.88

PROPERTY & EQUIPMENT

	Cost	Accumulated Depreciation	
Furniture & Equipment	45,000.00	27,375.00	
China, Glassware, Silver	8,850.00		
Total	53,850.00	27,375.00	26,475.00

TOTAL ASSETS $54,503.88

LIABILITIES AND OWNER'S EQUITY

CURRENT LIABILITIES

Accounts Payable	$ 800.00	
Sales Tax Payable	157.15	
Employee Taxes Withheld	138.36	
Accrued Expenses	751.00	
Total Current Liabilities		$1,846.51

OWNER'S EQUITY

Capital, Ann Dancer--December 31, 19X2	52,657.37

TOTAL LIABILITIES AND OWNER'S EQUITY $54,503.88

b. The net income amount may come from the statement of income or the worksheet; it is identical on either document.

c. The withdrawals amount comes from the worksheet.

d. The ending capital is computed.

3. Prepare the balance sheet (Exhibit 11.12):

a. With the exception of the accounts for owner's capital and owner's withdrawals, all of the amounts from the balance sheet section of the worksheet are used to prepare the balance sheet.

    b.   The ending capital amount for the balance sheet is brought forward from the statement of owner's equity.

Presentation of Monthly Operating Results

Tower Restaurant's income statement (Exhibit 11.10) presents the operating results for the 12-month period ended December 31, 19X2. Management may also require more detailed financial information; specifically, operating results for a given month.

A statement of income for any particular month could be prepared by analyzing the monthly activity of each income statement account in the general ledger. However, this approach is time-consuming and tedious. A better approach is to take the year-to-date information of the prior period and subtract it from this period's year-to-date information.

Using the Tower Restaurant as an example, the operating results for the month of December are easily calculated by subtracting the November year-to-date operating results from the December year-to-date operating results. This method is presented in Exhibit 11.13. For illustration, the December and November year-to-date operating results are presented on one statement of income. Computing on a horizontal basis, the December year-to-date less the November year-to-date produces the result for the month of December. A mathematical proof is possible by performing a vertical check on key amounts for the month of December, such as Gross Profit, Total Operating Expenses, Loss Before Fixed Charges, Total Fixed Charges, and Net Loss.

Rounding of Dollar Amounts

Many companies round the amounts on the financial statements to the nearest dollar. Larger companies will round to the nearest hundred dollars. Very large companies will report in the thousands of dollars; for example, an amount of $24,198,724.33 will be presented as $24,199 on the financial statements. The heading of the financial statements will indicate the rounding method used to report the financial data.

Posting the Adjustments for the Tower Restaurant

After the financial statements have been reviewed for accuracy, the adjusting entries that were journalized during the worksheet process may be posted by the bookkeeper.

Exhibit 11.14 shows the journalized adjusting entries, which have been posted to general ledger accounts in Exhibit 11.15. Notice that the general ledger balances are in agreement with the amounts on the financial statements, except for the Capital account. Net income (loss) and withdrawals are transferred to the Capital account by the process of closing entries, which is performed only at the end of the year.

Reversing Entries

The use of reversing entries is an optional bookkeeping procedure and is not absolutely required in an accounting system. The purpose

Exhibit 11.13 Tower Restaurant—Monthly Operating Results

	Year-to-date December 31	Year-to-date November 30	Month of December
Food Sales	$165,209.94	$162,590.75	$2,619.19
Cost of Food Sales	57,841.75	57,150.00	691.75
Gross Profit	107,368.19	105,440.75	1,927.44
OPERATING EXPENSES:			
Payroll	50,159.87	48,906.16	1,253.71
Payroll Taxes	5,154.75	4,788.75	366.00
Employee Meals and Other Benefits	5,074.18	5,039.18	35.00
Utilities	3,345.31	3,094.65	250.66
China, Glassware & Silver	1,800.00	1,650.00	150.00
Operating Supplies	3,008.11	2,898.66	109.45
Telephone	915.44	850.28	65.16
Office Supplies	923.14	923.14	
Credit Card Fees	1,868.75	1,868.75	
Cash Short or Over	137.66	137.16	.50
Repairs & Maintenance	2,489.34	2,489.34	
Total Operating Expenses	74,876.55	72,646.07	2,230.48
INCOME (LOSS) BEFORE FIXED CHARGES	32,491.64	32,794.68	(303.04)
FIXED CHARGES:			
Rent	9,600.00	8,800.00	800.00
Insurance	2,059.00	1,859.00	200.00
Depreciation	4,500.00	4,125.00	375.00
Total Fixed Charges	16,159.00	14,784.00	1,375.00
NET INCOME (LOSS)	$16,332.64	$18,010.68	($1,678.04)

of reversing entries is to simplify the recording of routine transactions such as cash receipts and cash payments in the next period. Without reversing entries, it would be necessary to refer to prior adjusting entries to properly record routine transactions in the next accounting period.

A good case supporting the use of reversing entries is the need to make an adjusting entry to accrue unpaid salaries and wages. For example, earlier in this chapter an adjusting entry was made for a particular business for unpaid payroll as of August 31. Recall that the calendar for August was as follows:

S	M	T	W	T	F	S
	1	2	3	4	5	6
7	8	9	10	11	12	13
14	15	16	17	18	19	20
21	22	23	24	25	26	27
28	29	30	31			

Exhibit 11.14   Tower Restaurant—Journalized Adjusting Entries

JOURNAL					Page *J6*	
Date 19X2	Description	Post. Ref.	Debit		Credit	
	(a)					
Dec. 31	Cost of Food Sales	501	718	00		
	Food Inventory	121			718	00
	Record storeroom issues to kitchen					
	(b)					
31	Employee Meals	607	35	00		
	Cost of Food Sales	501			35	00
	Record food used for free employee meals					
	(c)					
31	Operating Supplies	727	100	00		
	Supplies Inventory	131			100	00
	Adjust inventory account to physical					
	(d)					
31	Insurance	821	200	00		
	Prepaid Insurance	132			200	00
	Charge expired premium to expense					
	(e)					
31	Depreciation	891	375	00		
	Accumulated Depreciation -- F & E	157			375	00
	Record 1/12 annual depreciation					
	(f)					
31	China, Glassware & Silver (Expense)	721	150	00		
	China, Glassware & Silver (Asset)	149			150	00
	Record 1/12 annual depreciation					
	(g)					
31	Payroll	601	385	00		
	Accrued Payroll	231			385	00
	Record unpaid wages as of 12/31/X2					
	(h)					
31	Payroll Taxes	602	366	00		
	Accrued Payroll Taxes	232			366	00
	Record unpaid employer's taxes as of 12/31					

On August 31, employees were paid for the workweek of August 21 to 27. The payroll days of August 28 to 31 will be included in the paycheck for the first Wednesday in September. Therefore, on August

Exhibit 11.15 Tower Restaurant—General Ledger After Adjusting Entries

Title: Cash on Hand — Account No.: 101

Date	Explanation	Ref.	Dr	Cr	Balance
Nov 30		✓			1 000 00

Title: Cash--Regular Checking — Account No.: 102

Date	Explanation	Ref.	Dr	Cr	Balance
Nov 30		✓			25 792 16
Dec 31		S	2 693 99		
31		CP		10 262 92	18 223 23

Title: Cash--Payroll Checking — Account No.: 103

Date	Explanation	Ref.	Dr	Cr	Balance
Nov 30		✓			200 00
Dec 31		CP	730 35		
31		PR		730 35	200 00

Title: Accounts Receivable — Account No.: 112

Date	Explanation	Ref.	Dr	Cr	Balance
Nov 30		✓			185 00
Dec 31		S	248 65	185 00	248 65

Title: Food Inventory — Account No.: 121

Date	Explanation	Ref.	Dr	Cr	Balance
Nov 30		✓			4 875 00
Dec 31		CP	200 00		
31		AP	800 00		5 875 00
31		J6		718 00	5 157 00

Title: Supplies Inventory — Account No.: 131

Date	Explanation	Ref.	Dr	Cr	Balance
Nov 30		✓			1 100 00
Dec 31		J6		100 00	1 000 00

Title: Prepaid Insurance — Account No.: 132

Date	Explanation	Ref.	Dr	Cr	Balance
Dec 31		CP	2 400 00		2 400 00
31		J6		200 00	2 200 00

Title: Furniture & Equipment — Account No.: 147

Date	Explanation	Ref.	Dr	Cr	Balance
Nov 30		✓			45 000 00

Title: China, Glassware & Silver — Account No.: 149

Date	Explanation	Ref.	Dr	Cr	Balance
Nov 30		✓			9 000 00
Dec 31		J6		150 00	8 850 00

Exhibit 11.15 (continued)

Title: Accumulated Depreciation--F&E		Account No.: 157			
	Explanation	Ref.	Dr	Cr	Balance
Nov 30		✓			(27 000 00)
Dec 31		J6		375 00	(27 375 00)

Title: Accounts Payable		Account No.: 201			
	Explanation	Ref.	Dr	Cr	Balance
Nov 30		✓			(4 600 00)
Dec 31		CP	4 600 00		
31		AP		800 00	(800 00)

Title: Sales Tax Payable		Account No.: 211			
	Explanation	Ref.	Dr	Cr	Balance
Nov 30		✓			(1 216 75)
Dec 31		S		157 15	
31		CP	1 216 75		(157 15)

Title: Employee Taxes Withheld		Account No.: 215			
	Explanation	Ref.	Dr	Cr	Balance
Dec 31		PR		79 36	
31		PR		59 00	(138 36)

Title: Accrued Payroll		Account No.: 231			
	Explanation	Ref.	Dr	Cr	Balance
Dec 31		J6		385 00	(385 00)

Title: Accrued Payroll Taxes		Account No.: 232			
	Explanation	Ref.	Dr	Cr	Balance
Dec 31		J6		366 00	(366 00)

Title: Capital, Ann Dancer		Account No.: 301			
	Explanation	Ref.	Dr	Cr	Balance
Nov 30		✓			(74 324 73)

Title: Withdrawals, Ann Dancer		Account No.: 302			
	Explanation	Ref.	Dr	Cr	Balance
Nov 30		✓			38 000 00

Title: Income Summary		Account No.: 399			
	Explanation	Ref.	Dr	Cr	Balance

Exhibit 11.15 (continued)

Title: Food Sales		Ref.	Dr	Cr	Balance	Account No.: 401
	Explanation	Ref.	Dr	Cr	Balance	
Nov 30		✓			(162 590 75)	
Dec 31		S		2 619 19	(165 209 94)	

Title: Cost of Food Sales		Ref.	Dr	Cr	Balance	Account No.: 501
	Explanation	Ref.	Dr	Cr	Balance	
Nov 30		✓			57 150 00	
Dec 31		S	8 75		57 158 75	
31		J6	718 00	35 00	57 841 75	

Title: Payroll		Ref.	Dr	Cr	Balance	Account No.: 601
	Explanation	Ref.	Dr	Cr	Balance	
Nov 30		✓			48 906 16	
Dec 31		PR	868 71		49 774 87	
31		J6	385 00		50 159 87	

Title: Payroll Taxes		Ref.	Dr	Cr	Balance	Account No.: 602
	Explanation	Ref.	Dr	Cr	Balance	
Nov 30		✓			4 788 75	
Dec 31		J6	366 00		5 154 75	

Title: Employee Benefits		Ref.	Dr	Cr	Balance	Account No.: 605
	Explanation	Ref.	Dr	Cr	Balance	
Nov 30		✓			2 164 18	

Title: Employee Meals		Ref.	Dr	Cr	Balance	Account No.: 607
	Explanation	Ref.	Dr	Cr	Balance	
Nov 30		✓			2 875 00	
Dec 31		J6	35 00		2 910 00	

Title: Utilities		Ref.	Dr	Cr	Balance	Account No.: 712
	Explanation	Ref.	Dr	Cr	Balance	
Nov 30		✓			3 094 65	
Dec 31		CP	250 66		3 345 31	

Title: China, Glassware & Silver		Ref.	Dr	Cr	Balance	Account No.: 721
	Explanation	Ref.	Dr	Cr	Balance	
Nov 30		✓			1 650 00	
Dec 31		J6	150 00		1 800 00	

Title: Operating Supplies		Ref.	Dr	Cr	Balance	Account No.: 727
	Explanation	Ref.	Dr	Cr	Balance	
Nov 30		✓			2 898 66	
Dec 31		S	9 45		2 908 11	
31		J6	100 00		3 008 11	

Exhibit 11.15 (continued)

Title: Telephone — Account No.: 751

	Explanation	Ref.	Dr	Cr	Balance
Nov 30		✓			850 28
Dec 31		CP	65 16		915 44

Title: Office Supplies — Account No.: 752

	Explanation	Ref.	Dr	Cr	Balance
Nov 30		✓			923 14

Title: Credit Card Fees — Account No.: 753

	Explanation	Ref.	Dr	Cr	Balance
Nov 30		✓			1 868 75

Title: Cash Short or Over — Account No.: 754

	Explanation	Ref.	Dr	Cr	Balance
Nov 30		✓			137 16
Dec 31		S	50		137 66

Title: Repairs & Maintenance — Account No.: 761

	Explanation	Ref.	Dr	Cr	Balance
Nov 30		✓			2 489 34

Title: Rent — Account No.: 801

	Explanation	Ref.	Dr	Cr	Balance
Nov 30		✓			8 800 00
Dec 31		CP	800 00		9 600 00

Title: Insurance — Account No.: 821

	Explanation	Ref.	Dr	Cr	Balance
Nov 30		✓			1 859 00
Dec 31		J6	200 00		2 059 00

Title: Depreciation — Account No.: 891

	Explanation	Ref.	Dr	Cr	Balance
Nov 30		✓			4 125 00
Dec 31		J6	375 00		4 500 00

31, there are four days of payroll expenses not recorded in the accounting month of August.

The adjusting entry on August 31 provided for 4/7 of an average $7,000 payroll week, debiting Payroll Expense for $4,000 and crediting Accrued Payroll for $4,000.

After the journal entry was posted, the general ledger accounts appeared as follows:

Payroll Expense		Accrued Payroll	
8/31 AJE 4,000	(Wages 8/28–8/31)		8/31 AJE 4,000

Scenario When Not Using a Reversing Entry. The wages for the workweek of August 28 to September 3 will be paid on September 7.

	S	M	T	W	T	F	S
August	28	29	30	31			
September					1	2	3
	4	5	6	7			

↑
Payday for previous week
of Sunday to Saturday
(8/28 to 9/3)

Assume the payroll for the workweek of 8/28 to 9/3 is $7,000. On September 7, this routine transaction is entered in the payroll journal; the gross wages (payroll expense) will be recorded as $7,000 for the first week of September, and the ledger will appear as follows:

Payroll Expense		Accrued Payroll	
8/31 AJE 4,000	(Wages 8/28–8/31)		8/31 AJE 4,000
9/7 PR 7,000	(Wages 8/28–9/3)		

Not all of the $7,000 payroll expense applies to September; this payroll contains $4,000 applicable to August. A reversing entry provides a convenient method to avoid these accounting complications.

Scenario When Using a Reversing Entry. In review, the ledger accounts initially appeared on August 31 as follows:

Payroll Expense		Accrued Payroll	
8/31 AJE 4,000	(Wages 8/28–8/31)		8/31 AJE 4,000

Reversing entries are prepared at the beginning of the new accounting month. As the name implies, a reversing entry is the exact reverse of an adjusting entry. It contains the same account titles and amounts as the adjusting entry, except that the debits and credits are the reverse of those in the adjusting entry.

The reversing entry on September 1 is as follows:

Sep. 1	Accrued Payroll		4 000 00		
	Payroll Expense				4 000 00

After posting the reversing entry on September 1, the ledger accounts are as follows:

Payroll Expense		Accrued Payroll	
8/31 AJE 4,000	9/1 RJE 4,000	9/1 RJE 4,000	8/31 AJE 4,000
			Balance 0

After the payroll journal is posted on September 7, the general ledger account Payroll Expense will appear as follows:

Payroll Expense			
8/31 AJE	4,000	9/1 RJE	4,000
9/7 PR	7,000		

The postings of 9/1 and 9/7 now accurately reflect the $3,000 wages expense for September.

Which Adjusting Entries May Require Reversing Entries? Not all adjusting entries require reversing entries. Generally, any adjusting entry that will affect future cash receipts or cash payments should have a reversing entry in the next period. Adjusting entries that affect inventories, supplies on hand, and other items that require adjustment at each month's end may not require a reversing entry because the next month's adjusting entry will rectify the account balance.

The use of reversing entries depends on the accounting system and conventions of a particular business. Because of the unique nature of reversing entries and the fact that accounting policies vary from business to business, a universal rule is difficult to state. Generally, the following set of guidelines may be followed:

1. Search the prior month's adjusting entries and locate any entries that credit a liability account or debit an asset account. These are the entries that either increased a liability or asset account.

2. When such entries are located, it may be possible to determine whether a reversing entry is required.

Reversing Entries for the Tower Restaurant

The Tower Restaurant uses a simple method to determine those adjusting entries that will require reversing entries. Its policy is to use an "accrued" account to flag those adjustments that are to be reversed on the first day of the next accounting month.

Refer to Exhibit 11.14 and search for each adjusting entry that used some type of "accrued" account in its entry. The two entries that meet this parameter are the Accrued Payroll and Accrued Payroll Taxes entries. Note that these adjusting entries also increased liability accounts. The reversing entries are dated January 1, 19X3, and are as follows:

Jan. 1	Accrued Payroll			385	00				
	Payroll Expense						385	00	
Jan. 1	Accrued Payroll Taxes			366	00				
	Payroll Taxes Expense						366	00	

The reversing entries will not be posted until the next accounting period, which is January 19X3. In Tower Restaurant's case, the period ended December 31, 19X2, is also the end of its accounting year. Therefore, closing entries must be performed as of December 31, 19X2.

Closing entries are presented in the following chapter, which completes the accounting cycle with a discussion of the year-end accounting process.

Discussion Questions

1. What are the five sections that appear on a worksheet?

2. What is the purpose of a worksheet?

3. What is a trial balance?

4. What are the uses and limitations of a trial balance?

5. What are examples of a slide and a transposition?

6. What are the possible causes for the following trial balances being out of balance?

a.	Total debits = $98,678.98	Total credits = $98,078.98
b.	Total debits = $98,678.98	Total credits = $97,778.98
c.	Total debits = $98,678.98	Total credits = $98,660.08

7. What is the purpose of adjusting entries, and when are they recorded?

8. What is the purpose of reversing entries, and when are they recorded?

Problems

Problem 11.1
On August 1, 19XX, a lodging business paid $3,600 for a one-year insurance policy covering the period 8/1/XX to 8/1/X1.

a. What is the journal entry on August 1, 19XX?

b. What is the adjusting entry on August 31, 19XX?

c. What is the adjusting entry on September 30, 19XX?

d. What is the adjusting entry on October 31, 19XX?

Problem 11.2
On January 1, 19XX, a restaurant paid $4,800 for rent covering the period from 1/1/XX to 3/31/XX.

a. Journalize the payment on January 1.

b. Post to general ledger accounts on January 1.

c. Journalize and post the adjusting entries for January 31, February 28, and March 31. Update the account balances each month.

Problem 11.3
Journalize the following adjustments for the month ending April 30, 19XX. All adjustments are recorded monthly.

a. Depreciation on the building is $18,000 per year.

b. Depreciation on china, glassware, and silver is $2,400 per year.

Problem 11.4
The Supplies Inventory account on June 1 is as follows:

Supplies Inventory

6/1 Balance 800	

Purchases during the month of June were $300, $500, and $200. On June 30, a physical inventory of the supplies storeroom showed that $600 of supplies were on hand. What is the adjusting entry for June 30?

Problem 11.5
A restaurant operation uses a perpetual inventory system. The account Food Inventory shows a balance of $6,200 on June 1. During the month, purchases of storeroom food provisions totaled $20,000. Issues from the storeroom during the month totaled $18,000.

Problems *(continued)*

Of the $18,000 issued, free employee meals for the month totaled $500. Employee meals are charged on a departmental basis; for example, free meals to employees of the rooms department are charged to an account called Employee Meals—Rooms Department. The free employee meals of $500 will be charged as follows: $175 to Rooms Department, $225 to Food and Beverage Department, $100 to Administrative and General.

a. Journalize the issues for the month of June.

b. Journalize the free employee meals for the month of June.

c. On June 30, a physical inventory of the food storeroom showed that $8,000 of food provisions are actually on hand. Journalize the required adjusting entry.

Problem 11.6
Journalize the following adjustments for the month ending April 30, 19XX. All adjustments are recorded monthly.

a. The potential bad debts for the month are estimated at $450.

b. The unpaid wages as of the end of the month are estimated at $2,400.

c. The unpaid interest due on a note payable is estimated at $1,000.

d. Interest earned on a money market account is estimated at $500. This interest has not yet been received.

Problem 11.7
On January 1, 19XX, a hotel receives rent of $5,700 from an office tenant covering the period from 1/1/XX to 3/31/XX.

a. Journalize the receipt on January 1.

b. Post to the general ledger accounts on January 1.

c. Journalize and post the adjusting entries for January 31, February 28, and March 31. Update the account balances each month.

Problem 11.8
The bookkeeper for Founders Restaurant has completed the journals and postings to the general ledger accounts for the month of March 19XX. Your responsibility is to prepare a worksheet for the period ended March 31, 19XX, from the following general ledger summary. You should save the results of this problem to solve Problems 11.9 and 11.10.

A summary of the general ledger for the period ending March 31, 19XX is as follows:

Problems (continued)

GENERAL LEDGER—FOUNDERS RESTAURANT

Cash on Hand	$ 500.00
Cash—Checking Account	15,769.25
Food Inventory	5,106.00
Supplies Inventory	1,250.00
Prepaid Insurance	1,200.00
Furniture & Equipment	38,000.00
China, Glassware & Silver	7,500.00
Accumulated Depreciation—F & E	4,800.00 cr
Accounts Payable	8,900.25 cr
Sales Tax Payable	1,250.76 cr
Employee Taxes Withheld	525.00 cr
Accrued Payroll	0
Accrued Payroll Taxes	0
Capital, J. Baxter	49,650.94 cr
Withdrawals, J. Baxter	6,000.00
Food Sales	48,985.50 cr
Cost of Food Sold	10,186.00
Payroll	15,675.36
Payroll Taxes	1,254.03
Employee Benefits	785.50
Utilities	665.00
Kitchen Fuel	750.00
China, Glassware & Silver	600.00
Operating Supplies	563.25
Telephone	210.56
Office Supplies	456.98
Cash Short or Over	15.36
Repairs & Maintenance	825.16
Rent	4,500.00
Insurance	1,500.00
Depreciation—F & E	800.00

Instructions:

1. Set up a worksheet with the proper headings.

2. Copy all of the general ledger accounts and their balances on the trial balance section of the worksheet. Prove equality of debits and credits. As a checkpoint, the trial balance should equal $114,112.45.

3. Determine necessary adjustments following from these facts:

   a. The unpaid wages as of 3/31 are $875.

   b. Issues from the food storeroom for the month were $4,500.

Problems *(continued)*

c. Free employee meals for the month were $75 and are charged to the Employee Benefits account.

d. The expired portion of Prepaid Insurance is $300.

e. The employer's unpaid payroll taxes are $625.

f. A physical inventory of the operating supplies storeroom shows that $800 in supplies are on hand.

g. Monthly depreciation on the furniture is $400.

h. Monthly depreciation on China, Glassware, and Silver is $300.

4. Complete the worksheet. It is not necessary to journalize the adjustments for this problem. As checkpoints, the adjusted trial balance should equal $116,012.45, and net income should be $2,748.30.

Problem 11.9
Refer to the worksheet prepared in Problem 11.8. Your responsibility is to prepare the financial statements. The business year for Founders Restaurant is from January to December.

Instructions:

1. Prepare the statement of income, statement of owner's equity, and the balance sheet from the worksheet.

2. Management requests that all bookkeeping accounts appear on the financial statements, and all amounts are to be shown in dollars and cents.

Problem 11.10
Founders Restaurant uses reversing entries in its accounting system. Refer to the worksheet prepared in Problem 11.8. Analyze each adjustment of March 31 and determine which might require a reversing entry on April 1.

Instructions:

1. Journalize the reversing entries determined necessary.
2. Give the reason for your conclusion.

12
The Year-End Accounting Process

An accounting system uses forms and procedures to process financial data into usable financial information. Financial data refers to facts and figures, while financial information is a summary of the data in the form of financial statements and other reports useful in planning, control, and decision-making.

Earlier chapters demonstrated how financial data is documented and recorded in the journalizing and posting processes; once recorded, this data is further processed by means of a worksheet to produce monthly financial statements. The accounting practices involved in these activities are referred to as the accounting cycle because they are repeated on a daily or monthly basis.

Accounting for hospitality operations involves a fiscal year cycle with interim reports issued during the year. For accounting purposes, an operation may adopt its *natural business year* as its fiscal year. A natural business year is the 12-month period ending when the operation is least busy. Interim reports or statements refer to reports covering a time period less than one year—for example, a month or a quarter.

Chapter 12 will complete our discussion of the accounting cycle by addressing the year-end accounting process and answering such questions as:

1. What are the purposes of closing entries?

2. How are closing entries journalized using information from the income statement columns of the worksheet?

3. How is net income (loss) recorded in the general ledger?

4. What is a post-closing trial balance?

5. How is the general ledger set up for the next business year?

This chapter concludes the accounting cycle by discussing closing entries, the post-closing trial balance, and setup of the general ledger for the next year. The Tower Restaurant will continue to be used as a case study in order to demonstrate the year-end accounting process.

Exhibit 12.1   The Accounting Cycle

Daily	Monthly	End-of-Year
Analyze business transactions	Post journals to general ledger	Prepare the closing entries
Journalize business transactions	Prepare worksheet and adjustments	Post the closing entries
Post receivable & payable transactions to subsidiary ledgers	Prepare financial statements	Prepare post-closing trial balance

Before we consider the year-end accounting process, a review of the overall accounting system will help to reinforce your understanding of the various steps in the accounting cycle.

A Summary of the Accounting System

An accounting system includes the forms and procedures used in the accounting process, starting with the journalizing of business transactions, progressing toward the preparation of financial statements, and concluding with the closing of temporary accounts. The periodic activities in this system are often referred to as the accounting cycle. Exhibit 12.1 summarizes the major activities of the accounting cycle. These activities are represented in the following list:

1. Business transactions are analyzed from source documents.

2. Transactions are promptly journalized and, if applicable, posted to the subsidiary ledgers.

3. Journal entries are posted to the ledger accounts.

4. A worksheet is prepared. It begins with a trial balance of the general ledger accounts. Necessary adjustments are entered, and the amounts on the worksheet are crossfooted and sorted between income statement accounts and balance sheet accounts.

5. The financial statements are prepared from the worksheet.

6. The cycle described in steps 1 through 5 is repeated until the end of the accounting year.

7. At the end of the year, the temporary accounts are closed to end the current accounting year and to prepare for the beginning of the new accounting year.

An Introduction to Closing Entries

The major portion of year-end activities involves the preparation of closing entries. Closing entries clear and close the temporary accounts. An account is *cleared* by transferring its balance to another account. An account is *closed* when a closing entry brings its balance to zero.

The two main purposes of closing entries are:

- to bring the temporary accounts to a zero balance, and
- to record net income (loss) for the year in an equity account.

The term "temporary accounts" refers to the income statement accounts (revenue and expenses) and the Withdrawals account. These accounts are used to accumulate data for the current accounting year only.

Recall that the long form of the accounting equation is:

$$\text{Assets} = \text{Liabilities} + \text{Equity} + \text{Revenue} - \text{Expenses}$$

However, the revenue and expense accounts are closed at the end of the year and their combined balances transferred to an equity account. Therefore, the technical form of the accounting equation is:

$$\text{Assets} = \text{Liabilities} + \text{Equity}$$

All temporary accounts begin the new accounting year with zero balances, accumulate balances during the accounting year, and return to zero by means of closing entries at the end of the accounting year. Temporary accounts are also referred to as *nominal accounts*.

Balance sheet accounts (except Withdrawals) are permanent accounts because they maintain a perpetual balance as of a date, not just for a period of time. Permanent accounts are also called *real accounts*.

The balances of permanent accounts are carried forward to the beginning of the next accounting year. For example, if the Cash account has a balance of $5,000 at the end of the accounting year, this balance is carried forward to start the next accounting year.

Steps in the Closing Process

Closing journal entries are prepared at the end of the accounting year and are dated as of the last day of the year. The closing process can be performed using information from the income statement columns of the worksheet. The closing process involves the following steps:

1. Close all revenue accounts.
2. Close all expense accounts.
3. Transfer the net income (loss) to an equity account.
4. If a proprietorship is involved, transfer the Withdrawals account balance to the Capital account.

The closing of the revenue and expense accounts is accomplished with the use of a new nominal account called *Income Summary*. This account provides a place to summarize the revenue and expense accounts in order to arrive at net income or loss for the year. The resulting balance in the Income Summary account will equal the net income (loss) as shown on the worksheet.

The steps in the closing process are best explained by example.

Closing Entries for Motel Consultants

Motel Consultants is a proprietorship with a business year ending December 31. Its financial statements have been issued throughout the year on a monthly basis. After the financial statements have been prepared for the period ending December 31, 19XX, the year-end process is started.

The worksheet in Exhibit 12.2 will be used to prepare the closing entries.

Closing the Revenue Accounts

Revenue accounts normally have credit balances. Revenue accounts are cleared and closed by debiting each account for the amount of its balance. An offsetting credit is made to the Income Summary account.

Motel Consultants has only one revenue account—Sales. The closing entry is as follows:

Dec. 31	Sales	46,000.00	
	Income Summary		46,000.00

After this closing entry is posted, the Sales account would have a zero balance and the Income Summary account would appear as follows:

INCOME SUMMARY

	12/31 CE	46,000.00

Observe that the credit to the Income Summary account is equal to the total of the income statement credit column on the worksheet.

Closing the Expense Accounts

The closing of the expense accounts is performed in a manner similar to the revenue accounts. Since expense accounts normally have a debit balance, crediting these accounts will bring their balances to zero. The debit is to the Income Summary account.

Instead of closing each expense account individually, a combined or *compound* entry is used, which results in only one debit amount to the Income Summary account. The debit amount is the total of the individual amounts credited to each expense.

Motel Consultants has five expense accounts—Rent, Supplies, Telephone, Travel, and Depreciation. The closing entry for the expense accounts is as follows:

Exhibit 12.2   Motel Consultants—Worksheet

Motel Consultants
Worksheet
December 31, 19XX

	Trial Balance Dr	Trial Balance Cr	Adjustments Dr	Adjustments Cr	Adjusted Trial Balance Dr	Adjusted Trial Balance Cr	Income Statement Dr	Income Statement Cr	Balance Sheet Dr	Balance Sheet Cr
Cash	3160 72				3160 72				3160 72	
Accounts Receivable	1567 00				1567 00				1567 00	
Supplies Inventory	450 00			(a) 90 00	360 00				360 00	
Furniture & Equipment	2000 00				2000 00				2000 00	
Accum. Depreciation-- F&E		700 00		(b) 25 00		725 00				725 00
Capital, J. Daniels		2282 51				2282 51				2282 51
Withdrawals, J. Daniels	3 2687 26				3 2687 26				3 2687 26	
Sales		46000 00				46000 00		46000 00		
Rent	6000 00				6000 00		6000 00			
Supplies	870 00		(a) 90 00		960 00		960 00			
Telephone	480 63				480 63		480 63			
Travel	1491 90				1491 90		1491 90			
Depreciation	275 00		(b) 25 00		300 00		300 00			
Total	48982 51	48982 51	115 00	115 00	49007 51	49007 51	9232 53	46000 00	39774 98	3007 51
Net Income							36767 47			36767 47
Total							46000 00	46000 00	39774 98	39774 98

Dec. 31	Income Summary	9,232.53	
	Rent		6,000.00
	Supplies		960.00
	Telephone		480.63
	Travel		1,491.90
	Depreciation		300.00

Note that the debit to Motel Consultants' Income Summary account is equal to the total of the income statement debit column on the worksheet. After this closing entry is posted, the expense accounts would have a zero balance and the Income Summary account would appear as follows:

INCOME SUMMARY

| 12/31 CE | 9,232.53 | 12/31 CE | 46,000.00 |
| | | Balance | 36,767.47 |

The credit balance in the account now equals the net income shown on the worksheet.

Closing the Income Summary Account

A credit balance in the Income Summary account means that the company's total revenue exceeded its total expenses; thus, net income is the result. A debit balance in the Income Summary account means that the company's total expenses exceeded its total revenue; thus, net loss is the result.

INCOME SUMMARY

| Debit balance indicates *net loss* | Credit balance indicates *net income* |

Motel Consultants has a net income for the year ended December 31, 19XX. Therefore, a debit is required to close the Income Summary account. The Capital account is credited because it is increased by net income. The closing entry is as follows:

| Dec. 31 | Income Summary | 36,767.47 | |
| | Capital, J. Daniels | | 36,767.47 |

Note that the debit to the Income Summary account reconciles with the debit for net income in the income statement section of the worksheet.

After this closing entry is posted, the Income Summary and Capital accounts would appear as follows:

INCOME SUMMARY

12/31 CE	9,232.53	12/31 CE	46,000.00
12/31 CE	36,767.47	Balance	36,767.47
		Balance	0

CAPITAL, J. DANIELS

		12/31 Bal	2,282.51
		12/31 CE	36,767.47

Closing the Withdrawals Account

The purpose of this entry is to set the Withdrawals account to zero and to reduce the owner's Capital account by the amount of personal withdrawals from the business. Since Withdrawals has a debit balance, a credit is required to close this account. The Capital account is debited because the owner's withdrawals cause a decrease to the Capital account.

For Motel Consultants, the closing entry is as follows:

Dec. 31	Capital, J. Daniels	32,687.26	
	Withdrawals, J. Daniels		32,687.26

After this closing entry is posted, the Withdrawals account would have a zero balance, and the Capital account would appear as follows:

CAPITAL, J. DANIELS

12/31 CE	32,687.26	12/31 Bal	2,282.51
		12/31 CE	36,767.47
		Balance	6,362.72

Posting the Closing Entries

Exhibit 12.3 presents the general ledger for Motel Consultants after the closing entries have been posted. Each nominal or temporary account (revenue, expenses, Income Summary, and Withdrawals) has a zero balance. The permanent balance sheet accounts contain the final balances as of the end of the year, which will become the starting balances for next year.

The Post-Closing Trial Balance

After the closing entries are posted, a post-closing trial balance is prepared to retest the equality of debits and credits in the general ledger. This process helps to eliminate the possibility that an error occurred in posting the closing entries.

The post-closing trial balance is prepared from the general ledger and consists of the balance sheet accounts (with the exception of Withdrawals). Revenue, expenses, and withdrawals are not listed since they have zero balances.

The post-closing trial balance provides assurance that the accounts are in balance and may be used to set up the books for the next year.

Exhibit 12.3 Motel Consultants—General Ledger

Title: Cash					Account No.: 101
	Explanation	Ref.	Dr	Cr	Balance
Dec 31		✓			3 160 72

Title: Accounts Receivable					Account No.: 111
	Explanation	Ref.	Dr	Cr	Balance
Dec 31		✓			1 567 00

Title: Supplies Inventory					Account No.: 121
	Explanation	Ref.	Dr	Cr	Balance
Dec 31		✓			360 00

Title: Furniture & Equipment					Account No.: 131
	Explanation	Ref.	Dr	Cr	Balance
Dec 31		✓			2 000 00

Title: Accumulated Depreciation--F & E					Account No.: 141
	Explanation	Ref.	Dr	Cr	Balance
Dec 31		✓			(725 00)

Title: Capital, J. Daniels					Account No.: 301
	Explanation	Ref.	Dr	Cr	Balance
Dec 31		✓			(2 282 51)
31		CE		36 767 47	
31		CE	32 687 26		(6 362 72)

Title: Withdrawals, J. Daniels					Account No.: 305
	Explanation	Ref.	Dr	Cr	Balance
Dec 31		✓			32 687 26
31		CE		32 687 26	-0-

Title: Income Summary					Account No.: 399
	Explanation	Ref.	Dr	Cr	Balance
Dec 31		CE		46 000 00	
31		CE	9 232 53		(36 767 47)
31		CE	36 767 47		-0-

Exhibit 12.3 (continued)

Title: Sales		Ref.	Dr	Cr	Balance	Account No.: 401
	Explanation	Ref.	Dr	Cr	Balance	
Dec 31		✓			(46 000 00)	
31		CE	46 000 00		-0-	

Title: Rent Expense		Ref.	Dr	Cr	Balance	Account No.: 501
	Explanation	Ref.	Dr	Cr	Balance	
Dec 31		✓			6 000 00	
31				6 000 00	-0-	

Title: Supplies Expense		Ref.	Dr	Cr	Balance	Account No.: 509
	Explanation	Ref.	Dr	Cr	Balance	
Dec 31		✓			960 00	
31		CE		960 00	-0-	

Title: Telephone		Ref.	Dr	Cr	Balance	Account No.: 515
	Explanation	Ref.	Dr	Cr	Balance	
Dec 31		✓			480 63	
31		CE		480 63	-0-	

Title: Travel		Ref.	Dr	Cr	Balance	Account No.: 521
	Explanation	Ref.	Dr	Cr	Balance	
Dec 31		✓			1 491 90	
31		CE		1 491 90	-0-	

Title: Depreciation		Ref.	Dr	Cr	Balance	Account No.: 591
	Explanation	Ref.	Dr	Cr	Balance	
Dec 31		✓			300 00	
31		CE		300 00	-0-	

Exhibit 12.4 presents a post-closing trial balance for Motel Consultants, which has been prepared from the general ledger in Exhibit 12.3.

Setting Up Next Year's General Ledger

Next year's general ledger is set up to include all of the asset, liability, equity, revenue, and expense accounts that are expected to be used to record financial information. The chart of accounts or the previous year's general ledger may be used to set up the account titles and account numbers. The previous year's ending balances for the permanent balance sheet accounts are brought forward as of the start of the new accounting year. The post-closing trial balance provides the balances that are to be brought forward.

Assume Motel Consultants has no change to its chart of accounts for

Exhibit 12.4   Motel Consultants—Post-Closing Trial Balance

Motel Consultants
POST-CLOSING TRIAL BALANCE
December 31, 19XX

	dr	cr
Cash	3,160.72	
Accounts Receivable	1,567.00	
Supplies Inventory	360.00	
Furniture & Equipment	2,000.00	
Accumulated Depreciation--F & E		725.00
Capital, J. Daniels		6,362.72
Total	7,087.72	7,087.72

the accounting year January 1, 19X1, to December 31, 19X1. Its general ledger as of 1/1/X1 is presented in Exhibit 12.5.

Closing Entries for a Corporation

The closing process for a corporation is nearly identical to the method described for a proprietorship. The major difference is in those closing entries which affect equity accounts, because a corporation does not have the equity accounts Capital and Withdrawals. The closing entries for revenue and expense accounts are identical to those for a proprietorship. However, the resulting net income or loss contained in the Income Summary account is transferred to the Retained Earnings account rather than to a Capital account.

If the Income Summary account contains a net income, the closing entry is as follows:

Income Summary	xxx	
Retained Earnings		xxx

The effect of this entry is to close the Income Summary account and transfer the net income for the year to Retained Earnings.

Year-End Procedures for the Tower Restaurant

Thus far in the Tower Restaurant case study, December's business transactions have been recorded and financial data processed to produce the financial statements. The financial statements for the year ended December 31, 19X2, were presented in Chapter 11.

Before processing any financial data for the new accounting year beginning January 1, 19X3, the following year-end procedures must be performed:

Exhibit 12.5 Motel Consultants—General Ledger 1/1/X1

Title: Cash		Account No.: 101			
	Explanation	Ref.	Dr	Cr	Balance
Jan 1	B.F.	✓			3 160 72

Title: Accounts Receivable		Account No.: 111			
	Explanation	Ref.	Dr	Cr	Balance
Jan 1	B.F.	✓			1 567 00

Title: Supplies Inventory		Account No.: 121			
	Explanation	Ref.	Dr	Cr	Balance
Jan 1	B.F.	✓			360 00

Title: Furniture & Equipment		Account No.: 131			
	Explanation	Ref.	Dr	Cr	Balance
Jan 1	B.F.	✓			2 000 00

Title: Accumulated Depreciation--F & E		Account No.: 141			
	Explanation	Ref.	Dr	Cr	Balance
Jan 1	B.F.	✓			(725 00)

Title: Capital, J. Daniels		Account No.: 301			
	Explanation	Ref.	Dr	Cr	Balance
Jan 1	B.F.	✓			(6 362 72)

Title: Withdrawals, J. Daniels		Account No.: 305			
	Explanation	Ref.	Dr	Cr	Balance

Title: Income Summary		Account No.: 399			
	Explanation	Ref.	Dr	Cr	Balance

Title: Sales		Account No.: 401			
	Explanation	Ref.	Dr	Cr	Balance

Exhibit 12.5 (continued)

Title: Rent Expense					Account No.: 501
	Explanation	Ref.	Dr	Cr	Balance

Title: Supplies Expense					Account No.: 509
	Explanation	Ref.	Dr	Cr	Balance

Title: Telephone					Account No.: 515
	Explanation	Ref.	Dr	Cr	Balance

Title: Travel					Account No.: 521
	Explanation	Ref.	Dr	Cr	Balance

Title: Depreciation					Account No.: 591
	Explanation	Ref.	Dr	Cr	Balance

- Prepare closing entries to close the temporary accounts and record 19X2's net income in an equity account.
- Post the closing entries.
- Prepare a post-closing trial balance.
- Set up the general ledger for the new fiscal year.

Tower Restaurant's worksheet (as of December 31, 19X2) is used to illustrate the year-end process. This worksheet, which was prepared in the previous chapter, is reproduced here as Exhibit 12.6 for ease of reference.

Tower's Closing Entries

The closing entries process used by the Tower Restaurant is similar to that used by any business organization. The closing process is as follows:

1. Close all revenue accounts to the Income Summary account.
2. Close all expense accounts to the Income Summary account.

3. Close the Income Summary account and transfer the resulting net income as an increase to the owner's capital account.

4. Close the owner's withdrawals account and transfer the balance as a decrease to the owner's capital account.

Closing entries are easy to prepare and do not require extensive analysis. Simply stated, a temporary account is closed by an offsetting entry which reduces its balance to zero. For example, to close a temporary account with a $1,500 debit balance, the closing entry is a $1,500 credit.

The Income Summary account is a temporary account which summarizes the annual revenues and expenses. During the closing process, the revenue accounts will be transferred as credits to the Income Summary account and the expense accounts will be transferred as debits. Therefore, the Income Summary account may be conceptualized as follows:

INCOME SUMMARY

Total Expenses	Total Revenue

Closing the Revenue Accounts. The Tower Restaurant has only one revenue account—Food Sales. This account is closed with a debit and a corresponding credit to the Income Summary account. The closing entry is illustrated in Exhibit 12.7. At the time this entry is posted, the Income Summary account would appear as follows:

INCOME SUMMARY

	12/31 CE 165,209.94

Closing the Expense Accounts. Using a compound journal entry, each expense account is closed with a credit, and the sum of the expense accounts is debited to the Income Summary account. This closing entry is illustrated in Exhibit 12.7. At the time this entry is posted, the Income Summary account would appear as follows:

INCOME SUMMARY

12/31 CE 148,877.30	12/31 CE 165,209.94
	12/31 Bal 16,332.64

Closing the Income Summary Account. Because the Income Summary account indicates net income for the year, a debit is necessary to close the account. The corresponding credit is to the owner's capital account. This closing entry is illustrated in Exhibit 12.7. At the time this entry is posted, the Income Summary account would appear as follows:

Exhibit 12.6 Tower Restaurant—Worksheet

Tower Restaurant
Worksheet
December 31, 19X2

		Trial Balance		Adjustments		Adjusted Trial Balance		Income Statement		Balance Sheet	
		Dr	Cr	Dr	Cr	Dr	Cr	Dr	Cr	Dr	Cr
101	Cash on Hand	1000 00				1000 00				1000 00	
102	Cash--Regular Checking	18223 23				18223 23				18223 23	
103	Cash--Payroll Checking	200 00				200 00				200 00	
112	Accounts Receivable	248 65				248 65				248 65	
121	Food Inventory	5875 00			(a) 718 00	5157 00				5157 00	
131	Supplies Inventory	1100 00			(c) 100 00	1000 00				1000 00	
132	Prepaid Insurance	2400 00			(d) 200 00	2200 00				2200 00	
147	Furniture & Equipment	45000 00				45000 00				45000 00	
149	China, Glassware & Silver	9000 00			(f) 150 00	8850 00				8850 00	
157	Acc. Depreciation- F&E		27000 00		(e) 375 00		27375 00				27375 00
201	Accounts Payable		800 00				800 00				800 00
211	Sales Tax Payable		157 15				157 15				157 15
215	Employee Taxes Withheld		138 36				138 36				138 36
231	Accrued Payroll				(g) 385 00		385 00				385 00
232	Accrued Payroll Taxes				(h) 366 00		366 00				366 00
301	Capital, Ann Dancer		74324 73				74324 73				74324 73
302	Withdrawals, Ann Dancer	38000 00				38000 00				38000 00	
401	Food Sales		165209 94				165209 94		165209 94		
501	Cost of Food Sales	57158 75		(a) 718 00	(b) 35 00	57841 75		57841 75			
601	Payroll	49774 87		(g) 385 00		50159 87		50159 87			
602	Payroll Taxes	4788 75		(h) 366 00		5154 75		5154 75			
605	Employee Benefits	2164 18				2164 18		2164 18			
607	Employee Meals	2875 00		(b) 35 00		2910 00		2910 00			
712	Utilities	3345 31				3345 31		3345 31			
721	China, Glassware & Silver	1650 00		(f) 150 00		1800 00		1800 00			
727	Operating Supplies	2908 11		(c) 100 00		3008 11		3008 11			
751	Telephone	915 44				915 44		915 44			
752	Office Supplies	923 14				923 14		923 14			
753	Credit Card Fees	1868 75				1868 75		1868 75			
754	Cash Short or Over	137 66				137 66		137 66			
761	Repairs & Maintenance	2489 34				2489 34		2489 34			
801	Rent	9600 00				9600 00		9600 00			
821	Insurance	1859 00		(d) 200 00		2059 00		2059 00			
891	Depreciation	4125 00		(e) 375 00		4500 00		4500 00			
	TOTAL	267630 18	267630 18	2329 00	2329 00	268756 18	268756 18	148877 30	165209 94	103546 24	
	Net Income							16332 64			16332 64
	TOTAL							165209 94	165209 94	119878 88	119878 88

INCOME SUMMARY

12/31 CE	148,877.30	12/31 CE	165,209.94
12/31 CE	16,332.64	12/31 Bal	16,332.64
		12/31 Bal	0

Closing the Withdrawal Account. In the closing process, the Withdrawals account is credited and the Capital account is debited. This closing entry is illustrated in Exhibit 12.7. After this closing entry is posted, the Withdrawals account would have a zero balance, and the Capital account would be debited for $38,000.

Completing the Year-End Procedures

At this point, three steps remain in Tower Restaurant's year-end procedures: posting the closing entries, preparing the post-closing trial balance, and setting up next year's ledger.

Posting the Closing Entries. The closing journal entries are illustrated in Exhibit 12.7 and posted to the general ledger in Exhibit 12.8. After posting has been completed, the revenue and expense accounts in the general ledger have zero balances. The temporary equity accounts Withdrawals and Income Summary also have zero balances. The Capital account has been decreased for the owner's withdrawals during the year and increased for the operation's net income for the year just ended.

Preparing the Post-Closing Trial Balance. After the closing entries are posted, a post-closing trial balance is prepared to ensure the equality of debits and credits in the general ledger. The post-closing trial balance provides assurance that the accounts are in balance. It is prepared from the general ledger and consists of the balance sheet accounts (with the exception of Withdrawals).

Exhibit 12.9 presents Tower Restaurant's post-closing trial balance prepared from the balances shown in its general ledger (Exhibit 12.8).

Setting Up Next Year's Ledger. The general ledger account titles for this period are set up from Tower Restaurant's chart of accounts. The post-closing trial balance may be used to set up the books for next year. The permanent accounts have their balances brought forward for the next year. The temporary accounts start out fiscal year 19X3 with no balances, ready to accumulate data for the new accounting year.

Exhibit 12.7 Tower Restaurant—Closing Journal Entries

Date 19X2	Description	Post. Ref.	Debit	Credit
Dec. 31	Food Sales		165 209 94	
	Income Summary			165 209 94
31	Income Summary		148 877 30	
	Cost of Food Sales			57 841 75
	Payroll			50 159 87
	Payroll Taxes			5 154 75
	Employee Benefits			2 164 18
	Employee Meals			2 910 00
	Utilities			3 345 31
	China, Glassware & Silver			1 800 00
	Operating Supplies			3 008 11
	Telephone			915 44
	Office Supplies			923 14
	Credit Card Fees			1 868 75
	Cash Short or Over			137 66
	Repairs & Maintenance			2 489 34
	Rent			9 600 00
	Insurance			2 059 00
	Depreciation			4 500 00
31	Income Summary		16 332 64	
	Capital, Ann Dancer			16 332 64
31	Capital, Ann Dancer		38 000 00	
	Withdrawals, Ann Dancer			38 000 00

JOURNAL   Page J7

Exhibit 12.8 Tower Restaurant—General Ledger

Title: Cash on Hand Account No.: 101

	Explanation	Ref.	Dr	Cr	Balance
Nov 30		✓			1,000.00

Title: Cash--Regular Checking Account No.: 102

	Explanation	Ref.	Dr	Cr	Balance
Nov 30		✓			25,792.16
Dec 31		S	2,693.99		
31		CP		10,262.92	18,223.23

Title: Cash--Payroll Checking Account No.: 103

	Explanation	Ref.	Dr	Cr	Balance
Nov 30		✓			200.00
Dec 31		CP	730.35		
31		PR		730.35	200.00

Title: Accounts Receivable Account No.: 112

	Explanation	Ref.	Dr	Cr	Balance
Nov 30		✓			185.00
Dec 31		S	248.65	185.00	248.65

Title: Food Inventory Account No.: 121

	Explanation	Ref.	Dr	Cr	Balance
Nov 30		✓			4,875.00
Dec 31		CP	200.00		
31		AP	800.00		5,875.00
31		J6		718.00	5,157.00

Title: Supplies Inventory Account No.: 131

	Explanation	Ref.	Dr	Cr	Balance
Nov 30		✓			1,100.00
Dec 31		J6		100.00	1,000.00

Title: Prepaid Insurance Account No.: 132

	Explanation	Ref.	Dr	Cr	Balance
Dec 31		CP	2,400.00		2,400.00
31		J6		200.00	2,200.00

Title: Furniture & Equipment Account No.: 147

	Explanation	Ref.	Dr	Cr	Balance
Nov 30		✓			45,000.00

Exhibit 12.8 (continued)

Title: China, Glassware & Silver — Account No.: 149

	Explanation	Ref.	Dr	Cr	Balance
Nov 30		✓			9 000 00
Dec 31		J6		150 00	8 850 00

Title: Accumulated Depreciation--F&E — Account No.: 157

	Explanation	Ref.	Dr	Cr	Balance
Nov 30		✓			(27 000 00)
Dec 31		J6		375 00	(27 375 00)

Title: Accounts Payable — Account No.: 201

	Explanation	Ref.	Dr	Cr	Balance
Nov 30		✓			(4 600 00)
Dec 31		CP	4 600 00		
31		AP		800 00	(800 00)

Title: Sales Tax Payable — Account No.: 211

	Explanation	Ref.	Dr	Cr	Balance
Nov 30		✓			(1 216 75)
Dec 31		S		157 15	
31		CP	1 216 75		(157 15)

Title: Employee Taxes Withheld — Account No.: 215

	Explanation	Ref.	Dr	Cr	Balance
Dec 31		PR		79 36	
31		PR		59 00	(138 36)

Title: Accrued Payroll — Account No.: 231

	Explanation	Ref.	Dr	Cr	Balance
Dec 31		J6		385 00	(385 00)

Title: Accrued Payroll Taxes — Account No.: 232

	Explanation	Ref.	Dr	Cr	Balance
Dec 31		J6		366 00	(366 00)

Title: Capital, Ann Dancer — Account No.: 301

	Explanation	Ref.	Dr	Cr	Balance
Nov 30		✓			(74 324 73)
Dec 31		J7		16 332 64	
31		J7	38 000 00		(52 657 37)

Title: Withdrawals, Ann Dancer — Account No.: 302

	Explanation	Ref.	Dr	Cr	Balance
Nov 30		✓			38 000 00
Dec 31		J7		38 000 00	-0-

Exhibit 12.8 (continued)

Title: Income Summary	Explanation	Ref.	Dr	Cr	Balance	Account No.: 399
Dec 31		J7	148 877 30	165 209 94	(16 332 64)	
31		J7	16 332 64		-0-	

Title: Food Sales	Explanation	Ref.	Dr	Cr	Balance	Account No.: 401
Nov 30		✓			(162 590 75)	
Dec 31		S		2 619 19	(165 209 94)	
31		J7	165 209 94		-0-	

Title: Cost of Food Sales	Explanation	Ref.	Dr	Cr	Balance	Account No.: 501
Nov 30		✓			57 150 00	
Dec 31		S	8 75		57 158 75	
31		J6	718 00	35 00	57 841 75	
31		J7		57 841 75	-0-	

Title: Payroll	Explanation	Ref.	Dr	Cr	Balance	Account No.: 601
Nov 30		✓			48 906 16	
Dec 31		PR	868 71		49 774 87	
31		J6	385 00		50 159 87	
31		J7		50 159 87	-0-	

Title: Payroll Taxes	Explanation	Ref.	Dr	Cr	Balance	Account No.: 602
Nov 30		✓			4 788 75	
Dec 31		J6	366 00		5 154 75	
31		J7		5 154 75	-0-	

Title: Employee Benefits	Explanation	Ref.	Dr	Cr	Balance	Account No.: 605
Nov 30		✓			2 164 18	
Dec 31		J7		2 164 18	-0-	

Title: Employee Meals	Explanation	Ref.	Dr	Cr	Balance	Account No.: 607
Nov 30		✓			2 875 00	
Dec 31		J6	35 00		2 910 00	
31		J7		2 910 00	-0-	

Title: Utilities	Explanation	Ref.	Dr	Cr	Balance	Account No.: 712
Nov 30		✓			3 094 65	
Dec 31		CP	250 66		3 345 31	
31		J7		3 345 31	-0-	

Exhibit 12.8 (continued)

Title: China, Glassware & Silver			Account No.: 721		
	Explanation	Ref.	Dr	Cr	Balance
Nov 30		✓			1 650 00
Dec 31		J6	150 00		1 800 00
31		J7		1 800 00	-0-

Title: Operating Supplies			Account No.: 727		
	Explanation	Ref.	Dr	Cr	Balance
Nov 30		✓			2 898 66
Dec 31		S	9 45		2 908 11
31		J6	100 00		3 008 11
31		J7		3 008 11	-0-

Title: Telephone			Account No.: 751		
	Explanation	Ref.	Dr	Cr	Balance
Nov 30		✓			850 28
Dec 31		CP	65 16		915 44
31		J7		915 44	-0-

Title: Office Supplies			Account No.: 752		
	Explanation	Ref.	Dr	Cr	Balance
Nov 30		✓			923 14
Dec 31		J7		923 14	-0-

Title: Credit Card Fees			Account No.: 753		
	Explanation	Ref.	Dr	Cr	Balance
Nov 30		✓			1 868 75
Dec 31		J7		1 868 75	-0-

Title: Cash Short or Over			Account No.: 754		
	Explanation	Ref.	Dr	Cr	Balance
Nov 30		✓			137 16
Dec 31		S	50		137 66
31		J7		137 66	-0-

Title: Repairs & Maintenance			Account No.: 761		
	Explanation	Ref.	Dr	Cr	Balance
Nov 30		✓			2 489 34
Dec 31		J7		2 489 34	-0-

Title: Rent			Account No.: 801		
	Explanation	Ref.	Dr	Cr	Balance
Nov 30		✓			8 800 00
Dec 31		CP	800 00		9 600 00
31		J7		9 600 00	-0-

Exhibit 12.8 (continued)

Title: Insurance					Account No.: 821
	Explanation	**Ref.**	**Dr**	**Cr**	**Balance**
Nov 30		✓			1 859 00
Dec 31		J6	200 00		2 059 00
31		J7		2 059 00	-0-

Title: Depreciation					Account No.: 891
	Explanation	**Ref.**	**Dr**	**Cr**	**Balance**
Nov 30		✓			4 125 00
Dec 31		J6	375 00		4 500 00
31		J7		4 500 00	-0-

Exhibit 12.9   Tower Restaurant—Post-Closing Trial Balance

Tower Restaurant Post-Closing Trial Balance December 31, 19X2			
101	Cash on Hand	1 000 00	
102	Cash--Regular Checking	18 223 23	
103	Cash--Payroll Checking	200 00	
112	Accounts Receivable	248 65	
121	Food Inventory	5 157 00	
131	Supplies Inventory	1 000 00	
132	Prepaid Insurance	2 200 00	
147	Furniture & Equipment	45 000 00	
149	China, Glassware & Silver	8 850 00	
157	Accumulated Depreciation--F&E		27 375 00
201	Accounts Payable		800 00
211	Sales Tax Payable		157 15
215	Employee Taxes Withheld		138 36
231	Accrued Payroll		385 00
232	Accrued Payroll Taxes		366 00
301	Capital, Ann Dancer		52 657 37
	Total	81 878 88	81 878 88

Discussion Questions

1. When is the process of closing entries performed?
2. What are the purposes of closing entries?
3. What are the temporary general ledger accounts?
4. Why are the balance sheet accounts (with the exception of Withdrawals) not closed?
5. What is the purpose of the Income Summary account?
6. What is the purpose of the post-closing trial balance?

Problems

Problem 12.1

Journalize the closing entries using information from the partial worksheet for the Club Diner, a proprietorship. After journalizing, prepare a post-closing trial balance. A working T-account should be maintained for the Capital account to assist in the preparation of the post-closing trial balance.

The Club Diner
Worksheet
December 31, 19XX

	Income Statement		Balance Sheet	
	dr	cr	dr	cr
Cash			4,586.36	
Food Inventory			865.00	
Supplies Inventory			350.00	
Furniture & Equipment			7,500.00	
Accum. Depreciation--F & E				6,800.00
Accounts Payable				976.45
Sales Tax Payable				325.55
Capital, M. George				2,134.73
Withdrawals, M. George			12,500.00	
Food Sales		59,540.50		
Cost of Food Sold	18,750.68			
Payroll	10,945.35			
Payroll Taxes	1,069.67			
Supplies	524.25			
Utilities	3,185.92			
Rent	9,000.00			
Depreciation	500.00			
Total	43,975.87	59,540.50	25,801.36	10,236.73
Net Income	15,564.63			15,564.63
Total	59,540.50	59,540.50	25,801.36	25,801.36

CAPITAL, M. GEORGE

Problems (continued)

Problem 12.2

Journalize the closing entries using information from the partial worksheet for the Bus Diner, Inc. After journalizing, prepare a post-closing trial balance. A working T-account should be maintained for the Retained Earnings account to assist in the preparation of the post-closing trial balance.

The Bus Diner, Inc.
Worksheet
December 31, 19XX

	Income Statement		Balance Sheet	
	dr	cr	dr	cr
Cash			7,254.44	
Food Inventory			985.00	
Supplies Inventory			425.00	
Furniture & Equipment			8,500.00	
Accum. Depreciation--F & E				5,700.00
Accounts Payable				1,252.33
Sales Tax Payable				297.30
Retained Earnings				4,233.85
Food Sales		85,965.75		
Cost of Food Sold	24,986.22			
Payroll	39,882.11			
Payroll Taxes	2,678.14			
Supplies	792.78			
Utilities	3,645.54			
Rent	7,500.00			
Depreciation	800.00			
Total	80,284.79	85,965.75	17,164.44	11,483.48
Net Income	5,680.96			5,680.96
Total	85,965.75	85,965.75	17,164.44	17,164.44

RETAINED EARNINGS

SAMPLE CHART OF ACCOUNTS

The following pages present a sample chart of accounts which is intended to be used only as a guide to establishing an accounting system for recording business transactions. No attempt has been made to meet the specific needs of every property. The chart of accounts presented here is sufficiently flexible to allow individual owners or managers to add or delete accounts to meet the individual needs and requirements of their properties.

The sample chart of accounts uses a five-digit numbering system. The first two digits represent a department or cost center, and the last three digits indicate the account number. Suggestions for assigning the first two digits follow:

00 The whole hotel or motel; no specific department
10 Rooms Department as an entity; possible subdivisions include:
  12 Front Office
  14 Reservations
  16 Housekeeping
  18 Uniform Service
20 Food and Beverage Department as an entity; possible subdivisions include:
  21 Coffee Shop
  22 Specialty/Fine Dining Room
  23 Banquet
  24 Room Service
  25 Bar
  27 Kitchen
  29 Employee Cafeteria
30 Telephone Department
40 Gift Shop
45 Garage and Parking
47 Other Operated Departments
49 Rentals and Other Income
50 Administrative and General as an entity; possible subdivisions include:
  51 Accounting
  52 Data Processing
  54 Human Resources
  55 Purchasing
  57 Security
  59 Transportation
60 Marketing
70 Property Operation and Maintenance
75 Energy Costs
80 Management Fees
85 Fixed Charges

Suggestions for assigning the last three digits follow:
100–199 Assets
200–280 Liabilities
280–299 Equity
300–399 Revenue
400–499 Cost of Sales
500–599 Payroll and Related Expenses
600–699 Other Expenses
700–799 Fixed Charges

Assets

100 Cash
  101 House Funds
  103 Checking Account
  105 Payroll Account
  107 Savings Account
  109 Petty Cash
110 Marketable Securities/Short-Term Investments
120 Accounts Receivable
  121 Guest Ledger
  123 Credit Card Accounts
  125 Direct Bill
  127 Other Accounts Receivable
  128 Intercompany Receivables
  129 Allowance for Doubtful Accounts
130 Notes Receivable
  134 Receivable from Owner
  137 Due from Employees
140 Inventory
  141 Food
  142 Liquor
  143 Wine
  145 Operating Supplies
  146 Paper Supplies
  147 Cleaning Supplies
  149 Other
150 Prepaids
  151 Prepaid Insurance
  152 Prepaid Taxes
  153 Prepaid Workers' Compensation
  155 Prepaid Supplies
  157 Prepaid Contracts
  159 Other Prepaids
160 Noncurrent Receivables
165 Investments (not short-term)
170 Property and Equipment
  171 Land
  172 Buildings
  173 Accumulated Depreciation—Buildings
  174 Leaseholds and Leasehold Improvements
  175 Accumulated Depreciation—Leaseholds
  176 Furniture and Fixtures
  177 Accumulated Depreciation—Furniture and Fixtures

178 Machinery and Equipment
179 Accumulated Depreciation—Machinery and Equipment
180 Data Processing Equipment
181 Accumulated Depreciation—Data Processing Equipment
182 Automobiles and Trucks
183 Accumulated Depreciation—Automobiles and Trucks
184 Construction in Progress
185 China
186 Glassware
187 Silver
188 Linen
189 Uniforms
190 Other Assets
191 Security Deposits
192 Preopening Expenses
194 Deferred Expenses
196 Cash Surrender Value—Life Insurance
199 Miscellaneous

Liabilities

200 Payables
201 Accounts Payable
205 Dividends Payable
207 Notes Payable
209 Intercompany Payables
210 Employee Withholdings
211 FICA—Employee
212 State Disability—Employee
213 SUTA—Employee
214 Medical Insurance—Employee
215 Life Insurance—Employee
216 Dental Insurance—Employee
217 Credit Union
218 United Way
219 Miscellaneous Deductions
220 Employer Payroll Taxes
221 FICA—Employer
222 FUTA—Employer
223 SUTA—Employer
224 Medical Insurance—Employer
225 Life Insurance—Employer
226 Dental Insurance—Employer
227 Disability—Employer
228 Workers' Compensation—Employer
229 Miscellaneous Contributions
230 Taxes
231 Federal Withholding Tax
232 State Withholding Tax
233 County Withholding Tax
234 City Withholding Tax
236 Sales Tax

238 Property Tax
241 Federal Income Tax
242 State Income Tax
244 City Income Tax
255 Advance Deposits
260 Accruals
261 Accrued Payables
262 Accrued Utilities
263 Accrued Vacation
264 Accrued Taxes
269 Accrued Expenses—Other
270 Current Portion—Long-Term Debt
274 Other Current Liabilities
275 Long-Term Debt
278 Capital Leases
279 Other Long-Term Debt

Equity

For Proprietorships and Partnerships
280–287 Owner's or Partners' Capital Accounts
290–297 Owner's or Partners' Withdrawal Accounts
299 Income Summary

For Corporations
280–285 Capital Stock
286 Paid-in Capital
289 Retained Earnings
290–295 Treasury Stock
299 Income Summary

Revenue

300 Rooms Revenue
301 Transient—Regular
302 Transient—Corporate
303 Transient—Package
304 Transient—Preferred Customer
309 Day Use
311 Group—Convention
312 Group—Tour
317 Permanent
318 Meeting Room Rental
319 Other Room Revenue
320 Food and Beverage Revenue
321 Food Sales
322 Liquor Sales
323 Wine Sales
324 Cover Charges
325 Miscellaneous Banquet Income
326 Service Charges
328 Meeting Room Rental
329 Other Food and Beverage Revenue

330 Telephone Revenue
331 Local Call Revenue
332 Long-Distance Call Revenue
333 Service Charges
335 Commissions
336 Pay Station Revenue
339 Other Telephone Revenue
340 Gift Shop Revenue
350 Garage and Parking Revenue
351 Parking and Storage
352 Merchandise Sales
359 Other Garage and Parking Revenue
370 Space Rentals
371 Clubs
372 Offices
373 Stores
379 Other Rental Income
380 Other Income
381 Concessions
382 Laundry/Valet Commissions
383 Games and Vending Machines
384 In-house Movies
386 Cash Discounts
387 Interest Income
388 Salvage
389 Other
390 Allowances
391 Rooms Allowance
392 Food and Beverage Allowance
393 Telephone Allowance
394 Gift Shop Allowance
395 Garage and Parking Allowance
399 Other Allowance

Cost of Sales

400 Cost of Food Sales
401 Food Purchases
408 Trade Discounts
409 Transportation Charges
419 Other Cost of Food and Beverage Sales
420 Cost of Beverage Sales
421 Liquor Purchases
422 Wine Purchases
423 Beer Purchases
424 Other Beverage Purchases
428 Trade Discounts
429 Transportation Charges
430 Cost of Telephone Calls
431 Local Calls
432 Long-Distance Calls

440 Cost of Gift Shop Sales
441 Gift Shop Purchases
448 Trade Discounts
449 Transportation Charges
450 Cost of Garage and Parking Sales
451 Garage and Parking Purchases
458 Trade Discounts
459 Transportation Charges
490 Cost of Employee Meals
492 Bottle Deposit Refunds
495 Grease and Bone Sales Revenue
496 Empty Bottle/Barrel Sales Revenue

Payroll and Related Expenses

510 Salaries and Wages
511–519 Departmental Management and Supervisory Staff
521–539 Departmental Line Employees
550 Payroll Taxes
551 Payroll Taxes—FICA
552 Payroll Taxes—FUTA
553 Payroll Taxes—SUTA
558 Workers' Compensation
560 Employee Benefits
561 Vacation, Holiday, and Sick Pay
564 Medical Insurance
565 Life Insurance
566 Dental Insurance
567 Disability
569 Employee Meals
599 Payroll Tax and Benefit Allocation

Other Expenses

600 Operating Supplies
601 Cleaning Supplies
602 Guest Supplies
603 Paper Supplies
604 Postage and Telegrams
605 Printing and Stationery
606 Menus
607 Utensils
610 Linen, China, Glassware, etc.
611 China
612 Glassware
613 Silver
614 Linen
618 Uniforms
621 Contract Cleaning Expenses
623 Laundry and Dry Cleaning Expenses

624 Laundry Supplies
625 Licenses
627 Kitchen Fuel
628 Music and Entertainment Expenses
629 Reservations Expense
630 Data Processing Expenses
631 Hardware Maintenance
632 Software Maintenance
635 Service Bureau Fees
639 Other Data Processing Expenses
640 Human Resource Expenses
641 Dues and Subscriptions
642 Employee Housing
643 Employee Relations
644 Medical Expenses
645 Recruitment
646 Relocation
647 Training
648 Transportation
650 Administrative Expenses
651 Credit Card Commissions
652 Donations
653 Insurance—General
654 Credit and Collections Expense
655 Professional Fees
656 Losses and Damages
657 Provision for Doubtful Accounts
658 Cash Over/Short
659 Travel and Entertainment
660 Marketing Expenses
661 Commissions
662 Direct Mail Expenses
663 In-house Graphics
664 Outdoor Advertising
665 Point-of-Sale Materials
666 Print Materials
667 Radio and Television Expenses
668 Selling Aids
669 Franchise Fees
670 Property Operation Expenses
671 Building Supplies
672 Electrical and Mechanical Equipment
673 Elevators
674 Engineering Supplies
675 Furniture, Fixtures, Equipment, and Decor
676 Grounds and Landscaping
677 Painting and Decorating
678 Removal of Waste Matter
679 Swimming Pool Expense

680 Energy Costs
681 Electrical Cost
682 Fuel Cost
686 Steam Cost
687 Water Cost
689 Other Energy Costs
690 Guest Transportation
691 Fuel and Oil
693 Insurance
695 Repairs and Maintenance
699 Other Expense

Fixed Charges

700 Management Fees
710 Rent or Lease Expenses
711 Land
712 Buildings
713 Equipment
714 Telephone Equipment
715 Data Processing Equipment
716 Software (includes any license fees)
717 Vehicles
720 Tax Expense
721 Real Estate Tax
722 Personal Property Taxes
723 Utility Taxes
724 Business and Occupation Taxes
730 Building and Contents Insurance
740 Interest Expense
741 Mortgage Interest
742 Notes Payable Interest
743 Interest on Capital Leases
744 Amortization of Deferred Financing Costs
750 Depreciation and Amortization
751 Building and Improvements
752 Leaseholds and Leasehold Improvements
753 Furniture and Fixtures
754 Machinery and Equipment
755 Data Processing Equipment
756 Automobiles and Trucks
757 Capital Leases
758 Preopening Expenses
770 Gain or Loss on Sale of Property
790 Income Taxes
791 Current Federal Income Tax
792 Deferred Federal Income Tax
795 Current State Income Tax
796 Deferred State Income Tax

Glossary

A

ACCOUNT

A form in which financial data is accumulated and summarized.

ACCOUNT BALANCE

A summary of an account in terms of its resulting monetary amount; specifically, the difference between the total debits and the total credits of an account.

ACCOUNTING

The process by which quantitative information, primarily financial in nature, about economic entities is provided to external and internal users in order to aid decision-making.

ACCOUNTING CYCLE

The sequence of accounting procedures for a fiscal year; the accounting cycle comprises daily, monthly, and end-of-year activities.

ACCOUNTING EQUATION

The equation which states that assets equal liabilities plus equity.

ACCOUNTING SYSTEM

A system which consists of forms and procedures used to process business transactions—the ultimate objective of which is to produce reliable financial statements.

ACCOUNTING SYSTEMS DESIGN

The branch of accounting which focuses primarily on the information system of a hospitality organization.

ACCOUNTS PAYABLE

Unpaid invoices due to creditors from whom the restaurant receives merchandise or services in the ordinary course of business; they are also referred to as trade payables.

ACCOUNTS PAYABLE JOURNAL

A special journal used to record the receipt of all invoices, regardless of whether they will be paid immediately or at some later date; for some operations, entries to the accounts payable journal consist of only those invoices to be paid at a later date.

ACCOUNTS PAYABLE SUBSIDIARY LEDGER

A subsidiary ledger which provides detailed information about amounts owed by the business to its suppliers; it is also referred to as the creditors ledger.

ACCOUNTS RECEIVABLE

Amounts owed to a firm by its guests, usually through open account arrangements or nonbank credit cards.

ACCOUNTS RECEIVABLE SUBSIDIARY LEDGER

A subsidiary ledger which provides detailed information on amounts due the business from its customers; common types include the guest ledger, the city ledger, and the banquet ledger.

ACCRUAL ACCOUNTING METHOD

The method of adjusting the accounting records by recording expenses which are incurred during an accounting period but which (for any number of reasons) are not actually paid until the following period. (See Cash accounting method.)

ACCRUED EXPENSES

Unrecorded expenses which, at the end of an accounting period, have been incurred but not yet paid.

ACCUMULATED DEPRECIATION

A contra-asset account representing the cumulative amount of allocations to depreciation.

ADDITIONAL PAID-IN CAPITAL

The premium paid for stock in excess of its par value.

ADJUSTING ENTRIES

End-of-month entries in the general journal which are necessary to comply with the matching principle (accrual basis of accounting); adjusting entries are required for expired assets, unrecorded expenses, unrecorded revenue, and unearned revenue.

ADVANCE DEPOSIT

Amount paid to the business for goods and/or services it has not yet provided; an advance deposit represents a liability until the service is performed.

ASSET

Anything a business owns which has commercial or exchange value.

ATTEST FUNCTION

Reporting on the fairness and reliability of a company's financial statements—a function performed by independent certified public accountants.

AUDIT

A comprehensive investigation of the items that appear on the financial statements and in any accompanying notes with the purpose of expressing an opinion on the financial statements.

AUDITING

The branch of accounting most often associated with the independent, external financial audit, as conducted by independent certified public accountants.

B

BALANCE SHEET

A financial statement that provides information on the financial position of the hospitality business by showing the assets, liabilities, and equity on a given date.

BOOKKEEPING

The routine aspects of recording, classifying, and summarizing business transactions—only one part of the overall accounting function.

BOOK VALUE

The cost of an asset minus the amount of its accumulated depreciation; it is sometimes referred to as net asset value.

BUSINESS TRANSACTION

The exchange of merchandise, property, or services for cash or a promise to pay; business transactions initiate the accounting process.

C

CAPITAL ACCOUNT

A cumulative account which contains investments made by the owner in the business, plus the net income from operations of the business, less any net loss from operations of the business, less withdrawals of assets from the business by the owner for personal use.

CAPITAL STOCK

Collective term for various classes of common stock and preferred stock.

CASH

A category of current assets consisting of cash in house banks, cash in checking and savings accounts, and certificates of deposit.

CASH ACCOUNTING METHOD

The method by which the results of business transactions are recorded only when cash is received or paid out. (See Accrual accounting method.)

CASH PAYMENTS JOURNAL

A special journal used to record checks issued from the regular checking account.

CERTIFIED PUBLIC ACCOUNTANT (CPA)

A professional accountant who has met academic qualifications, satisfied state requirements, and passed the national CPA exam.

CHART OF ACCOUNTS

A listing of the titles (names) of all the accounts used by a particular business, serving as a "table of contents."

CITY LEDGER

A type of ledger used for all customers other than those classified as registered guests staying at the hotel.

CLASSIFYING

The process of assembling the numerous business transactions encountered by a business into related categories.

CLOSING ENTRIES

End-of-year entries in the general journal used to set the temporary accounts to zero and to record net income or loss for the year.

COMMON STOCK

Stock issued by a corporation which gives ownership interest and voting rights.

COMPENSATING BALANCE

A minimum amount that must be maintained in a checking account in connection with a borrowing arrangement.

COMPILATION

A report limited to considering financial statements for form, application of accounting principles, and mathematical accuracy—without expressing an opinion or any other form of assurance on them.

CONTRA ACCOUNT

An account which functions in an opposite manner to the regular classification with which it is associated; for instance, a fixed asset account is reduced by its associated Accumulated Depreciation account (a contra-asset account).

CONTROL ACCOUNT

A term describing either the Accounts Receivable account or the Accounts Payable account in the general ledger; the term refers to the relationship between the balances of these accounts and the totals of their associated subsidiary ledgers.

CONSERVATISM

The principle which asserts that assets and income should be fairly presented and not overstated, especially for those situations which involve doubt.

CONSISTENCY

The principle which states that once an accounting method has been adopted, it should be followed consistently from period to period.

CORPORATION

An incorporated business—a separate legal entity organized under law and distinct from its owners.

CORRECTING ENTRIES

Entries in the general journal used to correct previous entries which were erroneous.

COST ACCOUNTING

The branch of accounting which relates to the recording, classification, allocation, and reporting of current and prospective costs.

COST OF SALES

The cost of food and beverage merchandise held for resale and used in the selling process, not including any cost for labor or operating supplies.

CREDIT

To record an amount on the right side of an account; a credit is used to increase a liability, equity, or revenue account, and to decrease an asset or expense account.

CROSSFOOTING

The process of horizontally adding or subtracting numbers.

CURRENT ASSETS

Cash or assets which are convertible to cash within 12 months of the balance sheet date; to be considered a current asset, an asset must be available without restriction for use in payment of current liabilities.

CURRENT LIABILITIES

Those liabilities expected to be satisfied by the use of a current asset or to be replaced by another current liability within 12 months of the balance sheet date.

D

DAILY CASHIERS REPORT

An accounting document used to record cash register readings, cash count, bank deposits, and other transactions handled by the cashier.

DEBIT

To record an amount on the left side of an account; a debit is used to increase an asset or expense account, and to decrease a liability, equity, or revenue account.

DEPRECIATION

The periodic allocation of the cost of a fixed asset over its estimated useful life.

DIVIDEND

A distribution of earnings to owners of a corporation's stock. (See Stock dividends.)

DOUBTFUL ACCOUNTS

An account used to record the portion of accounts receivable judged to be uncollectible.

E

EQUITY

The claims of owners to assets of the business; equity represents the residual amounts after liabilities are deducted from assets.

EXPENSE

An account classification which includes day-to-day costs incurred in operating the business, expired costs of assets charged to expense by depreciation, and costs of assets (such as inventory) that are consumed in operating the business.

EXPENSE DICTIONARY

A special dictionary designed to enable controllers to classify expense items according to the proper account or expense group.

EXTERNAL USERS

Groups outside of the business who require accounting and financial information; external users include suppliers, bankers, stockholders, and investors.

F

FEDERAL INCOME TAX

The income taxes calculated on a firm's taxable income according to federal tax laws.

FEDERAL INCOME TAX WITHHELD

Taxes withheld from employees' gross pay that must be paid to the federal government.

FINANCIAL ACCOUNTING

The branch of accounting primarily concerned with recording and accumulating accounting information to be used in the preparation of financial statements for external users.

FINANCIAL ACCOUNTING STANDARDS BOARD (FASB)

An independent, non-governmental body that develops and issues statements of financial accounting standards.

FINANCIAL STATEMENT

Formal medium for communicating various kinds of accounting information to both internal and external users; examples include balance sheet, income statement, and statement of retained earnings.

FISCAL YEAR

The business year.

FIXED ASSETS

Long-lived assets of a firm that are tangible; for example, land, equipment, and buildings.

FIXED CHARGES

Expenses incurred regardless of the sales volume of the hotel; they are sometimes referred to as Occupancy Costs.

FOOTING

The process of totaling a column.

G

GENERAL JOURNAL

A two-column, general purpose journal; since each entry in a general journal requires individual posting, it is impractical for large volumes of repetitive transactions.

GENERAL LEDGER

Collective form of the bookkeeping accounts; in a manual system, the general ledger is composed of a separate page for each account.

GENERALLY ACCEPTED ACCOUNTING PRINCIPLES (GAAP)

Professional accounting standards which have received substantial authoritative support and approval from professional accounting associations and governmental agencies.

GOING-CONCERN ASSUMPTION

The assumption that a business will continue indefinitely and thus carry out its commitments; it is also known as continuity of the business unit.

GOODWILL

The premium paid in a purchase agreement that reflects the capacity or potential of a business to earn above-normal profits; goodwill reflects unrecorded intangible assets including the knowledge, skill, and teamwork of those employed by the company, as well as the company's name, reputation, location, and customer loyalty.

GROSS PROFIT

An intermediate income amount (the difference between net revenue and cost of sales) from which operating expenses and fixed charges are deducted to arrive at net income.

GUEST LEDGER

A type of ledger used for registered guests staying at the hotel, providing up-to-the-minute status on guest charges and payments made by guests; it may also be referred to as a front office ledger, transient ledger, or room ledger.

H

HISTORICAL COST

The principle which states that the value of merchandise or services obtained through business transactions should be recorded in terms of actual costs, not current market values.

I

IMPREST BASIS

Method of maintaining funds (for example, a cashier's initial funds or a payroll checking account balance) at a predetermined, fixed amount.

INCOME STATEMENT

A financial statement that provides information regarding the results of operations for a stated period of time.

INTERIM FINANCIAL STATEMENTS

Financial statements which are prepared during the business year; for instance, quarterly or monthly statements.

INTERNAL CONTROL

The policies, procedures, and equipment used in a business to safeguard its assets and promote operational efficiency.

INTERNAL REVENUE CODE (IRC)

A codification of income tax statutes and other federal tax laws, whose objectives are guided by large-scale political, economic, and social concerns.

INTERNAL USERS

Groups inside the hospitality business who require accounting and financial information, e.g., the board of directors, the general manager, departmental managers, and other staff.

INVENTORY

Stocks of food and beverage merchandise held for resale, stocks of operating supplies, and other supplies held for future use.

INVESTMENTS

Stocks or bonds failing to meet any or all of the conditions associated with marketable securities; investments also include cash restricted for use in connection with long-term borrowing arrangements and long-term notes receivable.

INVOICE

Statement issued by a seller containing relevant information about a purchase, including: parties involved; the transaction date; the method of shipment; and quantities, descriptions and prices of goods.

ISSUING

The process of distributing food and beverages from the storeroom to authorized individuals by the use of formal requisitions.

J

JOURNAL

An accounting document used to record business transactions.

JOURNALIZING

The process by which business transactions are recorded in a journal.

L

LIABILITIES

The claims of outsiders (such as creditors) to assets of the business; liabilities are sometimes called creditors' equities.

LIMITED PARTNER

A partner who does not actively participate in the management of the business, and is basically an investor whose liability may be restricted according to the terms of the partnership agreement.

LONG-TERM LIABILITIES

A term which describes any debt *not* due within 12 months of the balance sheet date.

M

MANAGERIAL ACCOUNTING

The branch of accounting primarily concerned with recording and accumulating accounting information in order to prepare financial statements and reports for internal users.

MARKETABLE SECURITIES

A category of current assets including stocks and bonds of large corporations and U.S. government bonds which are readily marketable and intended to be converted into cash should the need arise.

MATCHING PRINCIPLE

The principle which states that all expenses must be recorded in the same accounting period as the revenue which they helped to generate.

MATERIALITY

The principle which states that material events must be accounted for according to accounting rules, but insignificant events may be treated in an expeditious manner.

N

NET INCOME

The bottom line on an income statement which occurs as a result of revenue exceeding expenses.

NET LOSS

The bottom line on an income statement which occurs as a result of expenses exceeding revenue.

NONCURRENT ASSETS

Assets which are *not* to be converted to cash within 12 months of the balance sheet date.

NORMAL ACCOUNT BALANCE

The type of balance (debit or credit) expected of a particular account based on its classification; asset and expense accounts normally have debit balances, while liability, equity, and revenue accounts normally have credit balances.

NOTES PAYABLE

An account which includes any written promise (promissory note) by a business to pay a creditor or lender at some future date.

NOTES RECEIVABLE

An account for recording promissory notes made payable to the hospitality company.

O

OBJECTIVITY

The principle stating that all business transactions must be supported by objective evidence proving that the transactions did in fact occur.

OPERATING EXPENSES

All expenses incurred by a business (other than the cost of goods sold) which are necessary in its day-to-day activities.

ORGANIZATION CHART

A visual representation of the structure of positions within an operation, showing the different layers of management and the chain of command.

ORGANIZATION COSTS

Costs involved in the legal formation of a business; they are generally associated with forming a corporation.

OWNERSHIP EQUITY

Financial interest of the owner(s) in a business.

P

PAR VALUE

An arbitrarily selected amount associated with authorized shares of stock; it is also referred to as legal value.

PARTNERSHIP

An unincorporated business owned by two or more individuals.

PAYROLL JOURNAL

A special journal which basically serves as a check register for recording all payroll checks issued.

PERIODIC INVENTORY SYSTEM

An inventory system which does not use any formal methods for tracking receipts and issues; it requires physical counts of inventory on a periodic basis.

PERMANENT ACCOUNTS

Accounts which maintain a perpetual balance, i.e., they are not closed at the end of the fiscal year; permanent accounts are also called real accounts.

PERPETUAL INVENTORY SYSTEM

An inventory system in which receipts and issues are recorded as they occur; this system provides readily available information on inventory levels and cost of sales figures.

POST-CLOSING TRIAL BALANCE

A listing of the balance sheet accounts (with the exception of Withdrawals) and their account balances in order to retest the equality of debit and credit balances in the general ledger.

POSTING

The process by which journal entries are ultimately recorded in the bookkeeping accounts.

PREFERRED STOCK

Stock issued by a corporation which provides preferential treatment on dividends, but may not give the stockholder the privilege of voting.

PREPAID EXPENSES

Unexpired costs that will benefit future periods but are expected to expire within a relatively short period, usually within 12 months of the current accounting period; examples include prepaid rent (excluding security deposits) and prepaid insurance premiums.

PROMISSORY NOTE

A written promise to pay a definite sum of money at some future date, generally involving the payment of interest in addition to the principal (amount of loan); promissory notes may be characterized as negotiable instruments (legally transferable among parties by endorsement).

PROPERTY AND EQUIPMENT

A noncurrent asset category which includes assets of a relatively permanent nature that are tangible (such as land, buildings, and equipment) and are used in the business operation to generate sales; this category may be referred to as plant assets or fixed assets.

PROPRIETORSHIP

A form of business organization referring to an unincorporated business owned by one person (sole proprietor).

PURCHASE ORDER

An order for supplies or products, prepared by the operation and submitted to the supplier.

PURVEYOR

A firm which provides or supplies merchandise to hospitality operations.

R

REALIZATION

The principle which states that revenue resulting from business transactions should be recorded only when a sale has been made *and* earned.

RECEIVING

Accepting delivery of merchandise that has been ordered or is expected by the firm and recording such transactions.

RECEIVING REPORT

A report on items received, prepared at time of delivery.

RECORDING

The procedure of actually entering the results of transactions in an accounting document called a journal.

RESPONSIBILITY ACCOUNTING

The principle by which each department reports revenue and expense data separately from other areas of the organization; a given department is directed by an individual who is held responsible for its operation.

RETAINED EARNINGS

The portion of net income earned by the corporation which is not distributed as dividends, but is retained in the business.

REVENUE

Amounts that guests have been billed for products and services offered by the hospitality property.

REVENUE CENTERS

Areas within a hospitality operation which generate revenue through sales of products and/or services to guests; revenue centers include such areas as Rooms, Food and Beverage, and Gift Shop operations.

REVERSING ENTRIES

Beginning-of-month entries in the general journal which may be required due to certain types of adjusting entries recorded in the previous month; a reversing entry is the exact opposite of the adjusting entry to which it relates.

REVIEW

An opinion as to the fairness of the financial statements and an expression of limited assurance that no material changes to the financial statements are necessary for them to be in conformity with generally accepted accounting principles.

S

SALES & CASH RECEIPTS JOURNAL

A special journal used to record all of the sales and the cash receipts for the day; its primary input is the daily cashiers report.

SLIDE ERROR

An error caused by moving the decimal point of a number to the left or right of its correct position.

SPECIAL JOURNAL

A multi-column journal designed to record each major repetitive activity or event; a special journal is usually composed of separate columns for each type of transaction likely to occur repeatedly during the month, along with a sundry area for recording infrequent transactions.

STOCK DIVIDENDS

Dividends typically involving the issuance of common shares to existing common stockholders in proportion to their present ownership in the company.

STOCKHOLDERS

The owners of a corporation, also referred to as shareholders.

SUBSIDIARY LEDGER

A separate ledger that provides supporting detail of an account in the general ledger; examples include the accounts payable subsidiary ledger and the accounts receivable subsidiary ledger.

SUMMARIZING

The actual process of preparing financial information according to the formats of specific reports or financial statements.

SUPPORT CENTERS

Areas of a hospitality operation which are not directly involved in generating revenue, but instead provide supporting services to revenue centers; support centers include such areas as Administrative and General, Marketing, and Property Operation and Maintenance.

T

T-ACCOUNT

A two-column format (resembling a letter "T") in which debits are posted to the left side and credits to the right side.

TAX ACCOUNTING

The branch of accounting relating to the preparation and filing of tax forms required by various governmental agencies.

TEMPORARY ACCOUNTS

Accounts which begin the new accounting year with zero balances, accumulate balances during the accounting year, and return to zero by means of closing entries at the end of the accounting year; they are also referred to as nominal accounts.

TREASURY STOCK

Stock which has been reacquired by the company and is no longer considered issued and outstanding.

TRANSPOSITION ERROR

An error in which two digits in a number have been mistakenly switched.

TRIAL BALANCE

A listing of all of the accounts with their account balances in the order they appear in the general ledger; it provides a verification of the equality of debit and credit balances in the general ledger.

U

UNIFORM SYSTEM OF ACCOUNTS

A manual (usually produced for a specific segment of the hospitality industry) which defines accounts for various types and sizes of operations; a uniform system of accounts generally provides standardized financial statement formats, explanations of individual accounts, and sample bookkeeping documents.

V

VENDOR

A firm that sells wholesale merchandise. (See Purveyor.)

W

WITHDRAWALS

A temporary account (specifically, a contra-equity account) used to record personal withdrawal of business assets by an owner (proprietor or partner); it is sometimes called a drawings account.

WORKSHEET

A multi-column working paper used as a preliminary to the preparation of financial statements.

Index